BRITISH PRIME MINISTERS
IN THE TWENTIETH CENTURY

BRITISH PRIME MINISTERS
IN THE TWENTIETH CENTURY

Edited by
JOHN P. MACKINTOSH

VOLUME I
Balfour to Chamberlain

WEIDENFELD and NICOLSON

LONDON

Copyright © 1977 by John P. Mackintosh, Peter Fraser, José F. Harris, Cameron Hazlehurst, Kenneth O. Morgan, Trevor Lloyd, John Campbell, Alan Beattie

Reprinted 1979

Weidenfeld and Nicolson
91 Clapham High Street
London SW4

Designed by Behram Kapadia

ISBN 0 297 77291 0

Printed in Great Britain by
REDWOOD BURN LIMITED
Trowbridge & Esher

Contents

Contributors

John P. Mackintosh is MP for Berwick and East Lothian and Professor of Politics at Edinburgh University.

Peter Fraser is Lecturer in History, Dalhousie University, Nova Scotia, Canada.

José F. Harris is Lecturer in Social Administration at the London School of Economics.

Cameron Hazlehurst is a Fellow of the Institute of Advanced Studies, Australian National University and was previously a research Fellow at The Queen's College, and Nuffield College, Oxford. Previous publications include *Politicians at War, July 1914 to May 1915* and *A Guide to the Papers of British Cabinet Ministers, 1900–51*.

Kenneth O. Morgan is a Fellow and Praelector of Queen's College, Oxford.

Trevor Lloyd is Professor of History at Toronto University and has published *Empire to Welfare State: English History 1906–67*.

John Campbell is the author of *Lloyd George: the Goat in the Wilderness*, and is now working on a biography of F. E. Smith (Lord Birkenhead).

Alan Beattie is Lecturer in Political Science at the London School of Economics.

Introduction

John P. Mackintosh

The idea of producing this book occurred some time ago when there was considerable academic and public controversy over whether British government could validly be described as 'prime-ministerial' government. Since then the topic has come up at regular intervals, with the publication of such books as Richard Crossman's *Inside View* with proposals for changes in Whitehall such as the possibility of a Prime Minister's Department (see *The Times*, 24 August 1972 and *The Financial Times*, 25 August 1972), with the centralizing tendencies of Mr Heath who created the Central Policy Review Staff, with Sir Harold Wilson's establishment of a new Policy Unit and the retention of these institutions by Mr James Callaghan.

So the subject is not, and probably never will be, out of date. The idea was to produce an essay on each of a series of British Prime Ministers, concentrating particularly on three things: their handling of the Whitehall machine, their dealings with their own party inside the House and in the country, and their overall management of parliament. The intention was not to ask the author to examine whether the Prime Minister he was writing about was or was not 'prime ministerial' in these relationships, but to write a biographical evaluation concentrating on these themes. Any overall trends were to be allowed to emerge (if they existed), but it was hoped that the result would simply be a series of impressions of how different men tackled the same job.

It was hard to decide which period of Prime Ministers to cover. The British system of government has undergone sweeping transformations over the centuries, while retaining much the same outward form. The biggest change in modern history has been the advent of the mass electorate which made general elections a kind of plebiscite on the merits of the government of the day, which produced modern political parties and which made the government responsible to the people rather than to the House of Commons, thus vastly diminishing the role of that body.

But there have been other important consequential or subsidiary changes which also mark stages in the recent history of the British political system. One was when the executive took control of the time and procedure of the House of Commons, the decisive step being the alterations in the Standing Orders under Arthur Balfour in 1902. A second change was the development of the Cabinet secretariat which began with the Committee of Imperial Defence before the First World War, spread to the whole Cabinet during the war and became accepted as normal after Bonar Law became Prime Minister in 1922. Then there was the impact of the 1914–18 war which showed that the government could organize and control virtually the whole of industry if the electorate and their representatives agreed that that was in the public interest. A further important development occurred in 1944 when it became accepted that the government was responsible for the level of employment and the overall management of the economy.

Looking at these various stages in recent political history, it was clearly reasonable to choose a starting-point after the extension of the franchise and the growth of parties had created something like contemporary political conditions, but within this limit there was no obvious boundary. As a result, it was decided that the turn of the century was as good a point as any, commencing after the last member of the House of Lords to be Prime Minister, Lord Salisbury, had resigned. At the same time Balfour looked more like a modern Prime Minister in that his government did acquire virtually the present degree of control over the timetable of the House and he was able to face, with almost the same equanimity as Harold Macmillan in the 1950s, the simultaneous resignation of five Cabinet ministers on an issue of principle.

So this volume begins with a chapter on Arthur Balfour, aptly described by Peter Fraser as 'the last of the Victorians', and ends with one on Neville Chamberlain. Volume II will complete the survey with chapters on the Prime Ministers from Churchill to James Callaghan, there being only two omissions in the whole. There are no chapters on Bonar Law and Sir Alec Douglas Home. This is not because their periods as Prime Minister were unimportant – far from it – though both were short, Bonar Law serving for seven months and Sir Alec for twelve months, while the next shortest was Sir Anthony Eden, who lasted for one year and nine months. The brevity of the first two of these premierships would have made it hard to generalize about the features of Bonar Law or Sir Alec Douglas Home's treatment of their parties or the House of Commons as neither had time to establish a definite style of management, though in certain respects their reactions over even a few months of office are significant.

The interesting features of Bonar Law's period in office are the contrast between what took place and his own desire, often stated, to avoid all Lloyd George's methods of government. For instance, despite the Cabinet secretariat's being under suspicion as part of the Lloyd George system, it was so clearly necessary, given the volume of Cabinet business, that it was retained. Bonar Law wanted to put the clock back to the pre-1914 situation and leave departmental ministers, particularly the Foreign Secretary, to run their own offices, to handle their own spheres of responsibility, yet he found himself driven to take a major part in reparations negotiations with France. He had hoped for a less active, less 'dynamic' government and he did manage to return to a party-based system with a Conservative Cabinet in close touch with the Conservative majority in the House.

Yet events and the requirements of the office led or forced him to behave like most of the other Prime Ministers covered in this book. His biographer, Robert Blake, comments on his first session:

> It had been largely a personal triumph for him. He had carried nearly all the burden of the work. Indeed, it was somewhat ironical that he who had from the first proclaimed the importance of Cabinet responsibility and the abolition of one-man rule should have been forced to take so much upon himself.[1]

Later he was persuaded to give up his desire either to repudiate Baldwin's settlement of Britain's debts to the United States or to resign by the unanimous appeal of the Cabinet to continue (Baldwin had simply blundered in not getting the Cabinet's view before he accepted and announced the terms), but L.S. Amery's account of his methods in Cabinet show the way in which he normally exercised his powers:

> Bonar Law, under his diffident manner, was much more of an autocrat than Lloyd George and much more set in his ways. He was a businessman for whom an agenda was something on which decisions were to be got as soon as possible, not a series of starting-points for a general discussion. Sooner than let discussion roam afield or controversy be raised, he would cut things short by suggesting a committee.[2]

There is much in this that is similar to the description of Attlee's methods in Cabinet and while Bonar Law's sudden illness cut short his period as Prime Minister, there is every indication that he would have continued to put his own stamp on the administration, to dominate the House of Commons and to exercise much the same degree of control over the government as Lloyd George had done, though his intentions, manner and talents were so very different.

The interesting aspect of Sir Alec Douglas-Home's brief period as Prime Minister is very similar. He also followed a flamboyant personality, 'Supermac', who had rescued the Conservatives from the doubts and disarray that followed the Suez fiasco of 1956. Mr Macmillan gave the Conservatives their third successive electoral victory, and when he decided to resign there was a long-drawn-out, highly public and politically embarrassing struggle for the succession. When Sir Alec was finally chosen and asked to form a government by the Queen he faced somewhat the same problem as Bonar Law in that some leading Conservatives (Mr Iain Macleod and Mr Enoch Powell) refused to serve with him.

Yet he managed to form a government without any difficulty. His experience of office had been largely in foreign affairs (the exception was a short period as Minister of State in the Scottish Office) and he readily confessed to a relative ignorance of economic policy, but all the evidence suggests that Sir Alec established what must be accepted as the normal degree of control over his ministry. It was he who had earlier said, in an interview on the powers of the Prime Minister:

> Every Cabinet Minister is in a sense the Prime Minister's agent – his assistant. There's no question about that. It is the Prime Minister's Cabinet, and he is the one person who is directly responsible to the Queen for what the Cabinet does. If the Cabinet discusses anything it is the Prime Minister who decides what the collective view of the Cabinet is. A Minister's job is to save the Prime Minister all the work he can. But no Minister could make a really important move without consulting the Prime Minister, and if the Prime Minister wanted to take a certain step the Cabinet Minister concerned would either have to agree, argue it out in Cabinet or resign.[3]

His own view, looking back on his period as premier, was to confirm this account and none of his colleagues disputes that this was a

reasonable statement of the normal relationship they have experienced in the Cabinets in which they have served.

Sir Alec's dealings with his party and with the House of Commons
were distracted by one overriding consideration. Everyone knew that
there had to be an election within twelve months and he therefore had
an extra surge of loyalty from the rank and file, while in the House he
faced a rampaging opposition led by such an able in-fighter as Mr
Wilson, then at the height of his powers. Had Sir Alec been able to
postpone the election for even two months, the swing back to the
Conservatives which went on for most of his period in office might just
have given him victory, and had this happened there can be no guess as
to what his relations with the House of Commons would have
become. Leaders as diverse as Campbell-Bannerman, Attlee and Heath
have been transformed by electoral victories; they have been moved
from the position of men who seemed open to harassment, with
uncertain control of their parties, into an easy confidence and control
which allowed them to push aside questions which they did not care to
answer.

Thus, though both the Bonar Law and Alec Douglas-Home
premierships contain much that is of interest, the period in each case
was so brief and so dominated by the situation in which the
government was formed and by the problems of establishing a normal
political life-span, that they did not seem to merit the full treatment
given to the other Prime Ministers. On the other hand, there is a much
better case for the inclusion of Sir Anthony Eden (Lord Avon) in
Volume II. Not only did his government last for nearly two years but
there was time for his techniques in the roles covered by this book to
become evident and to merit some examination.

The study of Sir Anthony Eden is dominated by a discussion of the
Suez crisis, but it is not included just for this reason. Though Eden's
handling of the affair is often quoted as an example of prime-
ministerial government, as Robert Blake says, 'the same could be said
of Munich, of Chanak, of the outbreak of the 1914–18 war, and of
Disraeli's Near East policy in 1876–78.' Perhaps in the last two examples
the Cabinet played a more important role, but if so it may well have
been because there was more genuine division in these Cabinets than
there was in Eden's. Certainly, it took Disraeli a long time to get his
way and the issue of peace or war hung in the balance in Asquith's
Cabinet over several meetings, in both cases events helping the Prime

Minister. Eden went his way in 1956 much more clearly and definitely, being deflected only by outside events (such as Dulles' proposal for a Suez Canal Users' Association), but Blake is right to stress that 'Eden's relationship with his Cabinet did not differ from that of many of his predecessors'.

It is for this reason that this study was included. Eden had dealings with his party, his colleagues, the press and the House of Commons before the Suez issue arose. These modes were not deflected from a normal pattern by any special problems as he had been the 'heir apparent' to the leadership for fifteen years and, as he easily won a general election soon after he became Prime Minister, the Suez crisis, like all occasions of great stress, put pressure on these relationships and methods. There was no departure from the instinctive patterns of behaviour Eden had built up over thirty-two years in the House, and twelve as a Cabinet minister, but all were thrown into relief, the lights and shadows were brought out for everyone to see by a crisis which left a mark on every participant and which is properly regarded as one of the turning-points in British history when it became evident that a change of direction had actually taken place.

So this study contains chapters dealing with the thirteen British Prime Ministers who have had reasonable periods of office since the turn of the century excluding only two short, rather special premierships. It might have been thought that there was little need to go over this ground again. Since the controversy over 'prime-ministerial' government began in 1962, there has been the practical evidence of three longish occupancies of No. 10 Downing Street. Mr Macmillan has documented his period in office in a mammoth autobiography, as has Mr Wilson, while Mr Heath's methods have been widely discussed in the serious press.

The outcome of all this evidence and comment would seem to be a clear-cut confirmation, not of any exaggerated notions of a 'British Presidency', or of Prime Ministers' ignoring, hoodwinking or bullying their colleagues, but of the original proposition that:

The country is governed by the Prime Minister who leads, coordinates and maintains a series of Ministers, all of whom are advised and backed by the Civil Service. Some decisions are taken by the Prime Minister alone, some in consultation between him and the senior Ministers, while others are left to the heads of departments, the Cabinet, Cabinet Committees, or the permanent officials. ... There is no single catch-phrase that can describe this form of government, but it may be pictured as a cone. The Prime Minister stands at the apex, supported by and giving point to a widening series of rings of senior Ministers, the Cabinet, its Committees, non-Cabinet Ministers, and departments. Of these rings, the only one above the level of the Civil Service that has formal existence and acts as a court of appeal for the lower tiers is the Cabinet.[4]

In the case of Mr Macmillan, the features of his period as Prime Minister that lend support to this interpretation are well known. He took over when the Conservative party was badly shaken by the Suez episode and he re-established its confidence in the House, won over the media and then projected the government's image in a manner which gave him an increased majority in 1959. He was able to face the resignation first of a main prop of the ministry, Lord Salisbury, after three months and then three Treasury ministers after a year, dismissing the latter as 'little local difficulties'. Later, when he was worried by bad by-election results in July 1962, he sacked seven of his Cabinet. There have been controversies about these events, some commentators seeing an adverse reaction among some of the Conservatives to the 1962 sacking as more significant than the fact that they took place in the first instance, while others have tried to suggest that Macmillan was himself edged out, if not sacked, in 1963.[5]

But the overall impression of the lead he was able to give his government and of his main role in its changing policies towards Africa and towards the Common Market is clear, and now it is possible to read Macmillan's own estimate of his role and of the machinery of government at this time. Describing his management of the Cabinet, he says:

> The Cabinet must continue as it had always been, collectively responsible for all great decisions. ... In addition we must continue to work partly through a small inner group of Ministers, meeting occasionally, but chiefly through Committees of Ministers dealing with particular groups of subjects. That it was possible to operate the system and yet retain the confidence of the Cabinet as a whole was due partly to the generosity of my colleagues and partly to the

skill of Sir Norman Brook and my private secretaries in gaining their confidence.[6]

On the power of the Prime Minister he concluded that:

> A careful reading of histories and memoirs makes me feel that the power of a Prime Minister has steadily grown. Although he is only *primus inter pares*, the very complexity of affairs leads to the concentration of authority in his hands. ... In a Department, the burdens, however onerous, are to some extent limited. As Prime Minister one is answerable for everything. In a Department the ordinary life with one's colleagues and with the outside world goes on in a normal atmosphere and follows a more or less normal pattern. The Prime Minister's position is unique. Strangely enough it is also very lonely. I imagine a captain of a ship to have something of the same feeling.[7]

Harold Wilson modelled himself in many ways on Macmillan, but he seems to have been a little less clear about the long-term issues and about decision-making in this sense, though he was just as definite on questions of tactics, of appointments and of power. Wilson himself notes that:

> It was, and is, my strong view that, in modern Britain, the PM's grip on every major subject, particularly finance and economic affairs, industrial policies and industrial relations, foreign and Commonwealth affairs, including such major issues as Rhodesia and the Nigerian crisis, should be such that he can dictate, without a departmental brief, the main text of any speech he has to make, in Parliament or in the country. ... I find it hard to resist the view that a modern head of government must be the managing director as well as chairman of his team, and this means he must be completely *au fait* not only with developments in the work of all main departments, including the particular responsibility of No. 10, but also with every short-run occurrence of political importance.[8]

Wilson was quite clear that the task of coordinating and pushing through policies fell to him. At a Chequers week-end in 1965 he told his Ministers that:

> ... where Bills or White Papers were bogged down in Committees

with bureaucratic or legalistic difficulties or inter-departmental dissension, the issues should be brought to me for settlement, either by Cabinet or by *ad hoc* ministerial meetings under my chairmanship.[9]

Richard Crossman puts an interesting gloss on these comments. In his Godkin Lectures, he revealed that under Wilson, a Cabinet minister who lost his case in committee could only appeal to the full Cabinet with the consent of the chairman of the committee.

This is a great limitation on the power of the Cabinet Minister, the. fact that he has got to get the consent of the chairman. . . . He and the Prime Minister have ways of seeing that a Minister cannot get to the Cabinet even if he wants to.[10]

Crossman concludes his estimate of the Prime Minister's position by saying:

In the battle of Whitehall this man in the centre, this chairman, this man with a Department, without apparent power, can exert, when he is successful, a dominating personal control. This explains why a British Cabinet is always called a 'Wilson Cabinet' or a 'Macmillan Cabinet'. It is because every Cabinet takes its tone from the Prime Minister. The way the Prime Minister conducts it and administers it will give it its particular tone. Usually it is dominated by his personality.[11]

This was certainly the case under Wilson and he not only provided the tone and acted as spokesman and coordinator-in-chief but he took over whatever appeared to be the main issues of the day. Besides, like most modern Prime Ministers running the major lines of foreign policy when it involved dealings with other heads of states (summit meetings and Commonwealth conferences), he also took over the exploratory talks before Britain applied to join the Common Market and the main attempts to reach a settlement with the Rhodesian leaders; at one time he assumed responsibility for the Department of Economic Affairs; and he handled the negotiations in the five major labour disputes during his period as Prime Minister.

Unlike Wilson, Heath entered No. 10 Downing Street determined to be as different from Wilson as possible but, as had happened earlier when Bonar Law took over from Lloyd George, though the atmosphere in the upper reaches of the Heath government was very different, the degree of control exercised by the Prime Minister was as great as before, or even increased. Mr David Watt summed up his impressions of the first two years of the post-1970 Conservative administration thus:

> The fact is that the potentialities of the office have already been considerably extended by Mr Heath and they will almost certainly be expanded still further before he is done with it.[12]

It was certainly clear to members of the House of Commons that Mr Heath had established a very definite ascendancy over his colleagues, his party and, to a lesser extent, over the House as a whole. He did this by a mixture of qualities and methods. The main techniques were the traditional ones of the power of appointment and of patronage. Men who did not fit into his view of the future of the Conservative party and of the country were excluded from office, while lesser figures could now once again receive political honours. But perhaps Mr Heath's greatest weapon was his own determination. With a clear view of where he wanted the country to go and a great deal of preliminary policy preparation while in opposition, he held his party's nose to the political grindstone. Thus he never relented in his determination to drive through the Bill by which Britain would join the European Economic Community, though at times this involved real courage on some occasions when close divisions were predicted in the House. When he changed his mind, on devaluation (floating the pound downwards), on aid for certain declining industries, or on a prices and incomes policy, these new policies likewise were driven through the House.

In his handling of the machinery of government, Mr Heath made as much, or perhaps even more, use than his predecessors of Cabinet committees or 'task forces' (to use this terminology permits the inclusion of non-ministerial experts or a senior official) to produce proposals on particular problems. A good example was the task force he set up in early 1972 to devise a new policy for Ulster which excluded a number of ministers with strong views on the subject. While he tried to avoid giving the impression of constant activity which Mr Wilson generated, and also to avoid taking matters out of the hands of the appropriate minister, Mr Heath in fact improved the machinery of prime-ministerial control. The separate Civil Service Department was created by Mr Wilson, but Heath used it to make the Whitehall machine more responsive to his ideas on management and efficiency and he also created the Central Policy Review Staff. This is Lord Rothschild's 'think-tank', which advises any Cabinet minister but in reality is used by the Prime Minister more than by anyone else. Mr Heath also increased the No. 10 hold on government publicity. This began under Mr Macmillan with a special minister in charge; Mr Wilson shared the task with a group of personal aides in his political office but Mr Heath took on the job himself with the assistance of a senior civil servant. Finally – like previous premiers – he used the Cabinet secretariat and the Secretary to the Cabinet as principal assistants to the Prime Minister and through control of the Cabinet agenda and the choice of chairmen for the Cabinet committees and task forces, pushed a degree further the control Mr Wilson exercised by those methods.

In mid-1972 there was talk of creating a 'Prime Minister's department' sparked off by the publication of Sir Richard Clarke's lectures entitled *New Trends in Government*.[13] The idea was to combine the Cabinet secretariat, the No. 10 staff, the Civil Service Department, the Central Policy Review Staff and the section of the Treasury which prepared and supervised the five-year rolling programme of public expenditure into a single department. There was even talk of adding a section which would organize and coordinate all Britain's dealings with the Common Market. To have done all this would have once again increased the distance between the Prime Minister and his colleagues and have allowed him to operate more easily and rapidly as the managing director of Great Britain Ltd.

It must be emphasized that none of this would have altered the basic limits on the powers of a Prime Minister which are his need to carry most of his colleagues and of his party in the House of Commons with him and to avoid confrontations with entrenched and powerful pressure-groups at home or, in some cases, abroad; but the trends observable under Macmillan, Wilson and Heath show that very different men in this post all feel the need to grasp the levers of central control. Indeed, if they do not, no-one else can. And each has ended up trying to increase his effectiveness at doing this.

With this weight of actual evidence and range of agreement among observers, it might have been assumed that the controversy of the early 1960s could have been allowed to fade away and the issue regarded as settled. But dissentient voices on the other side have still been raised.

One which appeared to reject the entire concept of prime-ministerial government was Patrick Gordon-Walker's book, *The Cabinet*.

Mr Gordon-Walker begins by saying that 'nowadays the mode is to assert that the British system of government is being assimilated to the American and that in consequence the whole Cabinet structure is being or has been transformed.' After listing all the factors which have increased the power of the Prime Minister, he concludes:

> Although by the 1950s and 1960s the office of Prime Minister had risen greatly in status, although the Prime Minister had acquired an authority different in kind from that of his colleagues, he was still not independent of the Cabinet . . .
>
> A strong Prime Minister can be very strong. He can sometimes commit the Cabinet by acts or words. But he cannot *habitually* or often do so.
>
> A Prime Minister who habitually ignored the Cabinet, who behaved as if Prime Ministerial government were a reality – such a Prime Minister could rapidly come to grief. He would be challenged by his colleagues in the Cabinet and on occasion over-ridden. . . .[14]

He finally asks the basic question 'where does political authority lie?' and answers:

> I hope to have shown that the answer in Britain is – 'In the Cabinet and in the Cabinet alone.'[15]

A second very similar line of argument was put forward by Mr Ronald Butt in *The Power of Parliament*. The theme of the book is that recent academic and journalistic comment has underestimated the real influence, or power, as the title suggests, of the House of Commons. The explanation of the misunderstanding, according to Butt, is partly an over-estimate of parliament's influence between the 1830s and the 1880s, partly a failure to realize that the essential task of the majority in the House is to support and maintain a government and therefore an inability to appreciate the undercover or behind-the-scenes influence that elements in the majority can have on government policy.

While such a thesis has no direct bearing on the discussion about the powers of a modern Prime Minister, Butt goes on in his Conclusion Part II to make some general points on this issue:

... a Prime Minister must operate in a Cabinet ... and is restricted in his choice of colleagues ... however skilfully he may prepare the ground by private negotiations with colleagues or by the initiation of policies in Cabinet committees ... he cannot, in the last resort, steamroller wholly unacceptable policies through the Cabinet. ...[16]

Although the Prime Minister may be an initiator in certain key areas of policy, or take over the handling of a policy when it assumes emergency dimensions, it is obvious that he cannot oversee the whole area of government and that by far the larger part of policy initiation reaches the Cabinet from departmental ministers.[17]

He concludes that:

The reality of collective Cabinet responsibility is not disproved by the great power of the Prime Minister in modern conditions; by the support he (and other Ministers) receive from the parliamentary majority; or by the public presentation he receives as a 'President-type' figure at election periods and at other times of intense political activity. Prime-Ministerial power must be understood as varying with political circumstances and with the personal fortunes of the man who wields it.[18]

A third, somewhat idiosyncratic version of this position was put forward by Ian Gilmour. His underlying conviction is that British government has not responded to the challenges facing the nation in the last fifty years and though the source of the weakness is never pinpointed, it would appear to be, according to Gilmour, an undue number of internal constraints on decisive action. He concedes the apparent supremacy of the executive but, as he wishes to argue that it is crippled by indecision, he must conclude that the Prime Minister is unable or unwilling to act and that this is because he can be thwarted by the great departments of state acting through their representatives in the Cabinet. So he says:

There are in Britain virtually no institutions able to say 'no' to the executive. The Monarchy is above politics; the second Chamber has been paralysed; the House of Commons passes the Government's legislation; the law has been made subservient to the executive; local government has been subjected to Whitehall control; the press and television are hamstrung by government secrecy. Yet the negative principle in British government usually wins. British government says 'No' to itself. It is a paper tiger.[19]

As examples of a failure to act, he cites the Tory failure over the economy in the 1970s, appeasement in the 1930s, the failure to join the EEC in the 1950s, the inability to reform local government or the trade unions or to solve the Irish question. Mr Gilmour concedes virtually every aspect of the increased powers of the Prime Minister who, he accepts, 'is today much more powerful than any of his colleagues.'[20] 'Cabinet ministers are in the position of being tenants of the Prime Minister with no security of tenure. The power of appointment and dismissal confers an enormous preponderance of influence upon the Prime Minister.'[21] He notes that those who resign from a Cabinet are in a hopelessly weak position and that it is difficult and dangerous to challenge a party leader. But the real check is the need to carry the Whitehall departments: 'it is these citadels of power in Whitehall which bar the way to a Prime-Ministerial system. While the political landscape round the Prime Minister has been flattened by the disappearance of most other peaks of power, the Whitehall pyramids have maintained or increased their stature.'[22]

The general case against the proposition that the Prime Minister's powers have increased during the period covered by the present study is perhaps best summarized by A.H.Brown.[23] His conclusion is that 'as government becomes more complex and the range of governmental activity continues to expand, a Prime Minister has to run fairly hard simply to stay in the same place' in terms of his powers within the government. Mr Brown is not specific about the countervailing forces but casts doubt on all aspects of the Prime Minister's position, either by pointing to manifold other influences that might have to be considered or, where Prime Ministers have taken definite action, by claiming that these are special cases.

There are also some events in recent years which could be, and no doubt will be, cited as evidence in the next round of this perennial controversy. On the side of Mr Butt and those who claim that the House of Commons still provides an effective counter to executive power, there is the decision of the Labour government in 1969 to withdraw the Parliament (No. 2) or House of Lords Reform Bill. This was withdrawn after it had been debated for nine nights and only five out of eleven clauses had been passed. Then, on the side of Mr Gordon-

Walker and the continued authority of the Cabinet (which is also in part Mr Gilmour's point about the strength of the great departments), there is the defeat of Mr Wilson and his Secretary of State for Employment, Mrs Barbara Castle, over their desire to legislate on industrial relations in 1969. The rest of the Cabinet finally turned against the Prime Minister and he had to abandon the proposal.

What is the answer to these arguments? In the first place, the dispute has become very narrow. It can be sustained only by the critics suggesting that those who write about prime-ministerial government are alleging an American presidential pattern or a dictatorial system, a capacity to ride roughshod over ministerial colleagues, Whitehall and the Commons, or at least a hoodwinking or by-passing of the Cabinet. For instance, Mr Gordon-Walker feels that his task is to rebut a theory that the Prime Minister is 'independent of the Cabinet'[24] and to explain that 'a Prime Minister who habitually ignored the Cabinet ... would be challenged by his colleagues'[25] .... 'He cannot, like an American President, ignore their views.'[26] Mr Butt is, in his opinion, countering the case that the Prime Minister 'is ... able to make his Cabinet and his party in Parliament follow his policies and wishes',[27] so that 'the Prime Minister, for all practical purposes, is the Executive in Britain' with 'the members of the Cabinet little more than his dependents'[28] and that he can 'dispense with consideration for the views of his party....'[29] Mr Gilmour is rejecting the idea that the Prime Minister 'can now do what he wants'[30] and asserting, in contrast, that no Premier could 'always get his way with the Cabinet'[31] which 'is not the Prime Minister's Court'.[32] 'The ascendancy of the Prime Minister has not concentrated all decision-making in his hands.'[33] Mr Brown sets out to produce evidence which will 'make nonsense of the Prime Minister as a wielder of "autocratic" power',[34] who sets out to by-pass his Cabinet, a body composed entirely of 'lieutenants' whom he can manipulate without fear of denial or defeat.

In terms of these statements, the dispute has little point as such crude assertions are valueless and barely relevant to a system where the Prime Minister and his colleagues are drawn from the same party with the same mutual interest in political success. But these generalizations do conceal some important differences on specific issues and on the overall interpretation of British political institutions. Mr Gordon-Walker has an important point when he asserts that the Cabinet is the court of last appeal in the event of deep political divisions. If there is a split in a government or if the Prime Minister wants a new policy departure which might lead to a split, the matter will come to a climax or be resolved in the Cabinet. But it is quite a different matter to argue that the Cabinet takes all the important decisions. He realizes that in the Labour government of 1964–70, this was not the case and devotes a chapter of his book to considering why the policy of retaining bases and troops east of Suez was never discussed in the Cabinet until the devaluation of November 1967 made it inevitable. He comes up with no satisfactory explanation because, in fact, the decision to stay east of Suez was taken by the Wilson–Callaghan–Brown triumvirate when the Labour Cabinet was being formed (as was the decision not to devalue) and the Prime Minister was not prepared to have this policy reopened by the Cabinet. The same was true over devaluation – 'the un-mentionable' – and it was realized that to insist on talking about this question, as several able ministers would have wanted, would have been to challenge the authority of Mr Wilson, and none of his colleagues was prepared to do this.

On the question of the power of the Commons, the case mentioned above of the Parliament (No. 2) Bill is totally misleading. It was an exception because it started as an agreed constitutional reform which had, in propriety, to be taken on the floor of the House. Then the parties quarrelled and while the Conservatives did not oppose the Bill, they allowed some of their backbenchers to join government rebels in prolonging debate. As a result, the government lacked the normal party sanctions and felt unable to force through a guillotine motion. While they could not call on party loyalty as there was no direct party clash, filibustering by individual MPs went on. So the government never lost a division but progress was slow – fast by nineteenth-century standards, but the Labour government had other urgent legislation to bring forward and preferred to abandon the Lords Reform Bill rather than spend several weeks more on pushing it through.

The experience of the Heath government shows that there is no need to revise recent estimates of the influence of the House of Commons. When the Prime Minister decided to push through the Bill embodying Britain's terms of entry to the Common Market he seemed to be taking a great risk, but he was relying on the evidence that no government with a majority in the House had been beaten on a major issue of confidence in this century. The reaction among irritated Conservative anti-Marketeers came out when they defeated the government in December 1972 on an order bringing in certain immigration regulations dealing with both EEC and Commonwealth citizens; an issue on which feelings could be registered without endangering the government or its basic policies. On the whole, Mr Heath and his colleagues led their majority towards a disengagement with industry and then back into state aid and nationalization, towards a free labour market and back into a statutory incomes policy, towards a reduction of public expenditure and back to an increase of £700 million above the Labour party's targets and simply expected and got the loyal, a little reluctant, but sufficiently regular support of their majority in the House.

The points made by Mr Gilmour are most interesting, though there appears to be some confusion. The first evidence he cites is a list of the failures of the British executive, but the later implication is that these occurred because of internal contradictions within the political and institutional system, that 'British government says "No" to itself'. Further on, he argues that the basic internal conflict that paralyses action is the clash between the Prime Minister and the great departments of state. But if the list of failures is examined – economic policy in the 1920s, appeasement in the 1930s, failure to join Europe in the 1950s, failure to reform local government or the unions or to prevent the drift to civil war in Ireland – the explanations are very different. In the case of economic policy in the 1920s, neither the Treasury, the Board of Trade, the academic economists nor the politicians had solutions. They did not cancel each other out; they were united in total bewilderment and attachment to classical economic doctrines.

On appeasement, on the other hand, there was a clash between parts of the Foreign Office and between the Defence ministries and the Prime Minister, which the latter won overwhelmingly and easily, the outcome being one of the best examples of prime-ministerial power in this century. The failure to join Europe in the 1950s was due to an overestimate of Britain's world power and Commonwealth base that was shared by the Foreign Office and Conservative leaders and it would be hard to say which saw the light first, though throughout the 1960s, when it had come down on the European side, the Foreign Office pressed hard for British membership of the EEC. Our failure to join throughout the 1960s was due not to internal dissension but to General de Gaulle's veto. Again, it is difficult to blame divisions between or within Whitehall and the politicians for the Irish fiasco between 1918 and 1922 (or between 1969 and 1973). Above all, this was due to external problems based in Ireland, and chiefly in Ulster.

The two examples Gilmour quotes where there is more evidence on his side are local government and trade union reform. In the first case, reform proposals came up just after the war, but the Attlee administration could make no progress. By the 1960s, White Papers and Commission reports were produced but the Bills only went through in 1972 and 1973 to come into effect in 1974–5, though further changes or second thoughts due to the report of the Commission on the Constitution might yet alter the final result. On trade union reform, the Conservatives saw the problem but no Labour minister lasted long enough to tackle it. Mr Wilson appointed the Donovan Commission in 1965 and decided to legislate in 1969. His attempt had to be abandoned but was taken up by the Conservatives after 1970: their Industrial Relations Act was eventually passed.

It might seem as if, in these two examples, Gilmour has put his finger on a serious weakness in British government and, in so far as the Prime Minister of the day wanted action on these issues, it has been shown that he lacked power. But in both these cases, there were no divisions within Whitehall. All the departments wanted these reforms and none of them resisted pressure by the Prime Minister or his colleagues for change. The countervailing forces all came from outside or from party politicians. Over local government reform, the problem was that the public was uninterested, while the local party stalwarts were often councillors and deeply hostile to any change. As a result, no minister and no Cabinet was willing to move unless they had at least the agreement of the local authority associations and the latter were opposed both to change and to each other's possible lines of reform. This deadlock was only broken by the fact that the Labour government had to respond to the reports of the Royal Commissions it had established.

Trade union reform was an even more positive example of resistance from outside the machinery of government. It had its echoes inside as the adamant opposition of the TUC in 1969 encouraged Labour MPs to resist. It will probably never be established what was the decisive force in killing Mr Wilson's and Mrs Castle's proposed Bill. The Labour Chief Whip told the Cabinet that the Bill would not pass. The Cabinet swung against the Prime Minister but there is some evidence that he was prepared to proceed even with most of the Cabinet opposed and despite the report of the Chief Whip but was deterred when he realized that some senior ministers were prepared to carry their objections to the length of combining against him. What can be asserted is that had the TUC accepted the Bill, opposition inside the Labour party and inside the Cabinet could easily have been overcome by Mr Wilson.

Thus in both these cases, it was not powerful Whitehall departments or internal dissensions but external political pressure-groups, each with affiliations within the political parties, that prevented action in one instance by successive ministers of local government and in the other by the Prime Minister and his chief lieutenant on labour relations. These examples do raise the difficult question of how far, in certain respects or certain areas, government in Britain can achieve their objectives, of how far in this sense Britain is governable. They do not, to the same extent, question the power of the Prime Minister within the apparatus of government itself, though it is clear that when certain pressure-groups are really roused (particularly those that are built into the political parties) they can find sufficient potential centres of resistance within the Whitehall–Westminster machine to enable them to question and even thwart the most determined political leaders, including the Prime Minister of the day.

Perhaps the analysis of political power in Western systems of government has concentrated too much on the working of the systems themselves. The power of the American President is limited if he cannot win a war in Vietnam or prevent speculation against the dollar. Hitherto, these considerations have been largely left out of discussions of the balance of power between the President and Congress or between the White House and the various federal agencies. Similarly, the fact that Britain now has less influence in world politics than the United States has not normally affected comparisons between the relative authority of the Prime Minister and the President; this has been taken to refer only to their scope within their own political systems. But clearly this limitation has been too narrow if the power of each to enforce a prices and incomes policy has been excluded from the reckoning simply on the grounds that such a policy involves dealings with big business and the trade unions.

Thus some reservations must be made about the scope open to an able and determined Prime Minister in Britain if he locks in combat with major power blocks in the community, though this does not invalidate the descriptions of British government quoted above (p. 7) when the questions at issue are part of the normal run of British domestic and foreign policy. This distinction comes out when one turns to the comments of Mr A.H.Brown, which are all about the working of the political system. His characteristic is a genuinely academic inability to grasp the effects of power within a political system. For instance, he challenges the evidence that a Prime Minister can keep issues off the Cabinet's agenda and says there is a standard procedure for raising issues and that 'it is not in a Prime Minister's interest to keep matters off the agenda which his colleagues want to discuss.'[35] But Wilson did keep devaluation off the agenda, despite a widespread desire to discuss it, for two and a half years. In fact, no Cabinet minister would have contemplated asking for such a discussion as to do so was clearly to challenge the mainstream of government policy and the Prime Minister himself. It would be like a professor asking to raise 'student discipline' on the senate when the Principal had staked his reputation on a particular line of reprisals after a widely publicized student riot. ˙

Similarly, to say that widespread use of Cabinet committees under chairmen selected by the Prime Minister with reference, as under Wilson, to disputed issues to the Cabinet only with the PM's permission; to say that this strengthens the ministers on these committees more than the Prime Minister shows an unbelievable academic remoteness from reality. So does the argument that the Cabinet secretariat and its briefing help Cabinet members to assert their views more strongly against the Prime Minister or the departmental ministers concerned. But the point made by both Brown and Gilmour that the existence of departmental policies makes it harder for a determined Prime Minister or Cabinet minister to swing the official machine into line has some force. This is why Conservatives around Mr Heath complained of the flabbiness and unresponsiveness of the system, but this shows that they (and the Prime Minister) wanted and expected to impart an overall tone and direction to the government. There is evidence, mentioned above (p. 11–12) that machinery is being evolved to make this easier.

This series of essays on the record in office of British Prime Ministers in the twentieth century did not set out to prove any particular thesis. Each is an estimate of the man and his ministry; but what does emerge is that, however the policies and aptitudes of these men differed, they all implanted their personality, their tone, on their Cabinets and administrations. It makes sense to talk of Balfour's ministry or Chamberlain's period, and the successes or failures of these governments cannot be separated from the characteristics of the men who led them.

Notes

1. R.Blake, *The Unknown Prime Minister: The Life and Times of Andrew Bonar Law, 1858–1923* (London 1955), p. 480.
2. L.S.Amery, *My Political Life* (3 vols, London 1953–5) II, p. 246.
3. *Observer*, 23 August 1961.
4. J.P.Mackintosh, *The British Cabinet* (London 1962) pp. 451–2.
5. The controversy is dealt with in detail in the second edition of J.P.Mackintosh *The British Cabinet* (London 1968), pp. 432–3, where it is argued that Macmillan could easily have remained in office had he not thought he had to resign because of his health.
6. Harold Macmillan, *Pointing the Way* (7 vols, London 1972) V, pp. 22–3.
7. *Ibid.*, pp. 31 and 42.
8. Harold Wilson, *The Labour Government, 1964–70: A Personal Record* (London 1971), p. 45.
9. *Ibid.*, p. 137.
10. Richard Crossman, *Inside View* (London 1972), p. 57.
11. *Ibid.*, p. 68.
12. The *Financial Times*, 5 May 1972.
13. See the leading article in *The Times*, 24 August 1972, and *The Financial Times*, 25 August 1972.
14. P.Gordon-Walker, *The Cabinet* (London 1970; 2nd ed. 1972), p. 13.
15. *Ibid.*, p. 164.
16. R.Butt, *The Power of Parliament* (London 2nd ed. 1969), p. 450.
17. *Ibid.*, p. 451.
18. *Ibid.*, p. 454.
19. I.Gilmour, *The Body Politic* (London 1969), p..2.

20. *Ibid.*, p. 208.
21. *Ibid.*, p. 204.
22. *Ibid.*, p. 218.
23. A.H.Brown, two articles in *Public Law* (Spring and Summer 1968).
24. Gordon-Walker, *op. cit.*, p. 95.
25. *Idem.*
26. *Ibid.*, p. 96.
27. Butt, *op. cit.*, p. 445.
28. *Ibid.*, p. 446.
29. *Ibid.*, p. 455.
30. Gilmour, *op. cit.*, p. 206.
31. *Ibid.*, p. 207.
32. *Ibid.*, p. 217.
33. *Ibid.*, p. 220.
34. Brown, *op. cit.*, p. 30.
35. *Ibid.*, p. 50.

Arthur James Balfour

Peter Fraser

No British Prime Minister took office with more apparent advantages than Arthur James Balfour. Without any party crisis or general election, he quietly assumed the first place in the government when his uncle, Lord Salisbury, retired in July 1902. Balfour had been Leader of the House of Commons since 1895 with an overall Unionist majority of well over a hundred. The so-called 'khaki' election of 1900 had increased this majority, giving the Unionists 402 seats as against 184 Liberal, 2 Labour, and 82 held by Irish Nationalists, etc. Nor did Balfour have to fear opposition from the House of Lords, which was predominantly Unionist in sympathy. The two men who might have contested his claim to the premiership, Joseph Chamberlain and the Duke of Devonshire, in fact graciously acquiesced. The duke was privately annoyed that his prior claim, by nineteenth-century conventions, was not courteously acknowledged, and indeed there was something specious in *The Times*'s contention that a premiership held in the House of Lords had suddenly become out of the question. As for Chamberlain, it was contended that he did not have the qualities needed to lead the Commons, a function then perceived as more important than leading the government. Chamberlain had designs, and spoke earnestly. Balfour was not known to have any particular designs, and spoke urbanely. Some Conservatives regarded Chamberlain, the Liberal Unionist, as an 'alien immigrant' who could never be a real Conservative. It was no surprise, therefore, when following the practice of the time a Conservative party meeting endorsed the King's choice by electing Balfour Leader of the party, without any note of dissent.

Effective parliamentary opposition to the Unionists hardly existed, for the Liberals were hopelessly divided over the Boer War and the public squabbles between Lord Rosebery and Campbell-Bannerman.

But, oddly enough, lack of party challenge and a huge majority had confirmed Balfour in a style of parliamentary leadership which practically nullified his advantages. His management of the Education Bill of 1902 is an example of followership rather than leadership, redeemed by some brilliant improvisations. The Bill absorbed a vast length of parliamentary time, inflamed the country, and produced party splits and massive cross-voting. Its merits are largely due to the skilful use of Liberal votes to counter Tory rebels. And if Balfour did not readily claim the amenities of party discipline, such as the closure or threat of resignation, to further his own measures, he was no less parsimonious in supporting the measures of his colleagues. His premiership is largely a story of party misfortunes originating in divisions within his parliamentary party over issues which he either failed to clarify or left to chance. Serious splits in the Unionist party developed over the fiscal question and army reform, creating deadlocks and public disputes in parliament and the country and forcing Balfour into a more and more withdrawn and autocratic style of leadership.

It was Balfour's chief merit that he tackled great national problems which Salisbury had ignored. It was his tragedy that he lacked the popular touch or imaginative appeal to make his policies acceptable or even intelligible to the country. If Asquith was the 'last of the Romans', Balfour was the 'autumn rose' of the late-Victorian tradition of statesmanship. All accounts agree about his extraordinary personal charm, his verbal and dialectical brilliance, and his almost feminine gentleness and courtesy. He was a good listener, and 'Tell me, ...' would frequently preface his flatteringly attentive conversations. He combined impeccable aristocratic connections with intellect of a high order and a scientific bent. Tall and gangling, with a languid, precious air easily caricatured into the donnish, aloof personality with large forehead and pince-nez, he seemed 'above the greed and grind of common nature'. But he could be ruthless, and had surprised his critics and earned the title of 'bloody Balfour' by his implacable treatment of Irish extremists. His cold and detached mind enabled him to play the political game with hard and unyielding cleverness. Beatrice Webb saw him as 'strong-willed, swift in execution, utterly cynical, and honestly contemptuous of that pitiful myth "Democracy". He is pitiless: and whether they be hysterical Irishmen or whining unemployed, he would crush them between a flirtation with one of the Souls, and the reading of a French novel or German treatise.' Under the façade of a bored aesthete the real man kept a tight grip on the strings of power, persuading, charming, dividing his opponents while never yielding one iota of his own convictions. He followed others in describing his own tactics as 'dexterous', and no doubt approved of his public image as a skilled rapierist foiling the onsets of ordinary reasoners by subtlety and refinement of argument.

If, like his uncle, Balfour had been content with the ordinary kind of obstructive Conservatism – what Salisbury had described as seeing to it that things went to the devil slowly – he might have had an equally untroubled premiership. But Balfour's ambitious administrative policies touched the public on very sensitive nerves, in particular the sore points of protective tariffs and food taxes, voluntary enlistment and 'militarism'. To solve the real and pressing problems of fiscal policy and defence the country required a dynamic, popular leader of the type of Chamberlain or Lloyd George. Balfour had no sympathy with ordinary men, nor interest in their problems. Popular slogans and electoral programmes were nothing to him but objects for witticism and disdain. A recurrent theme in his private papers is the imbecility of his parliamentary followers – a prejudice which his private secretary, J.S.Sandars, knew well how to exploit. Here lay Balfour's weak spot: he was utterly unable to share even with the most distant empathy the feelings and prejudices that form the staple of politics. He tried to nurse his party like a sick patient, taking its temperature daily via the reports from his secretary and the Whips' office. He was easily panic-driven into giving way to popular cries. But he could no more understand the vagaries of opinion than he could predict the weather.

Not surprisingly, Balfour preferred to work behind the scenes, where his ingenuity could have full scope. The kernel of his Education Act, the clause concerned with the managers of denominational schools, was characteristically Balfourian in being immensely unpopular and immensely successful over the years. He brought the Irish Chief Secretary (Wyndham) into the Cabinet, and the resulting Irish Land Act succeeded where Gladstonian governments had failed in creating an Irish peasant-proprietary class. He broke the deadlock in the question of liquor licensing between the uncompromising exponents of local veto and the publicans, so that the social evil of the pub on every street corner was gradually mitigated, compensation being given from the profits of the trade. The efficiency of the House of Commons itself was greatly improved by the operation of the 'railway timetable' procedural rules which drastically curbed the rights of private members to air grievances and obstruct government Bills. No one had been more sceptical about the value of the rights of private members than Balfour.

Before considering the more public and more disastrous of Balfour's departures as Prime Minister it would be as well to take account of two important limitations on his freedom of action. One was the 'family' government he inherited from Lord Salisbury, variously called the 'Hotel Cecil' and the 'Byzantine succession'. The other was the inter-party 'compact' between the Conservatives and Liberal Unionists.

The Cecil 'cousinhood' formed the customary nucleus of the Conservative party. When Balfour took up the government his brother Gerald was already at the Board of Trade, and his cousin Lord Selborne was at the Admiralty. Lord Salisbury's heir, Viscount Cranborne, was Under-Secretary for Foreign Affairs, and was brought into the Cabinet as Privy Seal by Balfour in October 1903. The two brothers Lord Hugh Cecil and Lord Robert Cecil soon became militant free-fooders and did not obtain office, but the former was a prominent literary exponent of Conservatism and the established Church, who could be neither excommunicated nor reconciled to Balfour's mode of leadership, while the latter retained much personal influence. Balfour certainly went along with the idea that the Cabinet should be a coterie of friends and relatives. When Chamberlain resigned he was replaced at the Colonial Office by Balfour's close friend Alfred Lyttelton, a celebrated cricketer, whose sister is said to have been about to become engaged to Balfour just before her untimely death. Lyttelton was however far more able than his brother, whom Balfour made Chief of the General Staff. Another close friend, George Wyndham, brother of Balfour's alleged mistress Lady Elcho and former private secretary to Balfour himself, has already been mentioned as entering the Cabinet with the post of Irish Chief Secretary. Lord Lansdowne retained a commanding position in the Cabinet as Foreign Secretary, valued by

Balfour more for his good humour than his ability. 'I should not call him very clever,' he said in later years. 'He was ... better than competent ... I was always very fond of him. I was his fag at Eton, you know.' Finally, as if to emphasize the idea that outsiders were unwelcome, Balfour brought his ex-Chief Whip, Akers Douglas, into the Cabinet as Home Secretary. These men constituted the inner circle of the ministry. It should not, however, be assumed that they could be manipulated easily. Their effect was limiting rather than emancipating. Relatives have better opportunities for access and interrogation, and lifelong friends cannot lightly be ignored or dismissed. Balfour was only head boy in the prefects' common room. He had to retain the Cecils in the party, and he could never flout the sometimes unimaginative advice he got from his inner circle.

As for the compact with the Liberal Unionists, this constrained Balfour to play ball, so far as he could, with Joseph Chamberlain and Devonshire even after these had resigned from the government, for they possessed powerful parliamentary followings. Indeed a majority of Unionist MPs espoused Chamberlain's policy of tariff reform, which appealed to agricultural protectionists, and in the eyes of the public Balfour appeared to be tied to Chamberlain's erratic chariot. Devonshire carried great weight with the respectable middle classes, and even after his hostility to Chamberlain drove the duke into electoral negotiations with the Liberals (which failed) Balfour was still obliged to accommodate the fiscal views of the duke's followers under his policy of 'comprehension'. As a reinsurance Balfour made Chamberlain's son Austen Chancellor of the Exchequer in the government reshuffle, while Devonshire's heir Victor Cavendish became Financial Secretary of the Treasury. The two Liberal Unionist chiefs, now at war with one another, each professed to follow Balfour's personal leadership, but Balfour's fiscal formulations became submerged in the hubbub of warring tariff reformers and free-fooders. The Prime Minister became in fiscal and other cognate matters a kind of umpire, a constitutional monarch in his own party.

The policy of fiscal reform was originally one of an administrative kind which Balfour could readily support. The previous government had approved the Brussels Sugar Convention in March 1902 designed to prevent the 'dumping' of underpriced sugar in Britain by foreign growers. This was a sacrifice of the interests of home consumers and manufacturers in favour of the West Indies. It was also agreed in principle not to allow German trade discrimination against Canada on account of the gratuitous preference which Canada had conceded to British manufactures. To curb 'dumping' was not a serious offence to free-trade purists or 'Cobdenites', for if dumping became widespread the British electorate might blame it for creating unemployment, and the Labour movement might veer towards protectionist demands. Trade 'retaliation', which was Balfour's peculiar policy (though it could be traced back to Disraeli) was a more serious affront to Cobdenism. Imperial preference, even in the minimal form proposed by the Colonial Conference in August 1902, was politically even more explosive, for it implied food taxes. Food taxes existed and the actual proposal, taken up by Chamberlain as Colonial Secretary, was that the existing corn tax should be retained on foreign corn and remitted on Canadian corn. But, of course, Chamberlain was choosing the most favourable ground on which to perpetrate the ritualistic violation of a sacred principle. Even Balfour understood the potential sense of outrage in the public's reaction to the proposal when he steered it through the Cabinet in November 1902, for in his report to the King he emphasized the need to walk warily. But at this point Balfour made a fatal mistake. He presented Ritchie, then Chancellor of the Exchequer, with a loophole through which the decision could be jettisoned if Ritchie did not feel inclined to include it in his budget.

From Ritchie's correspondence with permanent officials of the Treasury and with his predecessor, Hicks Beach, it is clear that he was encouraged to regard the proposal as heralding a departure from free trade to protection, and that his refusal to embody it in the budget was a foregone conclusion. Though one of Balfour's few outside choices, Ritchie was no great asset to the government, and he soon became a disloyal conspirator. Believing that it was 'really a contest between free trade and protection' (as he wrote to Hicks Beach), Ritchie bided his time until the budget was so near that no successor could replace him. Balfour was now trapped. He asked Ritchie if he meant to resign on the issue, and was told (in Ritchie's words) 'I certainly meant to resign, and ... nothing would induce me to stay.' Ritchie had his way. But so too did Chamberlain, who took the game into his own hands and in his well-known speech of 15 May at Birmingham launched the policy of imperial preference into public discussion as one which would loom largely at the next election. That same day Balfour appeared to be acting in concert with Chamberlain when he explained to a large delegation of Unionists, many of them protectionists, that the corn tax, which had been totally abandoned, could not stand on its own but might be renewed in association with 'some great change in national policy'.

The government was now in a quandary, for Chamberlain had promulgated a policy which it had accepted but dared not announce. Balfour's choice was really between boldly endorsing the policy, and boldly going back upon it. Passions were far too strong on either side of the question, even in his own party, for any compromise. Those who went with Chamberlain wanted to link tariffs with social reform. Those who suspected Chamberlain tended to think, like Winston Churchill, that the policy 'must lead to the establishment of a complete protective system involving commercial disaster and the Americanization of English politics'. Certainly Chamberlain regarded imperial preference as the beginning of a great popular and forward-looking programme, and Devonshire objected to it for precisely this reason. Balfour now made the mistake of attempting to treat the policy as purely an administrative one, and tried to find some compromise formula of his own that would retain both Chamberlain and Devonshire while forcing the out-and-out free traders in the Cabinet to resign. Hence the somewhat ludicrous 'fiscal inquiry' pursued by the government during the summer of 1903 while sections of the Unionist party took up emotionally partisan positions. On 13 August Balfour presented to the Cabinet his own fiscal policy of retaliation, embodied in a treatise *Economic Notes on Insular Free Trade*, and while no decision was reached he was hopeful, as he reported to the King, that 'if (as he does not doubt) Mr Chamberlain shows a readiness to accept Mr Balfour's scheme, and to modify some of the plans which he has from time to time put forward rather hastily,' the majority of the Cabinet would support 'the moderate, yet important, suggestions' made by himself. At this point Balfour had not definitely abandoned imperial preference, but was about to make a determined effort to convert Devonshire to it.

That Balfour finally failed to retain the duke was a disaster to his government, but not entirely a deserved one. The duke, as he himself readily confessed, was somewhat deaf and occasionally inattentive. The discussion of imperial preference at the Cabinet of 19 November 1902 had been 'long and elaborate' but, no Cabinet minutes being kept, there was no record of the final resolution except for Balfour's letter to the King. Devonshire later asserted, writing to Chamberlain, that he had failed to understand that a decision 'was even provisionally taken', and that 'it must have been taken after very little discussion'. One is tempted to assume that he had fallen asleep. He therefore resented Chamberlain's Birmingham speech as an unwarranted departure, and soon he was falling prey to Ritchie's insidious approaches. Ritchie was now not only the head of a cabal within the Cabinet, but was prepared to carry his disloyalty to Balfour to the point of breaking up his ministry. He was being advised politically not only by Unionist free traders outside the government like Hicks Beach, Lord Goschen and Lord James of Hereford, but also by the 'mandarins' of the Treasury. Sir Francis Mowatt, the doyen of the civil service (just, luckily, retiring), wrote to Ritchie: 'I have known for the last two years that he [Chamberlain] contemplated an appeal to the country on protection coupled with preferential treatment, and old-age pensions thrown in as a bait to the working-class voter ...' Such villainy deserved, no doubt, any kind of opposition, and Mowatt counselled opposition from within the Cabinet. Chamberlain's speech, he insisted, 'was largely prompted by his desire to reverse your victory in the Cabinet. If you were to resign he would have succeeded, but if you remain ... your victory becomes more established every day, and, with it, your power to resist a policy which you regard as disastrous. ... It will be infinitely strengthened if you succeed in restraining your colleagues, or if, at all events, you remain with the colours when they desert them.' Ritchie looked beyond Balfour to a possible Devonshire–Rosebery ministry, and through Lewis Harcourt he was in touch with the Liberals. With two other Cabinet ministers, Balfour of Burleigh and Lord George Hamilton, he planned a concerted resignation, but only if Devonshire could be induced to go out with them.

The government's policy was to be agreed at a Cabinet on 14 September, and made public by Balfour at the annual conference of the party (the NUCCA) at Sheffield on 1 October. Devonshire's doubts, expressed in a copious correspondence with Balfour, elicited from the latter a written statement of fiscal propositions to be put before the crucial Cabinet, and Devonshire was indiscreet enough to show these to Ritchie, adding in his letter of 9 September: '... now that I see them in black and white, I feel that our position would be an impossible one if we were to assent to them ... I am afraid ... there is no alternative to the disruption of the government.' Devonshire arranged to see Ritchie the day before the Cabinet, and duly agreed to resign over the issue of imperial preference and consequent food taxes.

But the position had altered. Chamberlain also had now decided to resign, for the purpose of 'explaining and popularizing' the 'principles of Imperial union', but in writing this to Balfour he also suggested that Balfour press the policy of retaliation at the Cabinet 'although it will necessarily involve some changes' in the government. Balfour, understandably, did not read out this letter at the Cabinet, but followed its plan of dropping preference from the government's policy while insisting on retaliation. The dissentients offered their resignations, which Balfour accepted with decided promptitude. Chamberlain offered his, after Balfour had declared preference to be impracticable at that time, but since this was not a Cabinet decision Chamberlain's verbal declaration was not taken seriously. Days of confusion followed this meeting. Ritchie's formal letter of resignation was based, quite improperly, on an objection to food taxes, so rigidly was he set in his original design, which Balfour had foiled. He had to get Balfour's consent to alter his text. Devonshire decided to remain in office when it was finally brought home to him that Chamberlain was really going to resign. But Ritchie gave the old duke no peace. He accused Balfour of sharp practice, and Devonshire of breaking a compact. Goschen and Beach had called on him, he told the duke, to ask 'how it happened that I sent in my resignation when you remained, it having been impressed upon me, as I think I told you, that it was most essential we should act together.' The duke was not sure of the answer, lost his sleep, wrote abortive letters of resignation, and finally took the occasion of Balfour's Sheffield speech to resign decidedly.

The resignation of five Cabinet ministers and a Financial Secretary (Elliot) had no parallel in Victorian times, and seemed an absurd price, in the eyes of the public, for the tame fiscal policy outlined at Sheffield. Even the 'Sheffield minimum', as it came to be called, failed to gain the adhesion of the bulk of the Unionists. Most people took sides for or against Chamberlain, and the strife was carried into the constituencies by the Tariff Reform League, which began to exact pledges from sitting members or candidates. The minority supported the Free Food League, but while the 'free fooders' were insignificant in numbers they had respectable leaders, including Lord Hugh Cecil, Goschen, Hicks Beach, James, and now Devonshire. They could cause great embarrassment to Balfour by speaking on Liberal platforms and even, on occasion, by threatening to vote with the opposition. Balfour could do nothing to prevent this internecine struggle, for he accepted the principle that the selection of candidates should remain with the constituencies. Had he made his own fiscal policy the official policy of the party (as he had made it the policy of the Cabinet) it might have been otherwise. But in order to retain the Cecils and the free fooders, whom Chamberlain wished to 'eliminate', he kept the fiscal question an 'open' one in the parliamentary party. Needless to say, this rendered pointless the adoption of his policy by the Cabinet.

In one respect the ministerial reshuffle of October 1903 strengthened Balfour's position in the government. It enabled him to chair the Committee of Imperial Defence himself as Prime Minister, to create a secretariat for it so that it became a Prime Minister's department, and to alter the principle of its composition so that he could invite anyone to attend. The last change, away from an ex-officio composition which favoured the conservatism or departmentalism of the War Office and Admiralty, was justified by Balfour on the ground that by being able to invite Colonial representatives (Borden of Canada was soon to attend) the Prime Minister could create an institutional link with the self-governing Colonies which might evolve in the direction of imperial federation.

A demand for the reform of the Cabinet's Defence Committee, which had proved practically useless during the Boer War, greeted Balfour on his accession to the premiership. As formulated in a paper by H.O.Arnold-Forster which Balfour circulated to the Cabinet in October 1902 this was a demand for something like the German Great General Staff, only modified to suit the special needs of a maritime world-wide empire. The Defence Committee had been more a Cabinet committee to economize on military and naval estimates than an expert body concerned with strategic planning or war direction. Arnold-Forster wanted the addition of non-political experts and scientists, and the publication of the defence policies and defence needs of the empire as they were finally agreed. He rightly felt that imperial defence was largely a matter of persuading the public to pay for it. Balfour allowed this conception to be abandoned in favour of one which the War Office and Admiralty heads (Brodrick and Selborne) preferred. Thus the new Defence Committee of December 1902 was chaired by Devonshire and dominated by the political heads of the service departments and their intelligence staffs. But soon under Balfour's influence the Committee of Imperial Defence (as it came to be called in 1903) was undertaking ambitious strategic studies. Its chief concern was the defence of India, and the nature of the home army that would be needed to reinforce the Indian army in a war with Russia. For Balfour imperial defence could be defined in one word, 'Afghanistan', and indeed the completion of the Orenburg–Tashkent railway was soon to bring Russian forces to within four hundred miles of Kabul.

But Balfour's real problem over defence was political. The country was demanding a reduction of the army estimates, greatly inflated by the South African war, and it was impossible in England to contemplate conscription, the only means of obtaining cheaply a huge army with the capacity of expansion in wartime. Social changes had made the regular army's recruitment more difficult. The pay and conditions attached to long service overseas were relatively less attractive. Arnold-Forster's solution was to create a short-service army at home which would attract and train intelligent and sturdy recruits who after two years would pass into a reserve capable of being rapidly embodied in war. Balfour knew and approved this plan before he placed Arnold-Forster at the War Office, but his real reason for finally choosing this rather abrasive enthusiast was probably that as Parliamentary Secretary to the Admiralty Arnold-Forster was a committed exponent of the idea that the navy, not the army, was the proper instrument of home defence. He could therefore be supposed to favour drastic economies on the military side of home defence.

It is to Balfour's credit that he boldly and decidedly adopted the 'blue water' axiom that serious invasion was not to be feared. The doctrine was that if sea supremacy were maintained, enemy transports on the required scale would not be able to get through. If sea supremacy were lost, invasion would be unnecessary, since when food supplies were cut off the island would have to capitulate within weeks. These ideas were emphatically proclaimed by Admiral Fisher, then Second Sea Lord, and it was Fisher whom Balfour chose to implement them in association with Lord Esher. Esher was a long-standing friend of Balfour's as well as a confidant of King Edward, whom he advised especially on army matters. As a member of the Elgin commission Esher had regaled the King with personal impressions of the generals interviewed about the miscarriages of the Boer War, and had built up the conviction that a 'clean sweep' was needed at the War Office. Esher's minority report seemed likely to assuage public indignation when the findings were published, for it contained a drastic scheme for War Office reform. Balfour tried to induce Esher to take the War Office, before reverting to Arnold-Forster, but accepted Esher's alternative plan for a War Office Reconstitution Committee chaired by Esher which would exercise an unofficial, or perhaps one should say irregular, overlordship. A triumvirate of Esher, Fisher and Sir George Clarke (a 'blue-water' journalist and defence expert suggested by Fisher) set about an ambitious reform of the whole bureaucracy of defence which became one of the monuments of Balfour's premiership.

The conception of the Committee of Imperial Defence as a body of variable membership chosen by the Prime Minister, whom it directly advised, seems to have been Balfour's. The notion of a separate secretariat independent of the service departments and constituting a Prime Minister's department originated in memoranda by Lord Esher. Balfour at first resisted Esher's plea for an independent secretariat and wanted its personnel to be drawn from the intelligence branches of the Admiralty and War Office. Esher wanted a kind of imperial general staff directly under the Prime Minister, including officers representing India, possibly Canada, and other departments. He called it a 'Department of Scientific or Theoretical War Problems, wholly distinct from the Admiralty or the War Office, and subject to the authority of the Prime Minister himself. Balfour compromised, allowing the appointment of a permanent head of the secretariat (Sir George Clarke) but insisting that his subordinates should be on temporary secondments from the intelligence branches. The result was that Clarke became a kind of political aide to Balfour and was manipulated by Esher, who took over at critical junctures, such as when a secret sub-committee of the CID chaired by Esher reviewed aspects of Arnold-Forster's army scheme, or when after Balfour had resigned another 'conference' consisting essentially of Esher and Clarke instituted the well-known 'military conversations' with France. Nevertheless the permanent secretary of the CID lasted under the Liberal governments, and Hankey became a general aide to Asquith when the CID went into virtual abeyance during the First World War. Ironically, something like Esher's original conception was almost instituted as part of Lloyd George's Cabinet secretariat with Hankey still in the key role. Hankey was supposed to form a military secretariat, and set up a civilian counterpart, but he did not do so.

Unfortunately for Balfour, an unforeseen political storm drove the new CID secretariat into political courses from the moment of its formation in April 1904. Arnold-Forster was pressing on the Cabinet an army scheme which failed to produce dramatic economies. These in the War Minister's view would best come from the total abolition of the militia and volunteers. This almost incidental proposal was a political hornets' nest, for many Tories in Parliament and some ministers were militia officers, and for Liberals the militia ballot and the 'old constitutional force' of the volunteers were sacred cows, guarantees for the voluntary principle in military affairs and manifestations of that 'patriotic spirit' on which voluntaryism depended. Balfour withdrew his support from Arnold-Forster, whose scheme was postponed to the next session. In extenuation of this seeming weakness one might admit that the political situation was dangerously analogous to the fiscal crisis of the previous year, with the same suggestions of Unionist revolt and opposition exploitation of a popular cry. But Balfour was not content to drop the scheme which he had previously approved. He allowed Clarke as secretary of the CID to formulate alternative army schemes based on reviving the militia and expanding its numbers into a 'half-trained horde' (as Arnold-Forster called it) which would supplant the War Minister's home reserve as the means of reinforcing the Indian army in a war. A fortnight's annual camp, and part-time training, would be far cheaper than two years of intensive military training, so that Clarke's scheme would yield more men sooner for possible service in India. Arnold-Forster offered to resign, but Balfour could not afford another failure, and so through 1904 and 1905 he used the CID and its secretary to obstruct his War Minister in a disgraceful series of tortuous intrigues and deceptions.

Part of the problem was the class prejudice of what Esher called the 'officer caste'. Arnold-Forster's home short-service army offended professional prejudices, as his contempt for the militia offended the landed gentry. If given his own way, the War Minister would have wounded the susceptibilities of the career officers more seriously by instituting an elite general staff. Here Balfour's obstruction was again decisive. He agreed against Arnold-Forster's wishes to the appointment of Sir Neville Lyttelton as Chief of the General Staff and First Military Member of the new Army Council set up by the Esher Committee. Lyttelton was a poor choice and soon an acknowledged failure, but Balfour stubbornly refused to remove him. While he remained Arnold-Forster declined to form a general staff under him. Saddled with three other unassertive Military Members, Arnold-Forster was obliged to approve a plan for a general staff which would do little to attract brains into the army or higher command, or give staff officers a distinct career or even promotion on merit. His plan was passed finally just in time for Haldane, under the Liberals, to plagiarize it. In army matters therefore Balfour was actively responsible for thwarting the plans of his own War Minister, including an army scheme which would by 1914 have created a large trained reserve. He prevented the formation of the kind of general staff which might have made the army as professional as the navy. No doubt he did not wish to create a focus of rivalry with the CID. Also he became persuaded, in view of the intention of the Liberals to reduce the regular army, that the auxiliary forces should be preserved as the most likely source of men for the expansion of the regular army in wartime.

The conduct of foreign affairs during Balfour's premiership has been extensively covered by recent historiography, and this intricate subject does not lend itself to abbreviation. Certain generalities, however, seem well established. Balfour was, like his predecessors, a Prime Minister who dominated the Foreign Office. By bringing the CID to bear on strategic questions he was able to enter with confidence into commitments of a novel kind, especially the entente with France and the second Japanese treaty. Balfour became convinced that Russia was the real enemy of the British Empire, as an intangible power expanding almost imperceptibly, like a tide, and seemingly destined to encroach on Persia and India. At all events Russia seemed the only major power against which the British army might be engaged, and hence in the negotiations for the renewal of the Japanese treaty of 1902 which were carried on during the final stages of the Russo–Japanese war in 1905 Balfour successfully pressed for Japanese military assistance in India if Russia attacked Afghanistan. Such an attack was, he contended, rendered more likely by the terms of the proposed treaty, which guaranteed Japan against the attack of one power (not two as formerly) and hence might deter Russia from her Far Eastern ambitions in favour of ambitions in Afghanistan or Persia. It was a bold move to invite a Japanese obligation towards India, which perhaps might make a Liberal government feel that no British reinforcements needed to be provided for in strategic planning.

The German menace was perceived by Balfour and his colleagues as a naval one, at least before 1905. The Admiralty under Selborne, and elements in the Foreign Office, had been sufficiently aroused by German press hostility and by the type of vessels being built for the German navy to have identified Germany as the most dangerous potential enemy by 1902. Even Chamberlain, who had through his career taken France for an enemy and Germany for a friend and who had made a sincere effort to reach an understanding with Germany before the South African war, turned decidedly in the opposite direction in 1902. This reorientation affected thinking on naval ratios and facilitated the negotiations for an entente with France, but in the deliberations of the CID under Balfour there is no suggestion before 1905 that British military intervention on the Continent needed to be considered.

The CID devoted a great deal of time, on the other hand, to the problem of military reinforcements to India. The defence of the north-west frontier of India was a non-problem to those military experts who, like Sir Charles Dilke, thought the terrain of Afghanistan impassable by any large force. Much uncertainty surrounded the 'camel equations' involved. Balfour's choice was either to indulge the costly projects for strategic railways and a prospective battle-line in Afghanistan to meet a Russian advance, or to discourage railways approaching Afghanistan from either side and try to keep the area 'non-conductive'. He seems to have chosen the latter, though lack of financial means to meet Kitchener's escalating demands may have been the determining factor. Even so, the CID decided to make the military reinforcement which India would need the standard that should determine the size of the British army. By the scale of the armies engaged in the Russo–Japanese war Kitchener's demand for a reinforcement of some 100,000 men looked modest, but it was beyond the capacity of the regular army as organized and deployed over the empire. The 'striking force' which under Balfour was developed at Aldershot led by Sir John French was certainly far more immediately mobile than anything the Cardwell system could have produced, but it was small and without trained drafts to keep it in the field. Since he had defeated Arnold-Forster's army scheme, Balfour was obliged to use the CID, or rather the secretary of it supervised by Lord Esher, to discover an alternative source. Clarke submitted to Balfour many variant schemes for an 'imperial militia', which might provide 'second-line' troops with six months' training. And although Balfour failed to get any such scheme through his Cabinet, much less through Parliament, he was able to pass on Clarke's work (Clarke remaining as secretary of the CID) to the Liberals and to Haldane.

Doomed by the manifest trend of by-elections to defeat at the polls, and plagued by the defection of tariff reformers and critics of his handling of military affairs, Balfour had not by 1905 enhanced his party's respect for his leadership. In an attempt to neutralize the 'free food' cry he had given a pledge, speaking at Edinburgh on 3 October 1904, that if returned to power he would convene a 'free' Colonial conference, and if 'any large plan, of Imperial union on fiscal or other lines' were adopted, it would be submitted to the electorates of Britain and the Colonies before being implemented. Here was a 'double election' pledge which, in the eyes of Chamberlain and the tariff reformers, would muzzle them in the coming contests and destroy their appeal. Balfour's logic was that if the Unionists were going to lose the elections they ought to concentrate on fighting the policies of Liberals and socialists. He could not see the value to party morale and to the longer-term interests of Unionism of propounding some positive programme which would admittedly be defeated. Chamberlain cornered him at some after-dinner conferences, but in vain. Soon **the** opposition discovered that Balfour was not even prepared to defend the policies of the tariff reformers in the Commons. Private members' resolutions were met by the previous question only with increasing difficulty and exposed an opening rift in the Unionist benches. Finally a resolution was put down for 22 March 1905 condemning Chamberlain's 'general tariff' policy. The Cabinet of 21 March spent its whole time considering Balfour's objections to moving the previous question once more. 'In the eyes of most people,' Balfour reported to the King, 'this amounts to protection: and it would certainly be impossible to induce the party not to vote against it.' In parenthesis it ought perhaps to be pointed out that Balfour himself accepted the general tariff before a year was out. But on this occasion he 'absolutely refused to consent' and threatened to resign that afternoon. He got his way, and met the resolution by leading his followers out of the House as a theatrical gesture.

The tariff reformers had threatened not to support Balfour if he would not support them, and now they sent a deputation to him, headed by Chamberlain, to present a document signed by 142 MPs. It claimed that two-thirds of the parliamentary party favoured the Chamberlain policy, or would do if Balfour gave the word, while only 27 Unionists were totally opposed to any fiscal change. Four were unclassified, including Balfour himself. The result of the deputation was a very Balfourian fiasco. At a small conference on 16 May Balfour suddenly made what seemed an unbelievably generous bargain. He would not dissolve Parliament till the autumn of 1906, so that the next Colonial conference would meet 'automatically' that summer prior to any election. The results of the conference and the government's views on them could then be referred to the British electorate. Balfour even accepted that these might include the general tariff, to which he had 'no objection in principle'. Chamberlain for his part offered to give up his advocacy of tariff reform in the meantime and was willing to reenter the government as minister without portfolio.

Balfour had carefully assured himself that there was nothing in his previous speeches which explicitly precluded this compact. Had he stuck to it, things might have gone much more favourably for the Unionists. But he was frightened out of it by the free-fooders. Ritchie and others took the view that the plan contravened the 'double election pledge', which gave them in their own eyes the moral justification for threatening to join the Liberals in a vote of censure. This might, it is true, have put Balfour in a minority, which required a theoretical defection of about 34 Unionists to the opposition, but it was surely a risk worth taking, and perhaps no better example exists than this of Balfour's timidity in the face of any kind of party revolt. On 26 May he informed Chamberlain that he did not expect to remain in office until 1906.

For the remainder of his premiership Balfour retired into a more aloof style of leadership, as party meetings, deputations, or any such encounters with his followers merely aggravated the schism. He clung to office in order to complete the Japanese treaty, but his majority became precarious. Finally he was advised by Sandars to remonstrate with his supporters, even though Sandars believed that 'As a rule a party meeting is a method (for many reasons) to be avoided.' On 18 July therefore Balfour explained the government's programme and pleaded for better attendance at a meeting of some 260 Unionists, including Chamberlain, convened at the Foreign Office. Two days later he suffered an awkward parliamentary defeat and was hard put to it to explain why his government did not thereupon resign.

Balfour's last concern was to ensure the survival of the CID under the premiership of Campbell-Bannerman, its sworn enemy. Here Esher was indispensable. One idea, 'often discussed' between Esher and Lord Knollys, the King's secretary, was to create a 'permanent sub-committee' or 'permanent element' which would ensure continuity. Unfortunately the only salaried member of the CID, Lord Roberts, was proving a great embarrassment to Balfour by being associated with the movement for compulsory military service. He was summoned to Balmoral, where Esher, Balfour and Haldane were also present. The future of the CID, and the future composition of the prospective Liberal government, were discussed, and Esher was able to inform

Sandars that 'The King wants to strengthen *while you are in office* the permanent element'. It was perhaps a blessing for Balfour that Roberts finally insisted on resigning before the election, and also that Chamberlain's fiscal intransigence provided a pretext for not meeting the new session of Parliament and hence for resigning prior to a dissolution, a *non sequitur* whose logic Balfour explained to his colleagues in a Cabinet paper. Esher was called in to the conferences which Balfour held to consider how and when he should quit office, and on being asked to replace Roberts as a permanent member of the CID Esher insisted that Sir John French should be appointed also. The permanent element had materialized.

There is no evidence that Balfour anticipated that the permanent element would initiate the important military 'conversations' with France after his resignation but before the Liberal ministers had recovered from electioneering. He had approved in July the formation of a sub-committee, with power to summon officers. Esher had pressed him to enlarge this to cover 'naval and military expansion in the event of war', and one may fairly assume that after various modifications of the plan to preserve continuity the permanent element superseded the sub-committee, which never met. It is perhaps odd that Balfour never explored the most obvious combined operation, that of sending the Aldershot force to France or Belgium, especially in view of the treaty obligation to Belgium. It was this problem that the permanent element took up in December 1905. Admittedly the prospect of a German invasion of France seemed to be in the offing, as also a possible German violation of Belgium. The entente was not, of course, a military alliance, but, as the permanent element soon discovered, it was necessary to find out what the French would do in the event of an invasion through Belgium. This was the original point of the 'conversations', and the fact that Balfour had not seen it speaks volumes for the imperial, non-European orientation of his military policies.

When Balfour resigned on 4 December 1905 electioneering had, as it were, broken out. He had ranged against him on the fiscal question, which his party took to be the most important issue of the day, the majority of Unionist MPs, the bulk of the Unionist press, and both the NUCCA and the Liberal Unionist Association. It is a tribute to the great personal respect in which he was held, rather than an indication of the inherent power of a Prime Minister at this time, that he could thus oppose his party without greater symptoms of revolt. After the election, which tipped the balance of the party decidedly in Chamberlain's favour, a movement arose to displace Balfour from the leadership and to make the Conservative Central Office amenable to the will of the party. This failed because in the last analysis the party preferred an eminent leader to any particular programme, and this gives the clue to understanding the position of a Conservative Prime Minister at this stage of the constitution. Parliamentary eminence was of far more consequence than electoral appeal or legislative programme. Chamberlain represented the opposite approach, and was suspect with many Conservatives on precisely this ground. The influence of the Crown, especially in military and naval matters and in foreign affairs, could be a powerful adjunct to the authority of the Prime Minister, and through Esher and Knollys Balfour exploited this asset to the full. Over the actions of the most dominant members of his Cabinet, Chamberlain and Devonshire, he had little control, and even when these had resigned Balfour was never more than *primus inter pares* in his Cabinet. He got round this by taking decisions elsewhere, at the CID or at informal discussions with the ministers concerned. There does not seem to have been any regular inner Cabinet, which in view of the entrenched disputes is understandable. In matters of foreign policy and defence Balfour had a very free hand and could make dramatic and consistent progress. In matters of social policy and legislation he adopted a defensive stance, seeing a long-term antagonism between 'imperialism' in the best sense and 'socialism' (in the Continental sense). Ignoring the demand for a positive programme, he preferred to act as the exponent of the values of a vanishing patrician class fighting a rearguard against the general trend towards more popular forms of government. In the Tory tradition he has more in common with Lord Liverpool, the great administrator who staved off parliamentary reform, than with Peel or Disraeli. Only Balfour could have played this role in the twentieth century, and only Balfour would have thought of doing so.

Henry Campbell-Bannerman

José F. Harris
Cameron Hazlehurst

The premiership of Sir Henry Campbell-Bannerman fell between the publication of two classic works on the English political system – the first volume of Ostrogorski's *Democracy and the Organisation of Political Parties*, published in 1902, and Professor A.L.Lowell's *The Government of England*, which appeared within a few weeks of Campbell-Bannerman's retirement and last illness in April 1908. Both Ostrogorski and Lowell made observations on the powers and functions of contemporary Prime Ministers which largely determined the subsequent direction of 'prime-ministerial' studies.[1]

Ostrogorski remarked that a silent revolution had occurred in the relationship between the electorate and the leader of a party. The old-fashioned notion of local representation had gradually broken down and had been replaced by 'personal plebiscites' and 'a sort of popular Caesarism', whereby electors no longer chose their MP from among competing individual candidates but chose a Prime Minister from among the leaders of rival parties. In addition, Ostrogorski noted a similar change in the situation of a party leader or Prime Minister among his senior colleagues. He was no longer merely the 'first among equals', but 'a general in command of an army. He barely consults his staff, the front bench, and practically confines his confidences to an inner circle of a few lieutenants.'[2] This judgement was endorsed by Lowell, who emphasized the difference between the Prime Minister's *de jure* and *de facto* role. In Cabinet discussions, the Prime Minister was technically no more than a chairman and his office was formally non-existent until December 1905. Nevertheless, his control of political appointments, his determination of the agenda of public business, and his responsibility for interpreting Cabinet policy to the Crown gave him a power that was far superior to that of any of his colleagues. Whereas the resignation of a minister merely created a vacancy, the resignation of a premier involved the formation of a new Cabinet – the fate of a Prime Minister and his ministry were inextricably intertwined.[3]

Both Ostrogorski and Lowell based their observations primarily on the evolution of politics under Disraeli, Gladstone and Salisbury. But both claimed to be analysing current political trends as well as describing historical events, and both claimed that these trends were inherent in the system and not merely in the dominant personalities of particular Prime Ministers. It is, therefore, instructive to see how far the premiership of Campbell-Bannerman conformed to the constitutional theories of the leading political analysts of the day.

'C.B.', as he was widely called, had few of the obvious qualifications for the premiership – neither charisma, nor outstanding administrative competence, nor even personal dedication to public business and to the exercise of political power. Although he was one of the few survivors of the Gladstone-Rosebery regime of 1892–5, his ministerial experience was narrow. He had been an inoffensive Chief Secretary for Ireland and a conventionally Cardwellian Secretary for War. Among parliamentary Liberals his position prior to the King's summons was far from assured; for although he had led the opposition in the Commons since 1899 he had never been accorded the vacant leadership of the whole Liberal party. In the country at large he was renowned for his championship, if not actual leadership, of the 'pro-Boer' resistance to the South African war; and in parts of the Conservative press he was portrayed as a 'sentimental radical', an ignoble materialist, and the greatest anti-patriot since Charles James Fox.[4]

Apart from his consistent opposition to aggressive imperialism, however, Campbell-Bannerman was very little known outside Westminster and official Liberalism before 1905. Although he certainly trusted some of his colleagues more than others, he had never gathered round himself a faction or a personal political machine, nothing comparable with Joseph Chamberlain's Birmingham, the 'Hotel Cecil', or Rosebery's Liberal League. Nor was he closely associated with any of the celebrated Liberal interests or national groups – the nonconformists, land reformers, or the Celtic fringe, for example – although his sympathies lay to a certain extent with all of these movements. As a disciple of Gladstone his active radicalism was mainly directed towards 'constitutional' issues, such as the promotion of self-government and civil freedom; but even in these matters he was at once more progressive and more pragmatic than a true Gladstonian ought to have been. He was, however, rather out of touch with new cross-currents in early twentieth-century Liberalism, with the aspirations of Liberal imperialists, of 'Lib–Labs', and of social reformers and radicals like Charles Masterman and David Lloyd George. Apart from his basic allegiance to the party, Campbell-Bannerman was emphatically not a joiner; and as a leader in the Commons he constantly opposed the creation of divisive groups within the Liberal machine.[5]

Campbell-Bannerman's temperament and personal inclinations were predominantly those of an old-fashioned radical backbencher, rather than a Prime Minister and leader of a national party. Although he was usually identified with the 'business' Liberals, his active involvement in commerce had ended forty years earlier, and his outlook was that of a cultivated and cosmopolitan country squire. To Margot Asquith he was 'essentially a *bon vivant, a boulevardier* and a humorist', with whom she always enjoyed 'great laughs'; and W.T.Stead unkindly remarked that C.B. would be more useful to the party if he went on a vegetarian diet.[6] He liked non-political company and Continental travel, preferred yëllow-backs to blue books, and hated long sessions, late sittings, and bad parliamentary dinners. He disliked appeals to 'self-interest' in political argument, and deplored the raucous vulgarity of 'Jingoism' and 'Chamberlainism' as much as their political aims.[7] As a public speaker he was indifferent, and prone to gaffes. The verbal cartoons that graced his conversation and correspondence were lost on a public platform – although occasionally one of his more pungent phrases, such as the famous indictment of 'methods of barbarism', was chalked up on the score-board of contemporary political debate.[8] He was popular in the Commons and in the party, but his popularity was personal rather than political. He was liked and admired for his honesty, good humour, and freedom from rancour. But many, even of his warmest supporters, doubted his ability to rejuvenate Liberalism, to win a general election, or to form an effective government.

In almost every respect, therefore, C.B. lacked the conventional prerequisites for the capture of higher office, let alone the most glittering prize of all. He had no new political message, no widespread popular appeal, not even the wholehearted and consistent support of a majority of his party.[9] Instead of campaigning to make himself known to the electorate, he spent large parts of each year abroad, undergoing 'cures' and ministering to the needs of his invalid wife. He passed through the drawing-rooms and watering-places of Europe like a charming but secondary character in a Henry James novella. How, then, did such an amiable but essentially private individual rise to the rank of Prime Minister? How did he execute the functions of the office? And how, if at all, did he influence the evolution of the modern premiership in Great Britain?

C.B.s elevation to the leadership of the Liberal party in the Commons occurred almost by accident. Early in 1895 he had expressed the desire to escape from party politics by taking the vacant speakership of the House; and at the same time he openly doubted whether his health would permit him to hold office in any future administration. He occupied a peculiar and vital position, however, in Lord Rosebery's faction-ridden government, and both 'radicals' and 'imperialists' agreed that he could not be spared.

After Rosebery's resignation and ostensible retirement from politics in 1896 it was argued that only an ex-premier was entitled to lead the Liberal party while it was in opposition. The party leadership therefore lapsed; and the Liberals were led by Harcourt in the Commons and by Kimberley in the Lords. Harcourt was constantly embarrassed, however, by Rosebery's forays back into politics and by the ex-premier's persistence in making leaderlike speeches; and Harcourt publicly and indignantly renounced his impossible position in December 1898.

Harcourt's retirement gave rise to a rapid and far-reaching series of misunderstandings within the Liberal ranks.[11] John Morley published a letter of sympathy for Harcourt, thereby misleading his colleagues into believing that he also was withdrawing from public life. The way, therefore, seemed to lie open for the leadership of Asquith, who was acceptable to both radicals and imperialists, and was widely recognized as the outstanding Liberal debater and administrator of his generation.

However, leading Liberals, Asquith among them, agreed that, as a polite recognition of his seniority, the position should first be offered to Campbell-Bannerman.[12] C.B. surprised some of his colleagues by treating their invitation after the fashion of his Highland forebears as a 'call'. After some hesitation on grounds of ill-health, he accepted their offer; and his election as leader in the House of Commons was ratified by a meeting of Liberal MPs at the Reform Club in February 1899.[13]

Although there was strong residual support for Harcourt and Rosebery, Liberals in both camps welcomed the new leader as a man of the 'centre' under whom at least an outward show of party unity might be maintained. But, at the end of 1899, divisions in the party were accentuated by the outbreak of the South African war. C.B., who had sat upon the commission of inquiry into the Jameson Raid, was convinced that the conflict had been unnecessarily provoked by the Cape government and the Colonial Secretary. From the start, he condemned the inefficient prosecution of the war, although not until he learned of concentration camp methods against civilians in the Transvaal did he actively support the 'pro-Boers'. He carried with him a majority of the parliamentary party; but a vocal minority of leading Liberals – including Asquith, Grey, Fowler, and Haldane – followed the lead of Rosebery in supporting the government.[14] The imperialists were popularly vindicated at the polls in October 1900, when C.B.'s own massive majority was reduced at Stirling Burghs to a few hundred. He found himself in the unenviable situation of an opposition leader who had led his party to a crushing electoral defeat, and whose most able colleagues openly followed the lead of a rival statesman.[15] He appealed to Asquith to tone down his public adherence to Rosebery in order to preserve party unity;[16] but Asquith did not respond, and for a few weeks in the summer of 1901 the two factions publicly exposed their differences by pointedly and rather ludicrously dining apart.

Throughout the war not only the imperialists but moderate pro-Boers like Bryce, Ripon, and Herbert Gladstone clearly hoped for the restoration of Rosebery as a necessary prelude to the re-forging of a Liberal *via media*.[17] And, for nearly four more years, Rosebery continued to menace C.B.'s leadership by failing to convince his followers that he really intended, as he stated, to plough a lone furrow. C.B., by comparison, seemed as helpless as an upturned turtle; but his survival was ensured by a number of factors, some purely fortuitous and some the result of careful political calculation.

In the first place, Campbell-Bannerman behaved as though he would willingly efface himself if ever Rosebery wished to return to the party leadership. This readiness to step down was probably quite genuine. For reasons which are obscure to the historian, Rosebery had a reputation in some elements of the party as a force for unity; and C.B. was, above all, remarkable for his loyalty to the party.[18] But C.B.'s self-effacing attitude was entirely in accordance with self-interest, since it enabled him to avoid open rivalry with Rosebery and the imperialist faction. It was also, perhaps, a shrewd gamble, since Rosebery's taste for consistent intrigue was no greater than his stamina for government; and his vacillation proved to be C.B.'s most enduring political card.

C.B.'s greatest fear was that Rosebery would assume the leadership, not of the Liberals, but of a breakaway centre party of dissident imperialists, whose existence would irrevocably bifurcate the whole Liberal movement.[19] Certainly, there were several quasi-political coteries in the early 1900s which would have been prepared to support the kind of radical imperialism fleetingly propounded in Rosebery's Chesterfield speech in December 1901.[20] A new party organization seemed to be foreshadowed in the creation of an Imperial Liberal Council in 1900 and of Rosebery's Liberal League in 1902. The Liberal League has been described as 'a complete political machine', and it proved capable of putting nearly ninety candidates in the field in the 1906 general election.[21] Asquith, Haldane, Grey and Fowler became vice-presidents. But the League's most active leaders were as conscious as Campbell-Bannerman of Rosebery's capricious ways. They were all, in any case, much too cautious to abandon the mainstream of Liberalism for a body with a head tucked underneath its arm.

Although the Liberal imperialists despaired of recalling Rosebery, they were slow to perceive the gradual accretion of power which sheer survival as leader in the Commons gave to Campbell-Bannerman. Surrounded by influential and ambitious colleagues, C.B. in his manifest weakness had his own peculiar strength; and it is probable that if he had been clearly marked out at the beginning of 1902 as a future Prime Minister the imperialists would have taken positive steps to depose him. As it was, the fortunes of Liberalism seemed so low, and the next general election so remote, that a palace revolution seemed irrelevant and unnecessary. There was much talk, but little actual promotion, of a realignment in party politics in 1903 and 1904. When the Education Act and tariff reform began to rally opposition to the government it seemed futile to complicate the Liberal revival by raising policy-issues that were at least temporarily quiescent. Furthermore, it was Asquith rather than Campbell-Bannerman who led the rhetorical attack upon Chamberlain and was most strongly identified with the defence of the principles of free trade.

Nevertheless, C.B.'s steady leadership and damping down of party discord gradually won him increased support among the Liberal rank and file. The many faithful members who sought only to perpetuate Gladstonian ideas found in this 'capable, trusty, kindly, humorous man' the leader they were seeking;[22] and movements like the Young Scots Society and the powerful dissenting cohorts mobilized by Lloyd George demonstrated the existence of a staunch body of support for the old orthodoxies.[23]

C.B. and his Chief Whip, Herbert Gladstone, began unobtrusively to prepare for a general election when there was a marked by-election swing against the government in June 1903.[24] But there was no general anticipation of an imminent change of government before the beginning of 1904. C.B. avoided the formation of anything resembling a 'Shadow Cabinet'. In opposition, he confined political consultation to Grey and Gladstone and the remnant of 'ex-Cabs' who had held a Cabinet position in 1895; and he did not appoint Liberal 'policy committees', for fear of arousing among members false hopes of future office.[25] Partly for this reason, politicians and the press were slow to identify C.B. as the most probable next Prime Minister.

In October, Sir Henry Lucy, the Westminster barometer, thought that when Balfour resigned he would advise King Edward to call upon C.B.; but he predicted that the King would prefer Lord Spencer and that C.B. would get a consolation peerage as Secretary for War.[26] An administration led by Spencer seemed at that time by no means unlikely, for although this elderly Whig magnate took little active part in politics, he was personally unobjectionable to both Liberal camps. King Edward's dislike of C.B.'s foreign policy was well known, and it was recalled how in similar circumstances Queen Victoria had passed over Harcourt for Rosebery in 1894. Moreover, in October 1903 C.B. had reiterated his fears about his health; and in 1904–5 much of the political entertaining normally arranged by the opposition leader took place at Lord Spencer's house in St James's. In fact, however, Spencer secretly surrendered his claim by seniority to the premiership. Before his stroke late in 1905, he and C.B. had twice drawn up lists of a future ministry on the assumption that the premier had to be in the House of Commons.[27] Yet, although Balfour's resignation was expected at any time throughout the parliamentary session of 1905, it was not until June that W.T.Stead, with characteristic prescience, publicly tipped C.B. as the next Prime Minister with the greatest Liberal majority since 1832.[28] A few weeks later, C.B. met King Edward at Marienbad, and the King was apparently reassured by his moderation – particularly his acceptance both of the 'continuity' principle in foreign policy and of the Entente Cordiale.[29]

The Liberal imperialists for the first time became thoroughly alarmed at the impending prospect of a 'Little England' government, and admitted to themselves that the restoration of Rosebery was now a forlorn hope.[30] They realized that C.B. had become tremendously popular within the Liberal party and that the Irish trusted him.[31] But, they objected, he was 'not identified in the national mind with any fresh ideas, for indeed he had none'. They feared that, with Rosebery in retirement and Campbell-Bannerman in power, Liberal imperialism would have no spokesman of recognized authority in either the Commons or the Lords. Early in September, therefore, Asquith, Grey and Haldane decided to try to make use of C.B.'s popularity and unifying influence, but to deprive him of the substance of political power. Asquith and Haldane called upon Grey in his fishing-lodge at Relugas in north-eastern Scotland, and it was there agreed that Asquith as Chancellor of the Exchequer should lead the party in the Commons, while C.B. should hold the premiership in the relative obscurity of the House of Lords. The Woolsack was to go to Haldane and the Foreign or Colonial Office to Grey. It was also decided that Asquith, in 'as friendly and tactful a way as possible', should reveal this decision to C.B., and that Haldane, who had friends at Court, should enlist the support of the King. 'Unless our scheme were in substance

· carried out,' Haldane later wrote, 'we resolved that we could not join Campbell-Bannerman's government.'[32]

This arrangement – subsequently known as the 'Relugas compact' – proved easier to design than to enforce. As Lowell remarked three years later, an English premier in the upper house 'is in something of the position of a commander-in-chief who is not present with his forces in the field'.[33] Gladstone himself had recorded that a Prime Minister who depended on a deputy in the Commons was liable to expose himself to some 'very ugly tricks'. And, although Haldane successfully persuaded the King that C.B.'s chronic ill-health made it desirable for him to hold the premiership in the Lords, Asquith was less successful in his more delicate mission of broaching the matter with C.B., who made it plain that he expected and would accept the King's invitation to form the next government. C.B. tentatively proposed that Sir Robert Reid should be Lord Chancellor, Lord Elgin Foreign Secretary, and Asquith Chancellor of the Exchequer. At the same time he revealed that he had heard of a suggestion from Haldane that he should go to the Lords – a place for which he had 'neither liking, training nor ambition'. He did not absolutely rule out such a possibility; but Asquith realized, perhaps for the first time, that 'it would be with reluctance and even repugnance that Campbell-Bannerman would ever go to the Lords.' Asquith did not press the point; on this occasion, and during the next few weeks, he contented himself with urging the claims of Haldane and Grey – conceding, however, that in the making of appointments 'the future P.M. will have a perfectly free hand. ...' There is, in fact, no evidence to suggest that Asquith, having heard C.B.'s views on the subject, made any further attempt to fulfil his role in the Relugas compact or that he ever had any serious intention of refusing to hold office.[34]

C.B. meanwhile consolidated his position. In a series of speeches in the autumn of 1905 he had sketched out an ambitious programme of social reform, pleasing the radicals without committing his party on any particular issue. In mid-November he espoused Asquith's 'step-by-step' formula for progress towards Home Rule.[35] In a speech at Stirling on November 23 he reaffirmed Liberal support for eventual Irish self-government. This pledge provoked Lord Rosebery into finally renouncing his connection with C.B. – thus also unwittingly severing himself from Grey and Asquith – 'a singular illustration of how little mutual confidence really subsists between close political associates.'[36] Rosebery's speech in turn helped to persuade Balfour to resign without a dissolution, in the hope that strife among the Liberal factions would make it impossible for C.B. to form an effective government.

Late in November, leading Liberals had been debating the relative advantages of accepting office without a parliamentary majority and of refusing office until after the general election. Many of his followers urged C.B. that it would be unwise to expose Liberal weakness by forming a patched-up administration. But C.B. was convinced that, after so long in opposition, it was important to show the electorate that the Liberals could supply a representative and capable alternative government.

Early December 1905 seemed like a good opportunity for the execution of the Relugas compact. The incapacitation of Spencer left the Liberal leadership in the Lords vacant. But the scheme was frustrated by C.B.'s initial ignorance of the compact, and by the fact that of the three conspirators only Grey had any serious intention of carrying out the threat not to serve. Possibly if C.B. had realized that Asquith was a party to Haldane's intrigue he would have been more diffident about the problems of forming a minority government. However, he soon perceived that for Asquith the certainty of power weighed heavily against the obligations of friendship. He made no attempt to sound out leading Liberals during the last few days of the Conservative government, and did not come south from Scotland until Monday, 4 December, the very day of Balfour's resignation. On the Monday evening C.B. was shocked and hurt when Grey – 'all buttoned up and never undoing one button' – informed him that he could not hold office unless Asquith spoke for the party in the Commons and C.B. himself went to the Lords. This was C.B.'s first intimation of a conspiracy against him; but even so he was not particularly disturbed by the prospect of a government without Haldane or Grey.[37] He was, however, extremely anxious to include Asquith, who was an 'ex-Cab' and who for the past three years had been the Liberal party's leading apologist for free trade.

Asquith was the only one of the three conspirators in a strong bargaining position; but, although he urged C.B. to go to the Lords early on the morning of 5 December, he did not make that move a condition of his own acceptance of office. C.B. conceded that Asquith was better equipped to lead the Commons than he was himself; but

> after standing all the strain and stress of the last few years, he did not wish people to say he had run away when the pinch came – he could not bear the idea that anyone should think he was a coward.[38]

Later the same morning C.B. had an audience with King Edward, who advised him to take a peerage for the sake of his health. C.B. replied that this might eventually be necessary, but that he hoped to lead for a while in the House of Commons. He accepted the King's commission to form a government, still without knowing whether or not he would have Asquith's support. In fact, his fears were groundless, as Edward Grey had known the evening before, because several days earlier Asquith had cancelled the largest brief of his life on the obvious assumption that he would soon be holding office. Any lingering doubts that Asquith may have had about offering his services must have been dispelled by C.B.'s evident determination to form a government with or without his support. Later in the day of 5 December he accepted unconditionally C.B.'s invitation to become Chancellor of the Exchequer.[39]

Nevertheless, Asquith was clearly troubled, not by his relations with C.B. but by his obligations to Haldane and Grey. He made a 'personal appeal' to Campbell-Bannerman to break the deadlock by going to the Lords. C.B. prevaricated by saying that he must consult his wife; he may perhaps have remembered how he had once made a similar appeal to Asquith, but to no avail.[40] On Wednesday evening Lady Campbell-Bannerman came south from Scotland and urged her husband to remain firm. The next morning he told Asquith with some embarrassment that he intended to stay in the Commons, and instructed him to offer the War Office to Haldane, and the Foreign Office – which had been declined by Lord Cromer – to Grey.

Grey replied on 7 December that he could not surrender his independence nor give 'wholehearted cooperation' to a government that was not led by one of his own associates in either the upper or the lower house. He observed that 'it would be most undesirable for me to take office, feeling that my resignation might become necessary in a short time.'[41] He therefore rejected C.B.'s offer, while promising the government his loyal public support. This refusal – and a detailed account of the whole crisis – was leaked in *The Times*, probably at Morley's inspiration, on the following day.[42]

Asquith then despaired of Grey's capitulation. The initiative passed to Haldane, who found himself, through Asquith's defection, no longer the genius of a faction but the tenant of a wilderness shared only by Grey. On 6 December Asquith had written to Haldane, urging him that resistance to C.B. was no longer justified, since the first Liberal priority was now to win the general election for free trade.[43] On the following day Haldane received a letter from C.B., offering him either the attorney-generalship or an administrative office of Cabinet rank.[44] At this point, Haldane later recalled, his conscience began to trouble him. Was he really justified in refusing to give up his lucrative practice at the Bar – and thereby perhaps jeopardizing the cause of free trade – for merely personal reasons? He visited his friend Lady Horner, who in an 'illuminating hour' persuaded him that his duty lay in the service of his country. That evening he raised the matter with Sir Edward Grey. 'I put before him the thoughts which were passing through my mind, especially about resisting Protection. Were we not thinking too much of ourselves and too little of the public?' This discussion, Haldane maintained, planted seeds of doubt in the mind of Grey, and they were reinforced during the evening by persuasion from Arthur Acland. For the sake of 'the King and the nation', Haldane and Grey joined Campbell-Bannerman's government on the afternoon of Friday, 8 December 1905.[45]

The rest of C.B.'s Cabinet-making involved rather less private intrigue though no less public speculation. The appointment of John Burns, the ex-engineer from Battersea, as president of the Local Government Board, was widely interpreted as a sign of social change. But Burns had revealed himself as a very orthodox liberal economist in the debates on unemployment earlier in the year. A more significant and daring appointment was that of David Lloyd George, who had staked his claim to office as the representative of Welsh nationalism, nonconformity and radicalism, and now became President of the Board of Trade.[46] Sydney Buxton became Postmaster-General, having declined the Local Government Board; but Buxton, like C.B. himself, was a gentleman first, a radical second, and a politician a rather poor third. The other Cabinet appointments were markedly conservative, reflecting C.B.'s own rather passive conception of the functions of the state. Numerically the largest group were the six Gladstonian radicals; and the 'Whig' element in the party was grossly over-represented by the inclusion of five hereditary peers.[47] In religious complexion the ministry was predominantly unestablished. Ten nonconformists were balanced by six Anglicans, two free-thinkers and one Catholic. The Welsh nation was represented by Lloyd George, and Herbert Lewis who became a junior Whip. Herbert Samuel, an agnostic Jew, went to assist Herbert Gladstone at the Home Office.

Both inside and outside the Cabinet, Haldane's last-minute scruples about weakening a free-trade ministry proved to have been unfounded, since after so long in opposition there was no shortage of candidates for jobs. Even before the election C.B. had no difficulty in filling every vacant position, and was indeed embarrassed by the number of party members perforce turned empty-handed away. So pressing were the rival claims that an old and trusted supporter like James Bryce had to content himself with the Irish secretaryship, though he had hoped, not unreasonably, for the India Office; and Arthur Acland, whose mediation had been valuable in breaking the Relugas compact, got nothing – despite what he had understood as a definite promise from Herbert Gladstone.[48] The old 'inevitables' in the Cabinet were supported by a phalanx of younger men in junior posts: Churchill, Masterman, Runciman, McKenna and Lewis Harcourt among them. However, it did not escape notice that the combined ages of the Secretary and Under Secretary of State for India amounted to 131 years. And a sixty-year-old Under Secretary at the Foreign Office, together with a sixty-one-year-old Parliamentary Secretary to the Admiralty, and a sixty-year-old Financial Secretary at the War Office, dismayed some aspiring radicals as well as providing easy targets for Tory jibes about 'senescence' in the junior ranks of the ministry.[49] Nevertheless, whatever the particular disappointments and quibbles, it was soon clear that the very fact of being Prime Minister and thus controlling appointments had greatly enhanced C.B.'s personal power and the authority which he could wield in dealing with his colleagues.

C.B. had survived for so long as Liberal leader in the Commons by self-effacement rather than self-assertion, and by concealing rather than revealing the gradual increase of his power. These qualities were scarcely adequate for the successful execution of the role of Prime Minister; but many contemporaries observed that C.B. was subtly transformed by his accession to power. According to T.P.O'Connor, he was suddenly revealed as

> energetic, not easy-going; serious, not insouciant, with hot, not tepid conviction ... he was personally as well as officially the great outstanding personality of the new Ministry, dwarfing and submerging all the others.[50]

Once he had formed a ministry, C.B.'s primary task was to lead the Liberals to victory at the polls; and a general election was arranged for January 1906. C.B.'s election record was unpromising but his standing in the party and in the country was much higher than it had been in 1900 when the nation was divided by a controversial war. Moreover, several factors combined to make his electoral position much stronger than it had been five years before. The party machine and organs of propaganda were much more solidly behind C.B. than they had been in 1900, largely because of the efforts of Herbert Gladstone as Chief Whip. Gladstone was not an outstanding party manager but, like C.B. himself, he put a premium on party unity; and he strove to keep the Liberal Central Association, the National Liberal Federation and the parliamentary party loyal to C.B., even when privately urging his leader to appease Rosebery and Asquith.[51] In the subsidiary Liberal organizations, Roseberyites had made conspicuously little headway outside the Liberal League. The Liberal Publication Department under Augustine Birrell took a consistently anti-imperialist line; and all the regional federations had been recaptured by non-imperialists by 1903. However, Liberal Leaguers were not proscribed. At least forty-one who stood in the 1906 general election were endorsed by local associations, of whom almost half were assisted by cash from party headquarters.[52]

In 1903 Gladstone had negotiated a pact with Ramsay MacDonald – revealed only to the 'ex-Cabs' – which preserved Liberal candidates from three-cornered contests and helped to patch up the party's relationship with the working class. The pact with Labour had the additional advantage of reducing the number of demands to be met from Liberal election funds which were greatly depleted after the best part of twenty years of Tory rule.[53] Liberal organizations throughout the country were heartened by amicable arrangements with Labour and by the disarray of the Conservatives. And extra allocations of finance and party workers from the Central Association reinforced the local efforts of the rank-and-file movements of Liberal youth and Liberal women. The Women's Liberal Federation and the Women's National Liberal Association had by this time achieved an enrolment of one hundred thousand; and, after only three years' existence, the National League of Young Liberals was active in over three hundred branches. This surge of popular support was partly a response, and partly a stimulus, to the series of new policies and the 'progressive' image with which the Liberal party had been furnished by 1906.[54]

Backbenchers and younger radicals outside Parliament had begun to supply the fresh ideas and vigour which, notwithstanding his other valuable qualities, C.B. was unable to offer. The new radical movement was by no means homogeneous in aim or outlook. At one extreme it embraced a group of Liberal businessmen who were mainly concerned to promote state investment in public transport, scientific research, and 'Germanic' methods of higher education.[55] At the other extreme it included the *Daily News* Liberals, headed by Charles Masterman, who campaigned for the reform of the Poor Law, agricultural revival, taxation of site values, and equalization of local rates.[56] C.B. was not personally involved in these reforming movements, and, like John Morley, he was still inclined to explain all social and economic problems as the aftermath of an unjust war. But the fact that the *Daily News* was specifically committed to C.B.'s kind of anti-imperialism meant that the 'new Liberalism' also redounded more to his credit than to that of any other Liberal leader. Moreover, under pressure from Herbert Gladstone, he had tentatively incorporated certain new radical ideas into the official Liberal programme between December 1904 and January 1906.[57] His election address at the Albert Hall on 22 December 1905 outlined a programme of social improvement that included modernization of the Poor Law, the development of inland waterways, the 'colonization' of the English countryside, the relief of overcrowding, and measures to alleviate unemployment and the conditions of workers in sweated trades.

The radicalism of this manifesto was in fact rather illusory, since it put forward a definition rather than a solution for social distress; and by focusing primarily on problems of the 'land' it harked back to the Newcastle programme rather than forward to the 'national minimum' to be espoused by Churchill and Lloyd George. In addition, the fact that C.B. also promised a massive reduction of public expenditure suggested that neither he nor his colleagues fully understood the financial implications of large-scale social reform. Nevertheless, his speech was sufficient to persuade both contemporaries and historians that the Liberals in 1906 were a party committed to social change. C.B. recognized that the Liberal party had to explode the Labour claim to be the only friend of the workers; and, as Lord Crewe put it, the party was 'on trial as an engine for securing social reforms'.[58]

For reasons which are still a matter of controversy, however, 'social reform' was limited in popular appeal, even after the successive extensions of the franchise among the working class.[59] The Liberal Publication Department probably reflected the mood of the electorate when it produced for the 1906 election nine million leaflets on the fiscal question, six and a half million on the Tory record, two million on Chinese labour, and two million on social issues.[60] It seemed that the most crucial element in the improvement in C.B.'s electoral position was neither party solidarity nor promises of social improvement, but simply public disenchantment with ten years of Tory rule.[61] Since 1902 nonconformist opinion had been outraged by the transfer of denominational schools to the local rates; and many middle-class nonconformists who supported the South African war, or who had strayed into the Liberal Unionist camp, had for this reason returned to the Liberal fold. The swing against the Tories had become apparent in the by-elections of 1902 and 1903; and it was reinforced throughout the electorate by declining real wages, the Taff Vale judgement, the 'Chinese labour' scandal, and above all by the Unionists' espousal of imperial preference and tariff reform. The threat to free trade not only split the Tory party, but produced a number of *ad hoc* organizations – of which the Free Trade Union was the most influential – which powerfully augmented Liberal efforts in the constituencies. The political climate had in fact changed so drastically that to have championed the Boers and lost the 'khaki' election was no longer a liability by 1906.

The election of January 1906 was one of the last to be staggered over a period of several weeks. The turnout among registered electors was high; and widespread excitement seemed to pervade the voting public. In an intensive study of the campaign at both national and local levels, Dr Russell concluded:

> ... the Liberals were undoubtedly more *lively* in their presentation of their policies, than were the Unionists with theirs. The best songs, and the most compelling symbols were all on the Liberal side. Liberal propaganda was more intelligently conceived and more attractively presented, and perhaps, above all, the Unionists simply did not have the platform speakers to match Asquith, Haldane, Lloyd George, Churchill, Burns and others.[62]

The Liberals were undoubtedly the favourites. And, for the first time, Labour, fighting a parallel campaign with the Liberals on free trade, Chinese labour, and trade union rights, appeared as a significant political force. Few political commentators, however, were prepared for the extent of the landslide. The Liberals – who fought 121 more seats than in 1900 – returned 401 members, the LRC 29, the Unionists 157 and the Irish Nationalists 83. The government could therefore rely on a massive working majority and a substantial absolute majority over all possible combinations of opposition parties.[63] The ascendancy of the Liberals was exaggerated by the electoral system, and it was arguable that each successful Conservative candidate represented nearly two and a half times as many votes as each successful Liberal, despite the fact that two-thirds of Liberal victories were by majorities of 10% or more.[64] Nevertheless, government gains were remarkable not merely in the Liberal strongholds of Wales and Scotland and the West Country but in the traditionally Tory English counties (where Liberal agricultural workers found it easier to get to the polls in winter), and in the London boroughs.[65] Only Chamberlain's Birmingham, Orange Liverpool and the City of London held fast for Unionism.

Campbell-Bannerman therefore found himself at the head of the largest anti-Conservative majority for over eighty years. The Liberal back benches were filled with untried members – 220 were new to Westminster – reputedly bewildered by their wholly unexpected electoral success; and for the first time in English history there appeared to be a distinct cleavage between those who held the wealth and property of the nation and those who held the legally constituted political power. Contemporaries were apparently stunned by this *bouleversement* of political fortunes, and found it difficult to comprehend the significance of the events which had occurred. Sir John Gorst, the veteran Tory radical, predicted that 'the old Conservative party has gone forever and ... hereafter the Liberal and Labour parties will divide the supremacy in the state.'[66]

To anxious Conservatives and to eager reformers alike, the beginning of 1906 seemed an auspicious occasion for the launching of major social and political reforms. It was rumoured that the new Prime Minister was moving rapidly to the left; and the King's speech early in February promised a reduction of armaments, 'means for associating the people with the conduct of Irish affairs', and a total of twenty-two bills in the new session. Campbell-Bannerman soon established a command over the Commons that he had never enjoyed before; and in a highly charged debate on protection he publicly rebuked Arthur Balfour for failing to realize that politics in Westminster had taken a new and serious turn.

However, Campbell-Bannerman's government never really lived up to its early promise as an administration of reform. This was partly because, from the start of the Liberal regime, Balfour had declared his intention of blocking social revolution with his majority in the House of Lords. But it was also the result of powerful restraining forces among the Liberals themselves.

The vast majority of newly elected Liberal members were by no means the jejune radicals, unballasted by property and public responsibility, conjured by their critics. Dr Russell has calculated that 51 % of the Liberal candidates were 'carpet-baggers', compared with 39 % of the Tories. Though many of the new Liberals necessarily lacked parliamentary experience, a very high proportion had previously taken an active part in municipal life and other public duties, and most of them had been prospective parliamentary nominees longer than their Unionist opponents. Politically, the party was dominated by 'centre' Liberals, and socially by middle-aged members of the commercial and professional middle class.[67] 'There is no sign of any *violent* forward movement. ... The dangerous element does not amount to a dozen,' reported Herbert Gladstone to Campbell-Bannerman early in 1906 with undisguised relief.[68]

Even among reforming Liberals there was little overt unity of policy or long-term aims. The self-styled 'radicals' in the party – many of them 'explosive, disorganized, set upon action'[69] – ranged from Sir Christopher Furness, who waged a vendetta against Keir Hardie-ite socialism, to collectivist Liberals like Philip Whitwell Wilson, who voted with Labour on issues like 'the right to work'.[70] Members of the progressive Rainbow Circle split into those who wanted graduated taxation and deficit-spending and those who wanted economies in public expenditure and a reduction of the national debt.[71] About 180 Liberal MPs were affiliated to nonconformist churches and were concerned with education and Welsh disestablishment.[72] The largest single reforming group was that which advocated a tax or rate on the site-value of land; but this group was opposed by a 'cave' of Liberal businessmen and landowners, some of whom eventually withdrew from the party after land-valuation and assessment had been included in the budget of 1909. Reform was, therefore, a divisive as well as a unifying factor; and the new reformers fitted so uneasily into the Liberal framework that it is difficult to decide whether, for instance, some Liberal imperialists should be classed as 'radicals', and whether after 1906 they belonged to the party's 'right' or 'left'.

This confusion of aims stemmed largely from the fact that the Liberal revival had centred not around a new programme but round a vehement denunciation of Tory misrule. When it came to policy-formation, the Liberals were still reminiscent of a coalition of diverse and sometimes conflicting groups. Apart from the maintenance of free trade, they had no positive policy or principle with which to appeal for universal support. The young Winston Churchill, newly converted from Conservatism, was already flushed with a Disraelian vision of projecting the Liberals as the 'party of the nation'.[73] But many Liberal leaders were painfully conscious of the problems of conciliating 'men of substance' without losing support among radicals and reformers.

John Morley was convinced that only by alienating lower-middle-class Liberals could the government make material improvements in the condition of the working class. The trouble was, as Morley told Henry Fowler, 'if anybody thinks we can govern this country against the middle class, he is wrong.'[74] In March 1907, Richard Haldane remarked gloomily that 'this nation is "Left–Centre" not "Left"';[75] and a year later J.A.Spender interpreted Liberal by-election losses as a sign of public apprehension at expensive social reforms. 'The Government of course are in a cleft stick,' Spender wrote to James Bryce, shortly before C.B.'s retirement in 1908. 'They would suffer disastrously with their own supporters if they did not do these things, and they will suffer with the wavering elector if they do them. Now they have all the dragons on their hands at once, Church, Land and Liquor. It is not an ideal strategy but it was not easy to avoid.'[76]

Faced with divisions in the party and competing interests, C.B. adopted a strategy very similar to that which he had pursued in opposition. He consistently placed party unity before dynamic government or controversial reforms. It soon became clear that his radicalism in office, like W.E.Gladstone's, was focused almost entirely on constitutional rather than social issues – on self-government for the Boers, reform of the House of Lords and, to a lesser extent, female suffrage.[77] Towards social and economic innovations he was usually indifferent and sometimes actively hostile – believing, like Gladstone, that in the last resort civil freedom was the individual's best guarantee of material success. He accepted the need for secularizing education as the price of nonconformist support; and he agreed both to extend workmen's compensation and to give statutory protection to trade union funds. But he was anxious to confute the charge that his government was 'in the hands and at the mercy of Labour (which = socialism)' and to avoid legislation that appeared to discriminate in favour of the working class.[78]

C.B.'s failure to realize reforming expectations did not save him from accusations by right-wing Liberals of 'pandering to demagogism all round'. Lord Fitzmaurice complained about the increasing influence of hotheads like Winston Churchill, and that:

the National Liberal Club and the National Liberal Federation are allowed far too much influence in the councils of the party. The latter is simply the Trade Union of paid agents, often the worst judges of affairs.[79]

Criticism of this kind almost certainly reinforced C.B.'s own personal inclination towards a policy of studied inactivity; and after an initial burst of ministerial energy he seemed to relapse into the kind of genial lethargy that had characterized his earlier political life. Even his closest associates admitted that he was inclined to postpone decisions and to 'let things slide'.[80] It must also be remembered that C.B. was a constitutionally lazy man, who preached without practising the virtue of regular attendance at the House. By the end of 1905 he was also a chronically sick man, who in the opinion of his doctor ought never to have taken on both the premiership and the leadership of the Commons. During the summer of 1906 his nights were taken up with nursing his sick wife, whose death on 30 August left him suffering from physical exhaustion and severe nervous depression. Augustine Birrell later recorded: 'I have more than once seen him asleep during meetings of the Cabinet. His wife's death came too late to restore him to health.'[81] He suffered from two heart-attacks followed by prolonged convalescence in the autumn of 1907 and early in 1908; and the effective leadership of the government therefore passed to Asquith several months before Campbell-Bannerman's actual retirement in March 1908. At no time did C.B. have the physical and emotional energy with which Gladstone had hammered the problem of home rule and Asquith and Lloyd George subsequently challenged the House of Lords.

C.B.'s rather passive view of his own functions was seen not merely in his influence on policy but in his conduct of day-to-day affairs. Several of his colleagues later recalled that C.B.'s Cabinet was the most harmonious they had known. 'As head of a Cabinet,' Lord Morley testified, 'he was cool, acute, straight, candid, attentive to affairs, considerate.' But these qualities, though they maintained goodwill, militated against the prompt and orderly execution of business. Summarizing the defects of the Cabinet system under C.B., Haldane noted that 'the powerful orator secured too much attention. The Prime Minister knew too little of the details of what had to be got through to be able to apportion the time required for discussion.'[82]

Cabinet meetings were short and infrequent. There were no minutes or agenda; and C.B.'s brief reports to the King – which the sovereign found annoyingly meagre – were the only formal record of conclusions. It is impossible for the historian to know how well C.B.'s perfunctory letters conveyed to the monarch the gist of what occurred; but they suggest that – apart from questions of expenditure, which involved direct confrontation between the Treasury and the spending departments – there was surprisingly little Cabinet discussion of traditional affairs of state.

From the start of C.B.'s administration it was observed that a Cabinet of twenty-one members was too large a body for effective deliberation and the management of public affairs.[83] C.B.'s Cabinet was no larger than those of Salisbury and Balfour; but for nearly forty years there had been a tendency for Cabinets, whatever their party complexion, to decline in efficiency and to increase in size.[84] The creation of new departments, and the need for governments to represent an increasingly wide spectrum of interests, had destroyed the small, closely-knit and highly personal Cabinets which Walter Bagehot had seen in the 1860s as the keystone of the constitution and the seat of power. As effective organs of government, all Cabinets in the 1890s and 1900s were, therefore, in an advanced stage of putrefaction; and the Cabinets of Campbell-Bannerman, and later of Asquith, lay at the nadir of an administrative life-cycle of change and decay, awaiting the revitalizing energy and organization of Lloyd George and Maurice Hankey.

C.B. inherited from Balfour the Committee of Imperial Defence, a coordinating body of ministers, military and naval experts. After initial misgivings, C.B. soon appreciated the value of the CID as an extension of his own authority over the activities of the defence departments, although, in practice, Haldane rather than the Prime Minister was the regular chairman at CID meetings.[85] C.B. also continued the established practice of his recent predecessors in appointing *ad hoc* committees on inter-departmental problems over which he himself did not always preside. Land reform, the House of Lords, South Africa, and unemployment policy were considered in this way. But, as Dr John Brown has emphasized, the *ad hoc* committees tended to be 'ill-organized and uninformed'; and C.B. had no compunction about rejecting conclusions with which he disagreed.[86]

The existence of an inner Cabinet in Campbell-Bannerman's government was later attested by Margot Asquith and by the Under-Secretary for India, J.E.Ellis. To those excluded from its counsels, an inner Cabinet was, as Margot put it, 'the most hated and suspected thing in the world';[87] but, as Cabinets grew larger, a concentration of power among the Prime Minister's close associates was bound to occur. Nevertheless, it is not easy to determine which, if any, of C.B.'s Cabinet colleagues were closest to the heart of power. C.B. himself continued to confide most closely in Loreburn, Gladstone, Ripon, Bryce and Crewe. But these five scarcely constituted a powerful inner circle, being among the least influential and least dynamic members of the Liberal regime. Moreover, all C.B.'s colleagues agreed that he was quite impartial in his treatment of former political enemies and lifelong friends.[88] Morley believed that the CID was in some respects an inner Cabinet. But this was to mistake form for reality.[89] The group most clearly identifiable as an inner conclave is the handful of ministers who were aware of Sir Edward Grey's 'conversations' with Cambon during the Moroccan crisis of January 1906. These negotiations, which led to a tacit understanding on the French side that France would receive British assistance in the event of war, were revealed to Campbell-Bannerman, Ripon, Tweedmouth, Haldane, Fitzmaurice (Grey's Under-Secretary) and probably Asquith; but they were not made known to other members of the government till 1911. Both Campbell-Bannerman and Ripon had scruples about such secrecy; but the will of Sir Edward Grey prevailed. In this particular instance, a small group was acting as an incipient inner Cabinet; but there is no evidence to suggest that it had any kind of formal or permanent existence, or that the same group of ministers acted secretively in any other case.[90]

Delegation of power was far more characteristic of C.B.'s government than concentration. At the beginning of 1907 the Chancellor of the Exchequer's parliamentary private secretary reported that 'there are already signs of irritation at what some critics have described as the "Departmentness" of the present Government'.[91] Matters of high policy were increasingly decided, not by Cabinet discussion or by an informal clique, but by government departments and their ministerial chiefs. 'What strikes me most is how departmentalized the government is becoming,' wrote Lord Fitzmaurice in November 1907. 'The average member of the Cabinet seldom seems to me to know much of what is going on outside his own office.'[92] It was well known that in C.B.'s government decisions were frequently made and executed by individual ministers, and presented to the Cabinet as a virtual *fait accompli* to which other ministers could not very well object.[93] This shift of public business into the hands of departmental ministers was clearly a reflection of the growing specialization and volume of decision-making in a modern state. It put an unusually high premium on individual vigour and competence, and often allowed a determined minister, backed by a strong department, to ride roughshod over his Cabinet colleagues. In fact, for ambitious politicians and permanent civil servants, the nadir of Cabinet government during the first decade of the twentieth century was something of a golden age.

The clearest example of departmental independence in Campbell-Bannerman's government was the case of the Foreign Office under Sir Edward Grey. The circumstances of Grey's appointment had made it apparent that he had nothing but contempt for C.B.'s anti-imperialist views. Grey inherited from Lord Lansdowne a staff of Germanophobe permanent officials, whose views on foreign policy coincided with his own.[94] As soon as he entered the Foreign Office, he fostered Anglo-French 'military conversations', which were not at first revealed to C.B. At the Algeciras conference he supported 'hard line' French diplomacy without first consulting any of his Cabinet colleagues – subsequently defending himself with the slender excuse that they had all been away from London for the election campaign. When C.B. warned Clemenceau in April 1907 that English public opinion would not 'allow of British troops being employed on the Continent of Europe', Grey secretly reassured the French President that this prohibition would not apply in every case. Louis Mallet, one of Grey's permanent officials, privately denounced the stupidity of Clemenceau for raising the question 'apropos of nothing and with Campbell-Bannerman of all people' – as though the British Prime Minister were the last person in the world who ought to have known of British commitments in foreign affairs![95]

C.B.'s virtual exclusion from foreign policy was in marked contrast to the supervision which both earlier and later Prime Ministers exercised over the conduct of foreign affairs. Sir Charles Hardinge, Grey's Permanent Under-Secretary, testified early in 1908 that C.B. was 'the best Prime Minister there has been from an FO point of view and supports us in everything'.[96] C.B. was uneasy at the extent of England's commitment to the French; but he had no positive alternative to the policies devised by Grey. He was not a pacifist by conviction;[97] and, in spite of a sentimental preference for arbitration and disarmament, he believed that the maintenance of a revised 'two-power standard' was essential for national defence. Germany, with its expanding navy, was visibly the greatest threat to such a standard; and *faute de mieux* C.B. and his colleagues acquiesced in a diplomatic situation in which all European nations prepared for war.

If Grey enjoyed considerable autonomy in foreign affairs, Lord Elgin had rather less freedom at the Colonial Office. C.B. intervened decisively on the Transvaal Constitution question, rejecting both departmental advice and the proposals of a Cabinet committee comprising not only Elgin, but Lords Loreburn and Ripon, James Bryce and Asquith. In this case C.B. opted for the repudiation of the principle, favoured by the Liberal imperialists, of continuity of policy. By scrapping the Lyttelton Constitution, the Prime Minister conciliated the radicals in his own party as well as impressing the Boer leaders with a gesture of magnanimity.[98]

C.B. effectively exercised his personal influence on at least two other major issues. Late in March 1906 he intervened in a debate on the government's Trades Disputes Bill, and to the discomfort and great annoyance of most of the ministry's legal members advised the House to adopt an alternative Labour Bill instead. The second occasion was less public. A Cabinet committee on House of Lords reform recommended in mid-1907 a scheme for joint sittings between a delegation of peers and the whole House of Commons. The Cabinet at first accepted this scheme which was conceived by Asquith and Crewe. However, to C.B., the plan was neither sound in democratic theory nor safe for Liberal governments with small majorities. He thus took what J.A.Spender described as 'the rather unusual course of issuing a memorandum to his colleagues against the scheme of his own Cabinet committee'. And, notwithstanding the reluctance of Asquith, it was C.B.'s proposal for a suspensory veto which was eventually adopted as Cabinet policy.[99]

C.B.'s demonstrations of authority were exceptional. For most of the time he seemed indifferent to, or even unaware of, the change in the balance of decision-making power; and he made no personal or institutional adjustments to bring free-wheeling ministers under greater control. John Ellis wrote in April 1907:

> The [sagacity?] of the PM is still paramount (but) I think his driving power ... rather slackens. ... the Cabinet does not get its measures or plans ready prepared (perhaps Cabinets never do) and confusion and congestion arise in the H. of C. ....[100]

Several months later Lord Fitzmaurice remarked that:

> ... of course C.B. is not Mr Gladstone. He has none of that intimate general knowledge of affairs in nearly every department which Mr G. had. Indeed his weakness in this respect is frequently publicly seen and in office is lamentable.[101]

John Morley at the beginning of 1908 thought that C.B.'s retirement might weaken party unity, but would probably 'tend to the increase of Cabinet efficiency and *drive*'.[102]

If he did not supply a firm guiding hand in Cabinet, C.B. had the recognized virtue of being able to soften some of the fiercer antagonisms within the party. He took an unexpected opportunity to warn Haldane, through the Chief Whip, that 'any claim to separate recognition of the Liberal League would mean a reconstitution of the Government.'[103] In the management of the Liberal party, he owed more to his own personality than to the efficiency of the whips. George Whiteley, an ex-Tory, was an odd choice for Chief Whip who made his greatest impact by openly hawking honours in exchange for contributions to the party exchequer. The new chairman of the Liberal Publication Department, who had been hectored by the Chief Whip for voting against the government on military expenditure, complained 'He's a little bounder with not enough tact to ... cover a ... shirt button.'[104] Whiteley's subordinates irritated the Prime Minister by being at times 'too noisy and too frisky'.[105] And, although Asquith 'spoke highly of the efficient way [Whiteley] had managed the business of the House', he displayed little perturbation when Whiteley retired a few months after C.B.'s death.[106]

C.B. never 'played the part of a leader, a Prime Minister, a celebrity'. In fact, as his private secretary recorded, 'he was continually forgetting that he *was* Prime Minister.'[107] But unaffected geniality was no substitute for leadership. C.B. failed to give the Liberal party either impetus or direction. Admittedly he kept it busy. For eighteen months Parliament sat for more days and for more hours each day than it had in any comparable period under Balfour or Salisbury. The Speaker, writing in August 1907 of the strain on parliamentary staff, complained that all-night sittings, which previously had occurred about once or twice a session, had become twice-weekly events.[108] This was an exaggeration. The institution of a single sitting, running continuously from 2.45 pm to 11.30 pm, certainly imposed extra burdens not only on officials of the House of Commons but on those ministers who could not rely on an adequate understudy when they wished to dine. But, from April 1906, only unopposed or 'exempted' business was normally taken after 11.00 pm, and the Clerk of the House wrote in 1908 that 'the earlier hour of rising, notwithstanding the suspensions of the 11 o'clock rule from time to time made necessary by press of business, has been felt as a sensible relief.'[109]

By the autumn of 1907, the House of Lords had blocked a large part of the government's legislative programme; and the ministry was apparently drifting into a period of futile and aimless endeavour. C.B. was too ill to take a grip on events, set new goals, and revivify the administration. Yet his authority was unchallenged to the end; and in spite of the acknowledged ability of his successor, C.B.'s retirement and death deprived the Liberal leadership of an emollient wisdom it could ill afford to lose. For all his caution in policy, and lack of appetite for action, C.B. had exercised a remarkable influence over a Cabinet which might otherwise have languished in disharmony. His brief period of office demonstrated the validity of the central thesis of the constitutional scholars of the day. No matter how indifferent he was to the employment of his powers, the authority of the Prime Minister was, as Ostrogorski and Lowell observed, increasing. To a younger man than C.B., a man of definite purpose and strong will, the premiership offered massive opportunities to sway the destiny of the nation. It was hardly surprising, therefore, that C.B.'s departure from the scene should be recognized as a significant event. 'With his disappearance,' John Morley warned, 'will arrive a critical hour for our Party and our Principles.'[110] Many of Morley's colleagues did not share his apprehension about an Asquith premiership. But none of them questioned the political importance of a change of Prime Minister.

Notes

1. This study was completed in 1969, and first published in *History*, Vol. LX, October 1970. We have corrected a few errors of detail, amplified some points, and added references to later publications. John Wilson's *C.B.: A Life of Sir Henry Campbell-Bannerman* (London 1973) is a full-scale biography that is largely consistent with this account. For permission to see and quote from unpublished private papers, we are especially grateful to the Hon. Mark

2. Bonham Carter, Lord Gainford, Mr John Lehmann and Lord Ponsonby. M.Ostrogorski, *Democracy and the Organisation of Political Parties* (2 vols, London 1902) I, pp. 607–8.

3. A.Lawrence Lowell, *The Government of England* (2 vols, New York, 1912; 1st edition 1908), pp. 68–71; see also Sidney Low, *The Governance of England* (London 1922; 1st edition 1914), ch. ix.

4. 'The Late Prime Minister', *The Spectator* (25 April 1908), p. 656; Scrutator, 'The Pattern Englishman and His Record', *National Review* (January 1906), pp. 823–4.

5. Herbert Gladstone to C.B., 27 December 1901, *Campbell-Bannerman MSS* (cited hereafter as *C.B. MSS*) (Add. MS 41216, ff. 177–8).

6. *The Autobiography of Margot Asquith* (2 vols, London 1920, 1922) I, p. 164; T.P.O'Connor, *Sir Henry Campbell-Bannerman* (London 1908), p. 39.

7. C.B. to John Ellis, 10 November 1903, *C.B. MSS* (Add. MS 41214, ff. 131–4); C.B. to James Bryce, 29 October 1900 and 26 January 1903, *Bryce MSS*, Boxes E27 and P6.

8. J.A.Spender, *The Life of the Right Hon. Sir Henry Campbell-Bannerman, G.C.B.* (2 vols, London 1923) I, pp. 335–7 (cited hereafter as *Life of C.B.*).

9. As late as 7 December 1903, *The Times* estimated that, of the Scottish Liberal

MPs, one-third looked to Rosebery rather than to C.B. for leadership. On matters of foreign and imperial affairs, it has been calculated that 74 of the 211 Liberal MPs in 1905 were 'imperialist'. (See Timothy Boyle, *The Liberal Party and Foreign Affaiys, 1895–1905*, unpublished London University M Phil thesis, 1969, p. 302).

10. J. A. Spender, *Life, Journalism and Politics* (2 vols, London 1927) I, p. 66.

11. On this and the immediately following period see Peter Stansky, *Ambitions and Strategies*, The Struggle for the Leadership of the Liberal Party in the 1890s (Oxford 1964), pp. 275–94; and H.C.G.Matthew, *The Liberal Imperialists*, The Ideas and Politics of a Post-Gladstonian Elite (Oxford 1973), Part I.

12. *Life, Journalism and Politics*, I, pp. 69–70.

13. Stansky, *op. cit.*, pp. 287–92.

14. Jeffrey Butler, *The Liberal Party and the Jameson Raid* (Oxford 1968); see also Boyle, *The Liberal Party and Foreign Affairs, 1895–1905*.

15. The electoral defeat was not as crushing as has sometimes been suggested. The Unionist majority was reduced from 152 to 134.

16. Roy Jenkins, *Asquith* (London 1964), p. 126.

17. Gladstone to C.B., 17 December 1901, *C.B. MSS* (Add. MS 41216, ff. 171–2); Bryce to C.B., 26 December 1901, *C.B. MSS* (Add. MS 41211, ff. 184–5).

18. Bryce to C.B., 3 January 1902, *C.B.MSS* (Add. MS 41211, ff. 190–1).

19. C.B. to Gladstone, 24 February 1902, *C.B. MSS* (Add. MS 41216, ff. 197–8). 'From all I can learn,' C.B. concluded, 'the L. Imps will probably not desert, but they will remain and plot and sap.' C.B. strongly opposed organic union with the Unionist free fooders, to which the Liberal imperialists were attracted in 1903. (C.B. to Bryce, 7 December 1903, *C.B. MSS* (Add. MS 41211, ff. 250–1); Jenkins, *op. cit.*, pp. 141–2).

20. At Chesterfield Rosebery had called for a 'clean slate' in English politics and for the replacement of obsolete radicalism by 'national efficiency'. See L.S.Amery, *My Political Life* (3 vols, London 1953–5) I, pp. 223–9; and G.R.Searle. *The Quest for National Efficiency* (Oxford 1971) ch. IV.

21. M.Craton and H.W.McCready, *The Great Liberal Revival 1903–1906* (London 1966), pp. 10, 45–6; Matthews *op. cit.*, pp. 300–1, and *passim*.

22. R.B.McCallum, *The Liberal Party from Earl Grey to Asquith* (London 1963), p. 124.

23. Bryce to C.B., 3 January 1902, *C.B. MSS* (Add. MS 41211, ff. 190–1); David C.Elliot, *The Liberal Party in Scotland from the Midlothian Election to the First World War* (unpublished Harvard University PhD thesis, May 1950), pp. 83–8.

24. Gladstone to C.B., unsigned memorandum, 24 June 1903, *Herbert Gladstone MSS* (Add. MS 45988, ff. 45–6).

25. C.B. to Gladstone, 5 December 1904, *Herbert Gladstone MSS* (Add. MS 45988, ff. 132–3).

26. *National Review*, vol. 43 (August 1904), pp. 933–45; *Nineteenth Century* (October 1904), pp. 675–85. Lucy's detailed forecast of the distribution of jobs in the next Liberal administration had the distinction of being wrong in every case.

27. Lord Rendel's Memorandum of a Conversation with C.B., Easter Day, 1907, *The Personal Papers of Lord Rendel* (London 1931), p. 168.

28. *Review of Reviews*, June 1905, p. 573.

29. *Life of C.B. II*, pp. 174–9, 189.

30. Richard Burdon Haldane, *An Autobiography* (London 1929), p.156

31. Haldane to Asquith, 22 October 1905, *Asquith MSS*, 10, ff. 150–2; H.W.McCready 'Home Rule and the Liberal Party, 1899–1906', *Irish Historical Studies*, vol. XIII, no. 52 (September 1963), p. 345.

32. Haldane, *op. cit.*, pp. 157, 159.

33. Lowell, *op. cit.*, I, p. 72.

34. *The Autobiography of Margot Asquith* I, pp. 66–75; Asquith to C.B., 25 November 1905, *C.B. MSS* (Add. MS 41210, ff. 247–52). Italics added.

35. H.W.McCready, 'Home Rule and the Liberal Party, 1899–1906', p. 344.

36. Sir Almeric Fitzroy's Diary, 13 December 1905, in his *Memoirs* (2 vols, London ?1925) I, p. 274.

37. 'This friend of ours – such a wonderful intriguer and diplomatist we are told – has no more tact than a hippopotamus,' C.B. wrote scathingly of Haldane to Herbert Gladstone on November 20. (*Herbert Gladstone MSS*, Add. MS 45996, ff. 196–7.) Grey, C.B. was assured by Henry Labouchere, was 'an invention of the Press, and has no hold on Liberal opinion.' Morley, too, testified that 'Grey is grossly overrated'. (Peter Rowland, *The Last Liberal Governments: The Promised Land, 1905–1910* [London 1968], pp. 7, 13.)

38. *The Autobiography of Margot Asquith* II, p. 71.

39. Lord Craigmyle, *Letters to Isobel* (London 1936), pp. 258–9.

40. See above, p. 47.

41. Grey to C.B., December 1905, *C.B. MSS* (Add. MS 41218, ff. 44–5).

42. Wilfrid Scawen Blunt's Diary, 30 April 1908, in *My Diaries, Being a Personal Narrative of Events, 1888–1914* (2 vols, London 1919–20) II, p. 210.

43. Jenkins, *op. cit.*, pp. 150–2.

44. Rowland, *op. cit.*, p. 23.

45. Haldane, *op. cit.*, pp. 171, 181; R.F.V.Heuston, *Lives of the Lord Chancellors 1885–1940* (Oxford 1964), p. 199. Matthews, *op. cit.*, p. 118, suggests that no 'compact' existed, and that the Relugas policy had been abandoned by December. For a contemporary account which is consistent with our view, see T.Boyle, 'The Formation of Campbell-Bannerman's Government in December 1905: A Memorandum by J.A.Spender', *Bulletin of the*

Institute of Historical Research, XLV (November 1972).

46. 'Lloyd George represents three things: Wales, English Radicalism, and Nonconformists, and they are not three things which politicians can overlook.' (Churchill to Lord Hugh Cecil, 1 January 1904, Randolph S. Churchill, *Winston S. Churchill* II, Companion part 1, 1901–7 [London 1969], p. 284.)

47. Herbert Gladstone, Morley, Sinclair, Bryce, Reid and C.B. himself may be grouped in the first category. Lords Crewe, Ripon, Elgin, Tweedmouth and Carrington comprised the second.

48. A.K. Russell, *The General Election of 1906* (Oxford University DPhil thesis, 1962), p. 121; John Bowle, *Viscount Samuel, A Biography* (London 1957), p. 61.

49. Viscount Lee of Fareham, *A Good Innings* (3 vols, privately printed, 1939) I, p. 314.

50. T.P.O'Connor, *op. cit.*, p. 87.

51. Bernard Porter, *Critics of Empire, British Radical attitudes to colonialism in Africa, 1895–1914* (London 1968), p. 81.

52. *Liberal Magazine* (1903), pp. i–iii; Craton and McCready, *op. cit.*, pp. 45–6.

53. Frank Bealey, 'The Electoral Arrangement Between the LRC and the Liberal Party', *Journal of Modern History* XXVIII (1956), pp. 353–73; Frank Bealey and Henry Pelling, *Labour and Politics 1900–1906* (London 1958), ch. VI; Philip P. Poirier, *The Advent of the Labour Party* (London 1958), ch. X.

54. For Liberal organization in 1905, the best source is Dr Russell's unpublished thesis in the Bodleian Library, Oxford. The abbreviated published version is *Liberal Landslide: The General Election of 1906* (Newton Abbot and Hamden, Connecticut, 1973). There had been two women's organizations since a split over female suffrage in 1892.

55. See the memorandum from Sir John Brunner, Sir Christopher Furness, and others to C.B., 6 May 1904, *Herbert Gladstone MSS* (Add. MS 45988, ff. 96–102); and John Brown, *Ideas Concerning Social Policy and their Influence on Legislation in Britain, 1902–11* (unpublished London University PhD thesis, 1964), pp. 55–7.

56. See, for example, C.F.G. Masterman *et al.*, *The Heart of the Empire. Discussions of Problems of Modern City Life in England* (London 1902); new edition with introduction by Bentley B. Gilbert (Brighton 1973).

57. See the correspondence in the *C.B. MSS* (Add. MS 41217 *passim*).

58. Crewe to C.B., 19 November 1905, *C.B. MSS* (Add. MS 41213, ff. 337–8).

59. Henry Pelling, *Popular Politics and Society in Late Victorian Britain* (London 1968), ch. 1. Recent research suggests that Edwardian working-class organizations *did* in fact press for government-sponsored welfare policies, but that these did not always correspond to conceptions of social reform put

forward by radical members of the upper and middle classes (Pat Thane, 'The Working-Class and State Welfare 1880–1914', *Society for the Study of Labour History Bulletin*, No. 31 (Autumn 1975), p. 6.

60. Russell, thesis, p. 174.

61. Herbert Gladstone attributed the Liberal victory to (1) The Liberal–Labour pact. (2) Free trade. (3) C.B.'s South African policy. (4) Conservative outstay of welcome (a) inducing a wish for change and (b) arrears of industrial and social legislation. (5) Education. (Manuscript autobiography, *Herbert Gladstone MSS*. Add. MS 46118, f. 102.)

62. Russell, thesis, p. 355. The name of C.B. is conspicuously absent from Dr Russell's list of able platform speakers.

63. Craton and McCready, *op. cit.*, p. 21, estimate the government's absolute majority as 86, presumably by counting all Lib–Lab MPs with the LRC.

64. J.Rooke Corbett, 'Recent Electoral Statistics', *Transactions of the Manchester Statistical Society* (1906–7), pp. 37–63; *Report of the TUC Congress 1906*, pp. 46–7. Cf. Russell thesis, p. 500.

65. Henry Pelling, *Social Geography of British Elections, 1885–1910* (London 1967), p. 432.

66. Gorst to Bryce, 7 February 1906, *Bryce MSS*, Box P.6.

67. Russell, thesis, p. 170; J.A.Thomas, *The House of Commons 1906–11, An Analysis of its Economic and Social Character* (Cardiff 1958), pp. 18, 25, 31, 35, 44–5, 49.

68. Gladstone to C.B., 21 January 1906, *C.B. MSS* (Add. MS 41217, ff. 294–5); see also Morley to Lamington, 9 March 1906, *Lamington MSS*, in Stephen E.Koss, *John Morley at the India Office 1905–1910* (New Haven and London 1969), p. 74.

69. Charles Masterman's description, in Lucy Masterman, *C.F.G.Masterman* (London 1939), p. 73.

70. Ripon to C.B. 23 September 1906, *C.B. MSS* (Add. MS 41225, ff. 142–4); Whitwell Wilson, the Liberal MP for St Pancras, introduced the Labour party's 'Unemployed Workmen Bill' when Labour MPs were unsuccessful in the private members' ballot in March 1908.

71. The Rainbow Circle was a progressive economic and political discussion group, formed inside the National Liberal Club, which founded *The Nation* in 1907. Its members included J.A.Hobson, J.M.Robertson, Herbert Burrows, G.P.Gooch, Murray MacDonald, Russell Rea, Percy Alden, W.H.Clarke, and W.Pember Reeves. Its secretary for many years was Ramsay MacDonald. (J.A.Hobson, *Confessions of an Economic Heretic* [London 1938], pp. 94–5; Viscount Samuel, *Memoirs* [London 1945], p. 24.)

72. Elie Halevy, *A History of the English People in the Nineteenth Century* VI, 'The Rule of Democracy', trans. E.I.Watkin, Ernest Benn, 1961 (rev. ed.), pp. 64–5; see also Stephen E.Koss, '1906: Revival and Revivalism', in A.J.A.Morris (ed.), *Edwardian Radicalism 1900–1914* (London and Boston 1974).

73. Churchill to Bryce, 18 January 1906, *Bryce MSS*, Box C.

74. Morley to Bryce, 6 January 1908, *Bryce MSS*, Box P6; Morley to H.H.Fowler, 30 September 1906, in Edith Henrietta Fowler, *The Life of Henry Hartley Fowler, First Viscount Wolverhampton, GCSI* (London 1912), p. 505.

75. Haldane to Bryce, 12 March 1907, *Bryce MSS*, Box E28.

76. Spender to Bryce, 9 March 1908, *Bryce MSS*, Box E28.

77. See Ronald Hyam, *Elgin and Churchill at the Colonial Office 1905–1908. The Watershed of the Empire–Commonwealth* (London 1968), pp. 124–36; T.P.O'Connor, *op. cit.*, pp. 69–70; J.B.Mackie, *The Model Member; Sir Henry Campbell-Bannerman, Fifty Years Representative of the Stirling Burghs* (Dunfermline 1914), pp. 11–12; Constance Rover, *Women's Suffrage and Party Politics in Britain 1866–1914* (London 1967), pp. 121–2; Andrew Rosen, *Rise Up Women! The Militant Campaign of the Women's Social and Political Union 1903–1914* (London and Boston 1974), pp. 64–7.

78. C.B. to Gladstone, 23 January 1906, *Herbert Gladstone MSS* (Add. MS 45988, f. 213); C.B. to H.H.Asquith, 21 January 1906, *Asquith MSS*, 10, f. 200.

79. Fitzmaurice to Bryce, 11 October 1907, and 26 May 1907, *Bryce MSS*, Box E28.

80. Arthur Ponsonby to Bryce, 24 May 1907, *Bryce MSS*, Box E28.

81. Augustine Birrell, *Things Past Redress* (London 1933), pp. 245–6.

82. John, Viscount Morley, *Recollections* (2 vols, London 1919) I, p. 143; Haldane, *op. cit.*, p. 216.

83. *Annual Register* (1905), p. 237.

84. *The Spectator* (28 December 1907), pp. 1084–5. On Cabinet government in the mid-nineteenth century, see D.N.Chester, 'The Development of the Cabinet', *Parliamentary Affairs* 9 (1955–6), pp. 43–7.

85. Nicholas J.d'Ombrain, *The Military Departments and the Committee of Imperial Defence 1902–1914, A Study in the Structural Problems of Defence Organisation* (Oxford University DPhil thesis, 1970), pp. 225–7; see also the abbreviated published version, *War Machinery and High Policy, Defence Administration in Peacetime Britain 1902–1914* (London 1973), especially ch. VI.

86. John Brown, 'Scottish and English Land Legislation, 1905–11', *The Scottish Historical Review* XLVII, I, no. 143 (April 1968), p. 74.

87. Margot Asquith to J.St.Loe Strachey, 24 May 1915, *Strachey MSS*: 'I can't *think* why you so often mention the inner Cabinet. There is *always* an inner Cabinet. Gladstone, Dizzy, A.J.B., C.B. etc. etc. ...' Cf. Ellis to Bryce, 10 May 1909, *Bryce MSS*, Box E28.

88. Viscount Grey of Fallodon, *Twenty-Five Years 1892–1916* (2 vols, London 1925) I, p. 126.

89. Morley to Kitchener, 29 August 1907, *Kitchener MSS*, PRO 30/57/31; John Gooch, *The Plans of War, The General Staff and British Military Strategy c. 1900–1916*

(London 1974), shows the limits of CID influence on military questions.

90. George Monger, *The End of Isolation, British Foreign Policy 1900–1907* (London 1963) ch. 9; John P.Mackintosh, *The British Cabinet* (2nd ed.; London 1968), pp. 334–5; Samuel R.Williamson Jr., *The Politics of Grand Strategy, Britain and France Prepare for War, 1904–1914* (Cambridge, Mass. 1969), ch. 3.

91. Edwin Montagu to Asquith, January 1907 (copy), *Montagu MSS*.

92. Fitzmaurice to Bryce, 2 November 1907, *Bryce MSS*, Box E28.

93. *The Spectator* (22 February 1908), p. 284.

94. Zara Steiner, 'Grey, Hardinge and the Foreign Office, 1906–1910', *The Historical Journal* X, 4 (1969), p. 439.

95. Monger, *op. cit.*, pp. 325–6.

96. Michael L.Dockrill, *The Formulation of a Continental Foreign Policy by Great Britain 1908–1912* (unpublished London University PhD thesis, 1969), p. 20. In fact, C.B. did overrule both the Foreign Office and the Colonial Office when they protested early in 1907 against the Admiralty policy of scrapping obsolete ships and denuding distant waters of British 'police' forces. (See Arthur J.Marder, *From the Dreadnought to Scapa Flow, The Royal Navy in the Fisher Era, 1904–1919* I, 'The Road to War, 1904–1914' [London 1961], pp. 52–4.)

97. *Life of C.B.* II, pp. 156–7, describes C.B.'s aggressive reaction to the Dogger Bank incident of 1904.

98. See Hyam, *op. cit.*, pp. 98–136; there are further details confirming Hyam's account in the diaries of R.C.Lehmann, Liberal MP for Harborough, and C.B.'s private secretary, Arthur Ponsonby.

99. J.A.Spender and Cyril Asquith, *Life of Herbert Henry Asquith, Lord Oxford and Asquith* (2 vols, London 1932) I, p. 191; cf. Corinne Comstock Weston's 'The Liberal Leadership and the Lords' Veto, 1907–1910', *The Historical Journal* XI, 3 (1968), pp. 508–37.

100. Ellis to Bryce, 22 April 1967, *Bryce MSS*, Box E28.

101. Fitzmaurice to Bryce, 2 November 1907, *Bryce MSS*, Box E28.

102. Morley to Bryce, 6 January 1908, *Bryce MSS*, Box P6.

103. Rendel's Memorandum ... Easter Day 1907, in *The Personal Papers of Lord Rendel*, pp. 170–1.

104. R.C.Lehmann's Diary, 19 March 1906, *Lehmann MSS*.

105. C.B. to Lord Ripon, 9 October 1906, *Ripon MSS* (Add. MS 43518, f. 121). The Master of Elibank, as Scottish Whip, incurred special displeasure by mounting a personal campaign against socialism. (See Rowland, *op. cit.*, p. 87, and the Master of Elibank to Grey, 27 January 1908, *Grey MSS*, FO 800 [90].)

106. J.A.Pease's Diary, 7 April 1908, *Gainford MSS*.

107. Lord Ponsonby's Notes on C.B., in Francis W.Hirst, *In the Golden Days*

(London 1947), p. 259; see also Ponsonby's Diary, 10 October 1906, *Ponsonby MSS.*

108. Lowther to C.B., 20 August 1907, *C.B. MSS* (Add. MS 41242, ff. 256–8).

109. Sir Courtenay Ilbert, 'Supplementary Chapter', in Josef Redlich, *The Procedure of the House of Commons, A Study of its History and Present Form* (3 vols, London 1908) II, p. 207 and *passim*.

110. Morley to Robert Spence Watson, 22 March 1908, in Percy Corder, *The Life of Robert Spence Watson* (London 1914), p. 301.

Herbert Henry Asquith

Cameron Hazlehurst

Asquith's succession to the premiership was regarded by his contemporaries as a natural, almost an inevitable, event. For sixteen years he had been in the first rank of Liberal leaders. He might, had he striven for it, have had the leadership of the Liberal opposition in the House of Commons as early as 1898, when Sir William Harcourt retired. At that time, however, a bid for power would have been premature. Dignity and tactical sense pointed to the prior claim of Campbell-Bannerman. Not that C.B. emerged with undisputed title to the leadership; but, as Asquith himself observed:

> ... people have been so accustomed for more than a generation upon both sides to leaders who are obviously marked out for the post (Palmerston, Gladstone, Disraeli, Salisbury) that they are bewildered by the problem of choice.[1]

There was no such problem in 1908. As C.B.'s health waned, it was Asquith who took the chair at Cabinet meetings; and in the last weeks before C.B.'s resignation, Asquith deputized, with the approval of his colleagues and the King, for the ailing premier. Until Campbell-Bannerman formally relinquished his office, a month elapsed during which some of the duties of the head of the government were necessarily in abeyance.[2] But, as far as possible, the Chancellor assumed the responsibilities of the premiership. When he crossed the Channel to kiss hands, Asquith went to receive the formal recognition of a succession that was 'decisively settled by circumstances'.[3]

Although, late in 1907, there had been whispers of a move to draft the Foreign Secretary, Sir Edward Grey, no one challenged Asquith's succession. That he should follow C.B. seemed, in the event, unquestionable. Whether or not he would be an adequate replacement was another matter. 'I agree with you that Asquith must be the heir,' wrote Winston Churchill to Walter Runciman. 'I am sure,' Churchill went on, 'no better workman will have been installed since the days of Sir Robert Peel. As to the work which he will choose – that lies in the mists.' Churchill was 'full of hope' that the very fact of being placed on the pinnacle would bring forth Asquith's best qualities.[4] As for the new Prime Minister himself, he had no doubts about the special difficulties of his position. The Liberal party was in good heart, he told Lord Ripon, 'but has some stiff work before it, & must face the prospect of losing by-elections'.[5] To James Bryce, he confided on 28 April 1908:

C.B. leaves a gap which is not easily, & perhaps at all, capable of being filled. He was to the last, by negative as well as by positive gifts, an emollient and unifying factor in our party, and indeed in public life.[6]

How well equipped was Asquith for the premiership? He had been a Member of Parliament for more than twenty years. He had served Gladstone and Rosebery as Home Secretary. He was Campbell-Bannerman's Chancellor of the Exchequer. He owed his political fortunes not to birth or wealth, but to unmistakable ability. His credentials as a practical reformer, defender of free trade, and parliamentary craftsman of superlative skill were widely acknowledged. By loyal service as Campbell-Bannerman's chief lieutenant he had dispelled some of the fears engendered in radical circles by his earlier alignment with Rosebery and the Liberal imperialist wing of the Liberal party. As if anticipating Asquith's own doubts about his acceptability to all groups within the party, his first and most fulsome biographer, J.P.Alderson, had written in 1905:

Mr Asquith stands out today among Liberal statesmen as the one man who unites more than any other all sections of the Liberal party. He also enjoys the great advantage of possessing in a very large degree the confidence of the general body of the electorate irrespective of party.[7]

If there were those who would have balked at so unqualified an assessment, few would have denied Alderson's claim that the new Prime Minister had been 'a thorough, genuine, all-round Liberal, and a formidable fighter in the cause of progress'.[8] And, as he took up the supreme command of the great Liberal administration, Asquith sat securely at the head of a huge majority in the House of Commons and a Cabinet of exceptional talents.

Campbell-Bannerman bequeathed a strong ministry to his successor. Asquith's first act as premier was to consolidate his inheritance. With startling brusqueness he transferred the 'patently potty'[9] Lord Tweedmouth from the Admiralty to the Presidency of the Council, and dismissed Lord Elgin from the Colonial Office, the Earl of Portsmouth from the Under-Secretaryship at the War Office, and Edmund Robertson and Thomas Lough from junior posts at Education and the Admiralty. There was much to be said for each of these moves. Elgin, though a competent administrator, was a most reluctant and unpractised debater, as unforthcoming in the privacy of the cabinet as he was on the front bench.[10] Tweedmouth's disability was not silence but loquacity. Already afflicted by a 'cerebral malady' that was soon to render him unfit for any public duties, he had been the centre of a political scandal a month before Campbell-Bannerman's retirement. Having received a private letter from the Kaiser remonstrating about British naval policy, he had sent a reply which, it was rumoured in the press, contained details of unpublished naval estimates. It seems likely that the story leaked through Tweedmouth's own lips; and although he was able to rebut all implications of impropriety in his conduct of the correspondence, he 'gave the impression of a man who found himself in a difficulty of his own creation'.[11] Neither Portsmouth nor Robertson had made any particular blunder. But Asquith had tutored Portsmouth privately many years earlier and was well aware of his limitations; and Robertson, if he was not quite – as a Tory critic later wrote – 'profoundly ignorant of all naval matters [and] handicapped also by infirmities of age and parliamentary incompetence',[12] was certainly not so indispensable as to be allowed to continue blocking the path of younger, abler men. Lough, too, had offered little.

In Elgin's place at the Colonial Office, Asquith appointed Lord Crewe. The new Prime Minister had a high regard for Crewe's judgement, and was to rely upon his sober counsel and unostentatious influence as leader of the government in the House of Lords. At the Admiralty, Reginald McKenna, whose success as Financial Secretary to the Treasury had already won him advancement to the difficult office of the Board of Education, was installed in Tweedmouth's stead. What was notable about these changes was less the identity of the ministers concerned than the abrupt manner in which Asquith despatched the unwanted men, without explanation or apology. 'I venture to think,' wrote Elgin to Tweedmouth in bitter commiseration, 'that even a Prime Minister may have some regard for the usages common among gentlemen ... I feel that even a housemaid gets a better warning.'[13] Not until the creation of the coalition government in May 1915 did Asquith again dispense so brutally with the services of any of his colleagues.

The flutter of gossip which accompanied these disappointments was overwhelmed by the interest created by the other shuffles and promotions. Two men attracted the bulk of public attention: David Lloyd George who moved from the Board of Trade to the Exchequer, and Winston Churchill who stepped up to Lloyd George's vacant office and entered the Cabinet at the early age of thirty-four. A contemporary tale, emanating from John Morley, who himself had wistful inclinations for the chancellorship, alleged that Lloyd George 'put a pistol to Asquith's head and asked for the Exchequer with a threat of resignation'.[14] But there is no solid evidence that Asquith was ever required to submit to such crude pressure. Though he had been tempted to follow the precedents of Peel and Gladstone and combine the chancellorship with the premiership, his better judgement pointed to a different course. With Campbell-Bannerman's departure from the scene, the ministry's upper echelons were conspicuously weighted towards the old imperialist side of the party. The transfer of Haldane to the Treasury, therefore, was plainly out of the question. To humour the former pro-Boers and younger progressives, the promotion of Lloyd George was the obvious answer.[15] There was no doubt of the Welshman's radical sympathies; yet even the *Daily Mail* admitted that he had 'proved in office that he possesses in exceptional measure that practical business capacity, self-restraint, initiative, and large open-mindedness which, allied with the faculty of conciliation, are required of one who will control the national finances'.[16] In elevating Lloyd George, Asquith demonstrated from the beginning that he intended 'to be the leader, not of a section, but of the whole party'.[17] And in firmly attaching Lloyd George's future to his own, he laid the foundation of a partnership which was to be the cornerstone of his administrations through peace into war and coalition.

Despite his momentary display of inelegant butchery, Asquith did not cull the herd all at once. He surprised Herbert Gladstone with an encouraging invitation to remain at the Home Office.[18] The veterans Henry Fowler and Lord Ripon lingered on for a few more months. John Morley took a peerage and stayed until, after a score of false promises, he at last resigned on the outbreak of war. Into the vacancies at the lower levels came Charles Masterman and Jack Seely, both destined for quick promotion and unhappy interruptions to their careers. Jack Pease, who was promised the reversion to the office of Chief Whip, confirmed the wisdom of the premier's choice:

> Masterman was a most unpractical politician, he was an idealist who let loose below the gangway could do & had done mischief, but I was glad his tongue was tied & that he might see the difficulties of putting into practice his theories at the Local Govmt. Board. ... As for Seely, ... he had worked loyally with us, deserved his position through his work in the country & for the ability he had displayed, & as long as he was outside the ministry he had an influence which was capable of weakening the Govmt. in case of any disagreement.[19]

Whatever the reasons for their inclusion in the ministry, the new men, with the old, made a powerful team. To most students of Asquith's premiership, the ability of the Prime Minister to keep so gifted and divergently inclined a group in harness is seen as one of his major achievements. There were many occasions when conscientious differences were manifest. Over naval estimates, the House of Lords, and Ireland, schism seemed a recurrent danger. Disagreement on policy was sometimes aggravated by temperamental clashes. There was always an abundance of new ideas and plausible compromises to be appraised, as well as an intermittent stream of impractical schemes to be diverted. And presiding over so fertile a Cabinet, Asquith happily assumed the role of mediator rather than initiator. 'I have succeeded in getting back into more or less smooth water,' was a characteristic contemporary note. 'Happily,' he wrote on another occasion, 'not for the first (or perhaps the last) time, I was able to devise a form of saving words.'[20] The premier's calming influence was valuable. He did not play favourites in the Cabinet, and he contrived, at least until 1915, to appear loyal to all his colleagues which, according to J.A.Spender, was 'a very rare virtue in Prime Ministers'.[21] When, for example, Walter Runciman's Education Bill had to be withdrawn in December 1908, Asquith refused to accept Runciman's resignation. 'We cannot separate our fortunes in this matter,' the premier wrote, masking realistic calculation as an expression of sympathetic solidarity.[22]

It would be wrong, however, to overlook the fact that the stability and cohesion of the ministry owed at least as much to the unprompted behaviour of Asquith's colleagues, as to the Prime Minister's skill in reconciling them to each other. Morley's celebrated twenty-three resignations were not averted by Asquith's persuasion, but by his own undisguised preference for office. As Reginald McKenna cautioned Walter Runciman in October 1911, 'so long as a man retains office he retains the power to resign at his own time and for his own reasons'.[23] Two weeks later, when he unwillingly exchanged jobs with Winston Churchill, McKenna had an opportunity to heed his own advice. He threatened resignation; but he stayed, despite the fact that the Anglo–French military conversations, which he had strenuously opposed, were not terminated.[24] There is no need to take too seriously the self-righteous proclamation of Lloyd George, who told Crewe in February 1911:

> Frankly I think our naval expenditure an outrage on Liberal traditions & had it not been that I foresaw the disastrous effect of a split I should not have assented to them in 1909.[25]

Lloyd George, like most of his colleagues, had an unplumbed capacity for swallowing outrages on Liberal tradition. He relied on his ministerial salary, and enjoyed power too much to contemplate seriously a return to the back benches. And, although Edward Grey might hanker after trout-streams, Loulou Harcourt for unlimited game at close range, and Morley for his unread library, Grey believed that Walter Runciman, with his shipping interests, was 'almost the only man in the Cabinet who has a real perhaps even a preferable alternative to office'.[26] In any case, notwithstanding recurrent evidences of friction, as Grey was to tell Lloyd George in 1913, 'the personal relations of all of us have not only stood the long strain but have gained in attachment to an extent that must be very rare if not unprecedented in the history of Cabinets.'[27]

Certainly it must be conceded that, if Asquith's colleagues were sometimes a trial to him, they were also the staunch workhorses and stimulating innovators without whom his administration might well have been a stagnant interlude. He rightly resented the notion that he was 'a figurehead pushed along against his will and without his knowledge by some energetic colleagues'.[28] He went nowhere unwittingly; and as a braking influence he had few equals. Yet, what other contributions did he make? Not one of his colleagues has left unequivocally favourable testimony to his organization of government business. His Cabinet was the last in British history to operate without a secretary, agenda, or minutes. For want of an official record, ministers had to scribble their impressions in private journals or on odd sheets of paper. Carrington, Pease, Hobhouse and Burns wrote regular jottings on events. Harcourt, in particular, scandalized some of his colleagues by taking surreptitious notes while Cabinet meetings were in progress.[29] At least Harcourt's record was intended for personal use. From 1914 on, Asquith often divulged more of the proceedings to his young friend Venetia Stanley – sometimes in letters written while he was ostensibly presiding over a meeting of ministers – than to the King, who was the recipient of the only authorized account of Cabinet discussions.

Cabinet meetings during sittings of Parliament were held weekly in normal times, more frequently in times of crisis. Wednesday was the usual day. Informality of business arrangements gave to the Prime Minister an undefined power of initiating and ending consideration of particular subjects. And Asquith did not hesitate to postpone awkward decisions, refer contentious matters to committees, or settle disputes by private negotiation between the ministers most concerned rather than allow exhaustive deliberation by the Cabinet as a whole. It was not Asquith's custom to come to a Cabinet completely briefed and with a decision in his pocket. 'His powerful brain operated directly upon questions as they were put before him,' Augustine Birrell recalled, 'and he never seemed to go in search of them.'[30] Morley put it more harshly, speaking privately in 1912 of the premier's indolence and confidence 'in his ability to furnish at least some provisional solution when the situation created by neglect threatens to get out of hand'.[31]

When he chose to assert himself, Asquith had the mental equipment to dominate all his colleagues. But usually he used a light rein in preference to the cramping imposition of authority. 'He never spoke a word in Council if he could get his way without it,' Churchill remembered.[32] He did not press those of his ministers, like Morley, Grey and Harcourt, who did less than their share of parliamentary drudgery. There was, at least in the Commons, no shortage of eager men willing to shoulder extra burdens in the hope of greater recognition and preferment. Similarly, in the moulding of policy, especially social policy, the inventive and optimistic members of the Cabinet were given scope for self-assertion. Thus, when John Burns, in October 1908, appeared to be incapable of comprehending the gravity of the unemployment problem, he was 'outvoted and practically superseded by the appointment of a Cabinet Committee on Unemployment', consisting of Churchill, Lloyd George, Harcourt, Buxton, Gladstone, and McKenna, as well as Burns himself.[33]

By appointing *ad hoc* Cabinet committees, Asquith could relieve the whole Cabinet of tedious detail over such subjects as Colonial Office reorganization, franchise reform, or estimates. In selecting the personnel of such committees, he could exercise a discreet control over unwanted opinions or ensure that discussion was limited to those who had departmental responsibility or expert knowledge to contribute. Immediately after the general election of December 1910, for example, three special committees were nominated. A Foreign Affairs committee – apparently created to placate Lloyd George who had complained of being 'kept in the dark in regard to the essential features of our Foreign Policy' – consisted of the Prime Minister, Grey, Lloyd George, Morley, Crewe, and Runciman. Civil Service and Naval Estimates were given to the Chancellor of the Exchequer, with the Lord Chancellor, Churchill, Crewe, Burns, Buxton, and Pease. The heads of the big spending departments – Haldane, McKenna and Runciman – were to appear as witnesses. In addition, to 'ascertain [the] real facts bearing on finance of Home Rule', the Lord Chancellor, Birrell, Samuel, Grey, Haldane, Churchill and Lloyd George formed what was described as a committee of 'experts'.[34]

Little is known of the working of Cabinet committees or how long they lasted. A short life, no more than a couple of months, seems to have been typical. (The life of the Foreign Affairs committee, for example, seems to have ended by late July 1911.) When such groups were appointed to deal with particular bills, details were thrashed out 'in consultation with all the experts concerned and at command'.[35] Especially in uncharted fields like unemployment insurance, ministers could use the informal framework of a committee to consult with official and outside advisers. In April 1909 and again twice during April 1911 unemployment insurance was referred from the Cabinet in this way.[36] There was, however, no rule governing the use of committees. The army estimates escaped scrutiny in 1911 because, as the Cabinet was told, Lloyd George and Haldane (with Asquith's approval) had made a private 'deal'. The same thing seems to have happened the following year. When attention was drawn to the fact that Haldane's estimates had been presented to Parliament without ever being submitted to the Cabinet, the Secretary of State for War replied, amid laughter, that 'they had been about for some time'. Loulou Harcourt's slightly crestfallen rejoinder, 'about where?' was the nearest the Cabinet got to asserting its authority.[37] National Health Insurance was not assigned to a committee; but the Osborne Judgement and taxation problems arising out of the proposal to remove the pauper disqualification for old-age pensions were. The committee device, as Asquith employed it, was not only an administrative convenience but a way of both siphoning controversy out of the Cabinet and prolonging discussion of matters upon which public opinion, sectional interests, or forceful ministers sought quick decisions.

Asquith had no 'inner Cabinet'. He did, however, confide more readily in Crewe and Grey than in his other colleagues. In February 1912, Haldane told a friend that he, Grey, Lloyd George and Churchill 'generally dined together every week'.[38] And these four, though by no means constituting an inner Cabinet or enjoying the Prime Minister's exclusive favour, were demonstrably the most powerful individuals in the ministry. Still, Lloyd George and Churchill did not learn about the controversial Anglo–French military conversations until the whole Cabinet was informed in 1911. Knowledge of the military conversations was not confined to a permanent inner group. But there can be no doubt that care was taken to prevent news of the conversations leaking to ministers other than those who were directly involved in their inception or their subsequent continuation. The Committee of Imperial Defence was employed as a conveniently exclusive forum for the discussion of naval and military problems. In practice, especially after 1910, the CID was usually occupied with technical minutiae, and had little to do with major strategic questions. Since most members of the Cabinet assumed that defence was receiving expert examination in CID meetings, the War Office and Admiralty were left remarkably free to cooperate, or decline to cooperate, as they chose. Only with the appointment of Churchill's friend, Jack Seely, to the War Office in 1913 was any effective reconciliation of opposing departmental plans for a Continental war secured.[39]

The deliberations and conclusions of the CID were not, as of right, open to the Cabinet. In defence of restrictions, Morley wrote in July 1908: 'If every member of the Cabinet is to have permission for a roving exploration of the secrets of the CID the only result would be that the WO, the Admiralty, and the IO, would keep secrets to themselves, and the CID would find itself hamstrung. I think the PM (who is the master of the CID) should make his authorizations rather specific, limited and defined.'[40] Asquith did precisely this. Exclusiveness was further facilitated by the frequent absence of those ministers whom the Prime Minister had authorized to attend CID meetings. And, on occasions when the presence of particular people' – Morley or Harcourt, for example – was likely to be awkward, Asquith did not scruple to omit their names from the list of members to be summoned. The flagrant packing of one meeting, the famous gathering on 23 August 1911, provoked a major Cabinet storm. Attempting to justify the failure to invite Harcourt, Morley, and Lord Esher, Asquith called the meeting a sub-committee meeting. Harcourt was not slow to point out that no sub-committee had been appointed by the plenary committee. The true explanation, he believed, was that the meeting 'was arranged some time ago for a date when it was supposed that we should all be out of London . . . to decide on where and how British troops could be landed to assist a French Army on the Meuse!!!'[41]

This incident shook the faith of some of Asquith's colleagues in his candour and fair dealing with them. Jack Pease put it very simply, after two long and angry Cabinet meetings:

> Asquith, Grey, Haldane, Lloyd George, Churchill, thought they
> could boss the rest, but were mistaken ... on November 15 we won a
> great victory for a principle ... Asquith laid down the constitutional
> doctrine as to cabinet control in very effective words but majority of
> us felt he had been a party to a Defence Comtee arrangement ... &
> they had rigged an arrangement to go to war if necessity arose.[42]

What increased the disquiet of Pease, Harcourt, Runciman and
others was that Churchill and Lloyd George, who until 1911 had always
been relied upon 'for anti-war feeling', had suddenly

> become the really warlike element in our Government [and] have
> not only developed these new tendencies with rapidity but are
> characteristically given to rushes. The stability or balance of opinion
> of the cabinet cannot now be relied on by us ...[43]

There was no single member of the Cabinet to whom Asquith
always opened his mind; and there were some who rarely enjoyed his
confidences. Self-contained as he chose to be, it was, nevertheless,
impossible for him to remain ignorant of a fundamental shift in the
attitudes of Churchill and Lloyd George on defence questions. But,
because he 'left his colleagues more alone than a Prime Minister
should, and did not always communicate with them in writing as often
as he might have done',[44] he ran the risk of not detecting significant
movements of opinion before they were pressed upon him. There
were, of course, some subjects that were not ripe or not suitable for
general discussion. And on such questions as reshuffling the ministry
or going to the country, it was hardly surprising that he should reflect
alone before soliciting opinions, if indeed he genuinely heeded
comradely counsel. It is true that no dissolution took place without
Cabinet approval, as Asquith testified in his *Fifty Years of Parliament*.[45]
Hypothetical dissolutions were another matter. Cabinet was consulted
about the advisability of an election after the Lords' rejection of the
Licensing Bill in November 1908.[46] Late in 1913, however, only the views
of Grey, Crewe, Lloyd George and Haldane on a July 1914 election were
considered.[47] Grey (and possibly Crewe) was asked to advise whether a
dissolution would help to resolve the deadlock over naval estimates in

1914.[48] Lloyd George was consulted about a possible dissolution in 1913.[49] On none of these occasions did the matter come before the Cabinet. Grey appears to have been the sole confidant when the switch of Churchill and McKenna between the Home Office and the Admiralty was in contemplation in October 1911.[50] Such appointments were, of course, entirely the Prime Minister's prerogative.

Twice in the life of Asquith's government, over the reform of the House of Lords and Home Rule, a small negotiating committee of the Cabinet was deputed to explore the possibilities of compromise in conference with Tory front-bench delegates. That such constitutional conferences should more than once have been employed is an indication of the extraordinary nature of political life in this period. So deeply and bitterly divided were the principal parties from each other, and sometimes among themselves, that the normal constitutional machinery ceased for a time to function effectively. The breakdown of the political system, accompanied as it was by the periodic abandonment of conventional parliamentary courtesies, was caused partly by the uncompromising intention of Asquith and his colleagues to govern without the perpetual barrier of a Conservative House of Lords blocking major items of legislation. Partly, too, resistance was provoked by tactical error. Asquith's perpetuation of Campbell-Bannerman's practice of overloading the House of Commons' timetable had the double disadvantage of tiring his ministers and supporters and irritating the opposition. Alfred Emmott, the Chairman of Ways and Means from 1906 to 1911, recorded sadly on 12 March 1911:

> Poor Crewe collapsed on Friday week. Lloyd George still unable to be in the House ... McKenna & Harcourt both unable to conduct their election campaigns. On the top of all that the PM promises both Welsh Disest' & Home Rule for next year![51]

Paradoxically, it was in the middle of the first constitutional conference – born in deadlock – that a dramatic proposal of coalition, emanating from Lloyd George, was examined by the leaders of both great parties.[52] The struggle over the future of the House of Lords had brought out some of Asquith's best oratory and touched his deepest convictions. At the same time, by vacillation between limiting the

Lords' veto and reforming or abolishing the second chamber, he lost his grip on a section of the Cabinet and a vocal minority of the Liberal party in Parliament and the country. The situation was initially aggravated by Asquith's insensitivity to the balance of opinion in the Cabinet. He treated Grey's prolonged advocacy of a reformed upper house as an isolated eccentricity until McKenna, Runciman, and others went out of their way to demonstrate that Grey was not speaking or acting alone.[53]

Although he continued the work of social reform begun under Campbell-Bannerman, Asquith's radicalism went little deeper than that of his predecessor. His speeches on the constitutional crisis in 1910 and 1911 were a revelatory reminder of his own fundamental conservatism. 'We, the Liberal party,' he said at Manchester on 6 May 1911, 'are left to be the sole effective trustees of the principle of representative government.' He shrank with alarm from the referendum proposed by the Tories as an expedient device for resolving contentious issues. He had indeed toyed with the referendum heresy himself, but had overcome the temptation. His defence of the existing representative system – 'the great invention of modern political genius' – was thus not just a clever debating point; it was a testimony of faith. In the clash of debate and the enactment of legislation at Westminster he saw the guarantee of liberty and the hope for progress.

Where did Asquith seek to lead the nation? His conception of progress was limited. He gave intellectual assent to much of the new Liberalism: he gave it no passion or inspiration. When charged with exhausting the government's energies in 'tinkering the Constitution', he could retort with an impressive catalogue of legislative achievement, despite the frequently exercised veto of the Lords. Even J.A.Hobson was obliged to commend the 'new crystallization of Liberal policy' which could be observed by the end of 1909. Old-age pensions, wages boards, labour exchanges, public provision for the development of natural resources, enterprising policies for small holdings and town planning, taxes on unearned increments – all these, as Hobson admitted, exhibited 'a coherency of purpose, an organic plan of social progress, which implies a new consciousness of Liberal statecraft'.[54] And national insurance against unemployment and invalidity was still to come. But whose was the new consciousness? Asquith as Chancellor of the Exchequer had carried through major income tax reforms and had begun the planning of old-age pensions, land taxes, and a scheme of super-tax. But the more visionary innovators among his colleagues were impatient for a comprehensive strategy. 'Our real danger,' Lloyd George confided to Churchill in September 1910, 'is that the Government will drift along without any clear definite policy or purpose. I am perfectly certain that our more important associates have no plan of operations in their minds. This aimlessness, if persevered in, means utter disaster.'[55] Lloyd George's fears were at this time specifically focused on the current constitutional crisis; but even then his mind was at work on the future policy and prospects of the government.[56]

Asquith's deficiency was not simply that he had, as he once told an audience at the Empire Theatre, Oldham, 'too much of the old Adam of Cobdenism' in his blood.[57] He was lukewarm about state intervention; but, worse, he was as cautious about altering the traditional machinery of government as he was about changing conventional policies. Churchill had perceived by the end of 1908 that it would be possible to organize the planning and execution of public works, municipal and national, in a way that would significantly counteract fluctuations in employment. In June 1909 he proposed to Lloyd George the establishment of a Committee of National Organization, 'analogous in many respects to the Committee of Imperial Defence', chaired by the Chancellor of the Exchequer. Such a body could become responsible for forecasting the degree of unemployment, distributing Treasury funds between the various development bodies, and investigating the merits of proposals for constructive expenditure on roads, afforestation, canals or municipal relief.[58] The scheme came to nothing. There is no evidence that it ever reached Asquith; but so drastic an infringement of departmental boundaries was involved that it is scarcely conceivable that he or the Treasury would have approved it if it had come before them.

Asquith continued the practice of leaving departmental ministers substantially free from direction by the Prime Minister. However, the combination of a large busy Cabinet and the transfer of certain matters of high policy into the arena of the Committee of Imperial Defence and the Imperial Conferences, affected the position of the Prime Minister in relation to his colleagues.[59] Sidney Low thought in 1913 that:

> ... the Premier is acquiring the attributes of an Imperial Chancellor, and that he is performing certain duties to which the collective responsibility of the Cabinet cannot easily be applied.[60]

The peril of departmentalism and loose Cabinet coordination was emphasized in the preamble to Lloyd George's memorandum on coalition, written in August 1910:

> The head of a Department is supreme in that Department; not even the Prime Minister can effectively direct, guide and control his action; and, as for the rest of the Government, they are too concerned in the management of their own Departments to be able to give the necessary attention, even if it were possible for them to interfere with a colleague.

The industrial magnate Alfred Mond remarked, at about the same time, that ministers were so preoccupied with departmental trivia that they had insufficient time to devote to 'the working out and exposition of reasoned policy'.[61] What made the system more pernicious, according to Lloyd George, was that:

> No Party commands the services of more than half a dozen first-rate men, and it has to depend for the filling up of all the other posts in the Government upon the services of men of second and even third-rate capacity.[62]

Asquith, though likewise undeceived about the capacity of his team, did nothing to advance the cause of coalition. Nor did he point the way beyond what Lloyd George called 'carving the last few columns out of the Gladstonian quarry'.[63] After the general elections of January and December 1910, with the government henceforth dependent on Irish and Labour votes in the House of Commons, it was obvious that 'a wide programme of National reconstruction'[64] would encounter formidable obstacles. Crewe confessed in October 1910 that 'we have got pretty nearly to the end of our tether as regards great reforms on party lines ... and I don't see signs of the driving force which is to carry them.'[65]

Whatever else was demonstrated by the two general elections of 1910, it became clear that Asquith had not captured the imagination of the electorate, and that massive readjustment to the organization as well as the image of the Liberal party would be necessary if it were to aspire to a further lease of life.[66]

Where did Asquith fail? A cruel critic wrote in 1921:

> The truth is that Mr Asquith possesses all the appearances of greatness but few of the elements. He has dignity of language, trenchant dialectic, a just and honourable mind, but he is entirely without creative power. . . .
>
> He is a cistern and not a fountain.[67]

It was not enough that some of his colleagues bubbled over in generous compensation for his own deficiencies. For the Liberal party craved invigorating leadership and got instead a man whose 'understatement that amounted to taciturnity and a certain shyness and self-discipline, made even' friendly people think him inaccessible'.[68] No one ever accused Asquith of surrounding himself with a dense protective company of secretaries and assistants. On the contrary, he erred in not seeing the value of a personal staff to digest information and extend the range of his own executive arm. In 1913, the Prime Minister's personal secretariat numbered four, at a total cost to the exchequer of £1,017 a year.[69] From his diligent but unimaginative private office, Asquith received the routine competence that he expected, but not the stimulation that he needed. Nor, after the promotion of the melancholic yet effusive Edwin Montagu, did he get from his parliamentary private secretaries anything more than the most perfunctory gleanings of House of Commons gossip.[70]

It was also a legitimate criticism of Asquith that he overvalued the ministerial aptitude of men stamped in his own mould. He gave ample recognition to such un-Asquithian characters as Churchill and Lloyd George; but Lloyd George's idea – tentatively expressed in 1910 – of forming a government of businessmen was, at least in part, a sensible reaction to the undue prominence of lawyers and men of letters on the Liberal front bench.[71] Asquith persistently excluded from his Cabinet representatives of the large body of manufacturers, merchants, and financiers whose wealth and influence were so important in vitalizing the Liberal party at the constituency level. With the exception of Walter Runciman, Jack Pease and Percy Illingworth, his contacts with men of this type were minimal. With the ordinary Members of Parliament, the vast majority of his followers, he had practically no communication. He did not meet them socially. Though anything but a recluse, his entertaining – usually organized by the irrepressible Margot – and his excursions into society were confined to a select circle.

While he would have been the last person to tolerate discourtesy to parliament, Asquith, like Balfour and C.B., spent little time on the Treasury bench. The parliamentary correspondent of *The British Weekly* left this impression:

> He arrived at the proper moment to answer questions, scanning the prepared answers as he came in; and having given his replies, he went to his room, reappearing only when his intervention in debate was required. With an adroitness never surpassed he replied to questions intended to embarrass him, but his answers in many cases were so brief that they conveyed the impression of curtness.[72]

No machinery existed for the corporate expression of opinion by the Liberal party in the House of Commons. Experienced backbenchers like Sir Thomas Whittaker from time to time summoned emergency gatherings.[73] But the Liberal parliamentary party held only two official meetings between 1908 and 1914. Of these, Asquith attended one, in April 1908. In theory, the assembly met to 'determine who the Liberal leader shall be'; in practice it welcomed the new Prime Minister.[74] At the second gathering, in June 1909, the Budget League was formed. So far as Asquith was concerned, relations between the leadership of the party and the rank and file were a matter for the whips. He selected his Chief Whips with care, and reposed great confidence in them. Jack Pease, the Master of Elibank and Percy Illingworth brought, respectively, simple honesty, silky urbanity and Yorkshire nous to the premier's service. And it is a tribute to their talents that, in spite of the opaque focus provided by Asquith, they succeeded in binding the disparate elements of the party together through all the dissensions over the naval estimates, the 1909 Budget, the constitutional crisis, and Ireland. John Gulland, the bearded Scottish teetotaller who succeeded

Illingworth in January 1915, was overwhelmed by the strains of war politics. He would not have been chosen had more favoured candidates like J.H.Whitley or Wedgwood Benn been willing to undertake the task.[75]

The Liberal parliamentary party was a fragmentary and moody body held together less by affection for its leader than by a common antipathy to tariff reform and Unionism. It is often remarked that the party contained a large and potentially disruptive radical wing, that groups representing the Celtic fringe wielded great influence, and that the scores of nonconformist members were not disposed to forget the claims of conscience when their interests were at stake. Mr George Dangerfield, in his well-known study of *The Strange Death of Liberal England*, wrote of the Liberals as 'an irrational mixture of Whig aristocrats, industrialists, dissenters, reformers, trade unionists, quacks and Mr Lloyd George'.[76] Differences in social origin and occupation were, for the most part, less divisive than incompatible opinions. It is true that the 'troglodytes', some thirty in number, who opposed the 'socialistic tendencies' of the 1909 Budget included some very rich men. But there were many more wealthy Liberals who spoke and voted unhesitatingly in favour of the Budget and the rest of the government's reform legislation.

The largest single group of backbenchers was that which fought the continual compaign against rising naval and military expenditure. Just before Asquith became Prime Minister, the government had been dangerously close to defeat in the House of Commons by the reductionists. Asquith himself had to persuade the rebels to withdraw the amendment they proposed to move to the address on 5 February 1908; and Tweedmouth was obliged to lop £400,000 off the naval estimates.[77] In the following year the protests of the reductionists were torpedoed by the naval scare. Thereafter, from the introduction of the 1909 Budget until the Agadir crisis in 1911, all radical criticism, whether of estimates or foreign policy, was engulfed by domestic controversy. Instead of the six or seven score whose petitions had earlier shaken the Cabinet, only thirty-four could be mustered in the reductionist lobby in March 1910. Winston Churchill informed the King that 'the discussions have been lifeless, and enormous sums of money and vast programmes of reconstruction have been agreed to with an almost cataleptic apathy.'[78]

In the years following the Agadir crisis, Asquith, and especially Grey, were subjected to periodic questioning in the House by the eighty-strong unofficial Liberal Foreign Affairs Committee. In the autumn of 1911, in the words of Dr Dorey, 'the Radicals and their allies woke up to discover that Grey, trusted to look after foreign policy, had allowed it to go off the rails.'[79] The Liberal Foreign Affairs Committee, chaired in successive years by Noël Buxton, Philip Morrell and Arthur Ponsonby, attempted to arrest the anti-German tendency of government policy, and to elicit regular information on the whole range of foreign affairs. The 'severe economy of truth'[80] practised by the Foreign Secretary provoked searching inquiries into the nature of British commitments to other countries.[81] In answer to questions from two of the radicals, Sir William Byles and Joseph King, Asquith found it necessary to lend his own authority to the assurance that the government was in no way obliged by secret agreements to go to war should a European conflict develop.

Radical critics of foreign policy were relatively quiescent from the winter of 1912 until the Cabinet was once more riven by a naval estimates dispute in December 1913 and January 1914. However, even at the peak of their influence, the reductionists and the Foreign Affairs group rarely constituted a serious threat to the government. There was, after all, no point in turning out a Liberal government to put in a ministry of Conservatives who would spend more on armaments and be less reluctant to use them.[82] Nevertheless, Asquith could not afford to lose sight of the connection between opposition to spiralling defence expenditure and a more general hankering after economy. *The Economist* warned of the need to forestall 'a general protest against the burden of rates and taxes',[83] a reminder of Morley's dictum about the danger of trying to rule against the middle class. Such a protest came, in a minor way, in 1914. Seizing upon a technical defect in Lloyd George's Budget, Richard Holt, the Liverpool shipowner, led 'a combined remonstrance by businessmen and some survivors of the Cobden-Bright school of thought against the ill-considered & socialistic tendencies of the Government finance'. Holt summed up the views of his associates in a terse diary entry: 'We have certainly travelled a long way from the old Liberal principle of "retrenchment", and I deeply regret it.'[84]

In general, the discipline of the Liberal rank and file was as consistent as the party managers could wish. There was no permanently recalcitrant knot of dissentients. A snap division on the afternoon of 11 November 1912 on the report stage of a Home Rule Bill financial resolution was the only time when the whips were unexpectedly embarrassed by a shortage of obedient backbenchers. One hundred and four Liberals were absent unpaired, giving a Unionist majority of twenty-one. The Conservatives made what *The Liberal Magazine* justly termed 'a ludicrous attempt to pretend that the division represented the real feeling of the House, because certain Liberal members had criticized the financial proposals of the Home Rule Bill on certain points'.[85] The real trouble was slack whipping compounded by the accidental absence of the Chief Whip and his deputy, leaving the management of the House in inexperienced hands.[86] Many north-country and Welsh members had not returned from weekend visits to their constituencies. And as Richard Holt explained in his diary, 'Businessmen like myself must attend to their businesses.'[87] Such a defeat provided a temptation for opportunist Liberals to drive home criticisms of the government. The energetic radical MacCallum Scott enumerated three causes for complaint: '(1) Ministers absent. (2) The overcrowding of the session. Congestion of business. Overwork in Committees. (3) The uneasiness about the Finance of the Irish Bill.'[88] In particular there was mounting criticism about the pressure of work in the House, and Asquith adroitly turned this to account as an added reason for proceeding without delay to the enactment of Home Rule.[89]

Complaints about the declining opportunities for effective backbench participation in the process of government were already, in Asquith's period, the conventional wisdom of the textbooks. The Estimates Committee, set up in 1912, was a feeble experiment in parliamentary control that lapsed on the outbreak of war. And such procedural devices as were left to the private member were as ruthlessly abolished or circumvented by Asquith as by any of his predecessors. When plagued by questions, mainly from Conservatives, after the Curragh incident, Asquith simply announced that he would answer no more.[90] The government was obstructed at the same time by its own supporters who exploited the loophole that permitted the blocking of debate on any subject by putting down a notice of motion on that subject. Standing Orders were accordingly altered to give the Speaker discretion to ignore blocking notices.[91]

Commenting on Asquith's frequent resort to the closure in 1912 and 1913, Sidney Low remarked:

> It may or may not be true that the 'closure by compartments' method 'stifles the voice and paralyses the action of the House of Commons', and that it is causing the House of Commons to be regarded as a mere automatic machine for registering the edicts of a transient majority.[92]

These quotations, exhumed with understandable relish by the opposition, were from Asquith's own speech in July 1904 on the proposal to closure the Licensing Bill by stages. Asquith probably did not enjoy devouring all parliamentary power and initiative; nor was he prepared to admit that the power of the private MP had actually diminished between the 1880s and 1914.[93] But the imbalance of strength between the Cabinet and the private member was not, in any case, caused by the rule of procedure; the rules themselves were a consequence of the determination of the government to legislate. Austen Chamberlain, reflecting on the snap division of November 1912, recalled that:

> Asquith said in the Parliament Bill debates that the real protection of the minority against the forcing through of several highly contentious measures in a single session was that the attempt to do so would break down the limits of physical endurance, and that is just what happened. He had overworked his men and sooner or later was bound to reap the penalty which he had himself foretold.[94]

Immediately after the snap defeat, a junior whip, William Wedgwood Benn, was given a free hand by Percy Illingworth to improve the technical machinery for summoning and recording the movements of members. Benn devised a system of intelligence-gathering and control that made a repetition of the November 1912 incident almost impossible. Extra telephones, a pneumatic message tube, and a two-tiered 'scoring board' were installed; and a vigilance committee was formed to observe the movements of the opposition. According to Benn, the underlying principle of the reorganization was to aim at the maximum leave of absence for government supporters, rather than the maximum attendance – a shift of emphasis grounded in shrewd insight into backbench temperament.[95]

The government's majority was, in fact, more frequently endangered by the unrecorded wanderings of the faithful than by deliberate acts of opposition. Dissent as a way of life was congenial only to a tiny minority. Radical consciences were, it must be admitted, rarely still for long. They erupted on many issues. Over imperial policy, Dr Bernard Porter has argued persuasively that between Vereeniging and Sarajevo 'Radicals had learnt to come to terms with the African Empire. ... They criticized the way Britain was administering it, but not the fact that she did administer it.'[96] Thus twenty-six Liberals defied front-bench advice and voted against racially discriminatory provisions of the South Africa Act.[97] Nearly as many voted to reduce the salary of the Foreign Secretary in protest against the Czar's visit in 1909. Twenty-three registered their objection in 1910 to the failure of the government to transfer the revenues of the duchies of Lancaster and Cornwall to the public exchequer. Eight deplored the Press and Seditious Meetings Act and other restrictive legislation in India. An amendment to the Welsh Church Bill in December 1912 produced eleven votes against the government whose majority fell from the usual one hundred to fifty.[98] These irritating disturbances usually subsided quickly and were not always taken as far as the division lobbies, though dissent was disseminated widely in ably written radical journals.[99] Manifestations of reaction against the reforming drift of Liberal legislation were even fewer. About thirty, mostly wealthy, men turned out to vote against various clauses of the 1909 Budget dealing with the land taxes. But the third reading of the Finance Bill went through with only two Liberal votes against it, and a handful of abstentions. None of these episodes represented a specifically anti-Asquith demonstration. Nor did they suggest any possibility that he had lost enough of the party's confidence to be in danger of deposition.

Until the disillusion which spread in the Liberal ranks when the government seemed to have lost control of the Irish situation in 1914, there was only one occasion when Asquith's own position was in jeopardy. Before the general election in January 1910 he had given the impression to the country that he had a guarantee from the King to create sufficient peers to pass the Budget into law. When it was revealed that no such assurance had been given, the disappointment and annoyance among Liberal supporters was intense. The whips found their men 'more plain than polite' about the way they had been misled.[100] In addition, having lost his independent majority, Asquith was impelled to negotiate for support in the Commons from the Irish Nationalists, thus further exposing the government to criticism for 'sordid' bargaining. A number of ministers advocated the resignation of the government. Some of the Prime Minister's colleagues feared that if the situation were not saved promptly, Churchill and Lloyd George might be tempted to resign and lead the disaffected forces. 'They will say,' Runciman predicted at the end of March, 'that the time has come for him to show that the Government is in earnest and the sovereign must be approached. All the Radicals and the Irish will demand this step; Asquith will decline to do it; the cry will go forth "Make way for some one who will".'[101]

During March and April 1910, as Lucy Masterman recorded:

The Party got extremely depressed. A large number of members had great difficulties in their constituencies, the executives of the Associations resigning right and left, and I believe the Government's reputation never stood so low as at that moment. Asquith, I was told, wandered about utterly wretched and restless, like a man conscious that he is facing a situation too big for him. Private members brought pressure to bear on the Whips.[102]

After a fortnight of gradual stiffening, Asquith disproved Runciman's gloomy prophecy and reunited Cabinet and party with an unambiguous approach to the King and a firm declaration of intent in parliament.

Very early in his ministerial career, Asquith sketched out what might be taken as the intellectual basis of his political style. 'In this country,' he contended, 'public opinion and popular conviction when they are profoundly stirred are too strong a force to be manipulated by the most cunning devices of politicians.' Democracies, like individuals, he said, had moods. At times there was a disposition to push on 'full steam ahead'; at other times the inclination might be for half speed. And there could be 'moments of reaction, very temporary, very transient, when they almost seem to stand still.'[103] Holding a view like this, it is not surprising that Asquith eschewed attempts to sway audiences with rhetoric, and that he remained extraordinarily unconcerned – even by the standards of his contemporaries – at the image he presented to the newspapers; or that the electoral implications of the growing disposition in the Labour party towards independence should have apparently troubled him so little.

Yet the year of Asquith's accession to the premiership saw the beginning of a new understanding of what Graham Wallas called 'Human Nature in Politics'. William Trotter, in pioneering articles in *The Sociological Review*, William MacDougall in his *Social Psychology*, and Wallas, all contributed to a formal exposition of the non-rational factors in political life which were instinctively being exploited by Joseph Chamberlain, Lloyd George, Churchill, and other flamboyant characters. 'Advertisement and party politics are becoming more and more closely assimilated in method,' Wallas observed.[104] Sometimes, Wallas noted, 'a man of exceptional personal force and power of expression . . . may fashion a permanent and recognizable mask for himself'.[105] Asquith's mask was grave and unexciting. Only on rare occasions was he enticed by the spirit of his surroundings into communion with his hearers. Only once in his premiership was he caught up in the colour, gaiety, and manufactured enthusiasm of a staged political event. Sir Henry Norman, organizer of the Budget League, exhibited the Prime Minister and his entourage at Bingley Hall, Birmingham, on 17 September 1909, 'to yelling multitudes like a travelling circus; there were dinners and suppers on boards; flowers and champagne; cheers and mobs, as per programme'.[106] *The Morning Post* reporter detected, at one point in Asquith's speech that evening, that 'the face which admirers like to call sphinx-like was corrugated by a smile'.[107] There was no repetition of the Bingley Hall carnival.

The work of the Budget League deserves some further comment. In its six months' active existence, this *ad hoc* organization experimented and pioneered in the techniques of political persuasion. Inspired by

Churchill, its chairman, and organized by Henry Norman, the League mobilized all the resources of Liberal journalism, platform talent, and administrative acumen into a massive propaganda campaign to counteract the hostile claque of the Conservative opposition and its Budget Protest League. Asquith took little direct part in the League's work. He addressed three meetings, recorded a brief speech to be played on gramophones mounted in a fleet of ten vans, and held a reception for Liberal editors. In all these activities, however, there were glimpses of the possibilities of a new kind of political leadership.

The Bingley Hall meeting, if the overflow crowd was counted, was thought to be 'the largest political meeting under a roof in modern times'.[108] A conference of Liberal editors and correspondents, provincial and metropolitan, was the first, and – so far as can be ascertained – the last occasion before 1914 when an attempt was made to coordinate the flow of information between press and party. Lloyd George, Churchill, Pease and Norman conferred with twenty-four newspapermen, including A.G.Gardiner, C.P.Scott, J.A.Spender, Robert Donald, and H.W.Massingham, exchanging ideas, and agreeing at the end to the creation of machinery for the more effective dissemination of articles, speeches, cartoons, and pungent para- graphs.[109] The Budget gospel was spread in areas where paid speakers or dutiful MPs did not penetrate by the recording of speeches by Lloyd George and Churchill as well as the Prime Minister. The gramophone, though not unknown at elections, had not previously been employed on anything like this scale.[110]

That all this could have gone on under Asquith's eyes – indeed, Norman was appointed by the Prime Minister and, subject to the concurrence of a committee of MPs, was left unfettered in the choice of arguments and techniques – is an indication that Asquith was less contemptuous of the manipulative arts than he pretended to be. He never made himself accessible to reporters, but he did not ignore the press. He knew very well that his principal colleagues had close contacts with editors and political correspondents. He knew too that Liberal party money was invested, through nominees, in the *Westminster Gazette* and the *Birmingham Gazette*.[111] Admittedly, he habitually confused the editor of the *Daily Express* with the Chilean Naval Attaché;[112] but he took the Liberal editors seriously enough, at least once, to read out to the Cabinet a letter signed by Donald of the *Daily Chronicle*, Gardiner of the *Daily News*, Parke of the *Star*, and Hirst of the *Economist*, urging reductions in naval and military expenditure. 'The PM,' according to Pease, 'dwelt on the strength of the view and referred letter to [the naval estimates] Committee to consider.'[113]

As with the press, so with the party organization, Asquith's superficial indifference to details was underpinned by a realistic appraisal of where the strength lay, and an assurance of competence and loyalty from the permanent officials and Chief Whips. Edwin Montagu complained in June 1908 that the Liberals had 'too many conflicting and rather impotent spending institutions'.[114] Little could be done about independent organizations like the National Liberal Federation and the Free Trade Union. But, within a few months of Montagu's letter, the Liberal League had collapsed, thus removing one divisive influence. And, before the 1910 elections, Pease created a network of regional Liberal federations to supplement the patchy party framework and revive registration work. He devolved responsibility to the provinces, installing more trained agents who were answerable to the Liberal Central Association. Unlike the LCA, the National Liberal Federation was not controlled by the government. Under the presidency of Sir John Brunner from 1911 to 1913, it was notably susceptible to the influence of Francis Hirst, especially in bringing radical feeling to bear on Churchill's 'fatal and provocative' naval building programme, and Grey's foreign policy.[115] Because Hirst was in close touch with members of the ministry, the NLF was used by some ministers, in effect, as an auxiliary force in the policy struggle that was taking place in the Cabinet. It was fortunate for Asquith that throughout the six years of his peacetime premiership Sir Robert Hudson, as secretary of both the NLF and the LCA, could guarantee that the NLF's autonomy would not go beyond limits acceptable to the leader of the party. Hudson, his biographer contended, 'kept the confidential organization in touch with the rank and file in the country, and placed the party machine in a position in which it was safe from capture by any section'.[116]

For the whole of Asquith's premiership, the Chief Whip, following the traditional practice, was responsible for planning the parliamentary timetable, managing the government supporters in the House of

Commons, and, in addition, supervising the extra-parliamentary organization, the selection of candidates and the accumulation and disbursement of the party fund. By the middle of 1914, with some prompting from the Master of Elibank and Lloyd George, Asquith had admitted that the Chief Whip's multiple functions could no longer be performed effectively by one man. A proposal to create a new post of party organizer in the country, leaving the Chief Whip nothing but parliamentary work, was accepted in principle but overtaken by the Home Rule crisis and the outbreak of war.[117]

Perhaps the ultimate peacetime test of Asquith's statesmanship was the imminent threat of civil war that confronted the government in July 1914. Whether a bolder course in 1912 or 1913 might have averted the final bitter disputes about the exclusion of Ulster is a question to which historians can return no clear answer.[118] What is beyond question, however, is the very great damage done to Asquith's personal position in 1914. His relations with Bonar Law and other Conservative leaders deteriorated to a state of frigid formality that would have been imprudent at any time but was culpably hazardous when civil war, then European war, threatened. Even those of his colleagues who had been least openly critical of his leadership in the past were to be heard complaining that he had 'no power of action'.[119] Much depended on his nerve. Faced with the prospect of armed rebellion, 'there never was a time,' Christopher Addison wrote, 'when it was more important for Asquith to sit tight and maintain the rights of Parliament.'[120] For a short time, after the Curragh incident, Asquith's unequivocal pronouncement about the necessity for civil control of the army pleased the Liberal back benches. Opposition invective 'welded Liberals & Labour together to an extraordinary degree, and even moderate Liberal Imperialists are coming out strongly in protest.'[121] Charles Trevelyan described Asquith's assumption of the War Office as 'the greatest coup of the whole of this remarkable business'.[122] Within weeks, however, the initiative had slipped from the premier's hands. In May, the Chief Whip warned the Cabinet that, quite apart from disaffection among the rank and file, the sheer exhaustion of Liberal MPs would make it impossible to secure the attendance of enough members to ensure the safety of the government if there were an autumn session.[123] And, two months later, not only the government's majority but the whole political structure was on the verge of disintegration as rebellious forces threatened to take up arms in Ireland.

The outbreak of war in Europe and the British decision to stand by France rescued Asquith from the desperate uncertainty of the Irish situation.[124] For the first few months of war, the nation was united in the struggle against Prussian militarism and apparently content with Asquith's leadership. The government benefited from a surge of patriotic ardour, skilfully intensified by the speeches of Lloyd George and Churchill, and the ubiquitous face of Lord Kitchener. 'The unattackable K',[125] as Walter Runciman described him, was appointed to the War Office and given large powers over strategy, munitions, and recruiting. To Kitchener, and to Churchill at the Admiralty, the day-to-day direction of the war effort was entrusted. Asquith himself kept in closest touch with his principal colleagues. But the Cabinet, although it met frequently, exercised little control over major strategic questions.

Asquith had realized at the beginning of the war that, if the Liberal government split, it might be necessary to invite the Conservatives, and possibly the other parties, into a coalition. When, by the spring of 1915, it was obvious that Germany would not quickly be defeated, the idea of a national government was again in the air. The petulant resignation of Fisher, the First Sea Lord, at the same time as a parliamentary storm was gathering over the alleged shell shortage, made it impossible for the Conservative leaders to keep their followers in check and prevent an open attack on the government. Asquith agreed with Bonar Law and Lloyd George that a coalition, unattractive as it was to them all, was the imperative solution. But the suppression of political opposition at home was no substitute for victory in Europe or the Dardanelles. The Liberal rank and file did not welcome the abrupt termination of the government which they had supported for so long. Labour leaders joined the new government with deep misgivings. And the Conservative front-benchers entered the coalition with little enthusiasm and only a grudging allegiance to Asquith as Prime Minister.

Asquith never managed to weld the disparate elements of the coalition into a harmonious team. Indecision during 1915 and early 1916 over strategy, and especially over conscription and Britain's financial role in the war, angered the Tories. The abandonment of free trade and voluntary service strained Liberal loyalties. And Asquith's own dominance, over the ministry and over parliament, declined with the increasing paralysis of the supreme command. As early as November 1914, he had recognized that the major decisions of war policy could not effectively be taken by a group of twenty men, most of whom had extraneous departmental responsibilities. A small war council was created; and on it Arthur Balfour joined Asquith, Lloyd George, Churchill, Grey, Kitchener, the First Sea Lord, and the Chief of the Imperial General Staff. But neither the responsibility nor the powers of this body were ever properly defined. In less than four months five new members had been added. Yet Asquith did not infringe the formal authority of either the Cabinet or the Secretary of State for War and First Lord of the Admiralty.

As Prime Minister, Asquith was not only unassertive but inadequately informed. Maurice Hankey, secretary to the war council, pointed out on 17 May 1915, that there was 'literally no one in this country who knows, or has access to, all the information, naval, military, and political, on which future plans must be based'.[126] Though the bodies which succeeded the war council – the Dardanelles committee and the war committee – were better organized, they too suffered from imprecise duties and powers. Rather than establish a single body with supreme authority over day-to-day affairs as well as over future policy, Asquith sought, with decreasing success, to coordinate the various overlapping authorities by informal consultation with his senior colleagues. Had the government been blessed by military triumphs, its inefficiency might have been tolerated. But bloody failure on the Somme and elsewhere provoked a growing clamour for stronger leadership. After the resignation of Churchill and Carson late in 1915, and still more after Kitchener's death in June 1916, a masterful exertion of authority by the Prime Minister would have been opportune. But Asquith seemed incapable of seizing the initiative. And, as his own grasp weakened, so did his reliance on the sustaining presence of Lloyd George grow.

At the end of 1916, when Lloyd George, Carson, and Bonar Law were pressing for reform, even the faithful Crewe admitted that 'no member of the Government was undisturbed by a conviction that a prompt change in methods was demanded'.[127] Further, Arthur Balfour, whose loyalty Asquith had come to take for granted, urged that 'a fair trial should be given to the War Council à la George'.[128] Indeed, Lloyd George's rise to power was probably as much a consequence of the disillusion of Asquith's friends as it was of intrigue by his critics. For Lloyd George himself shrank from the supreme responsibility of the premiership. In urging a small, powerful war committee, he wished to remedy Asquith's executive inadequacy. But he believed that Asquith still retained considerable influence in the House of Commons and with the Liberal party in the country. Any government without Asquith, it seemed, would be in a precarious position.

Asquith was not overthrown by a palace revolution. Nor did he resign on the calculation that no one else could be successful in forming a government. His resignation, Professor Trevor Wilson has written, was 'a despairing act of recognition that the process of retreat and surrender could go no farther, and that the time had come to abandon a position from which dignity and authority had already departed'.[129] Momentarily, Asquith was in a despairing mood. Had he acted resolutely in his own interest he could have clung to the premiership and restored his waning influence. Instead, thinking that Lloyd George, Carson and Bonar Law had conspired to topple him, he gave up the struggle.

Eight and a half years in office had exacted a heavy toll on Asquith's fibre; the last months of contention and criticism also seem to have undermined his morale and unbalanced his judgement. He attributed the discredit of the ministry not to its own widely acknowledged defects but to the 'daily vindictive, merciless attacks in the columns of the newspapers'.[130] This was a far cry from his earlier characteristic affectation of disdain for the press. It is difficult to avoid the conclusion that the strain of the war, accentuated by insobriety, ill-health and private grief, had rendered him unfit to continue at the head of the nation's affairs. It was a melancholy end.

Assessments of Asquith's premiership have usually contrasted the six years of peacetime leadership and achievement with the shorter, and less successful, war period. As an anonymous reviewer of his memoirs wrote: 'Asquith had the misfortune to outlive his epoch. He lived to an epoch and to a crisis for which his gifts were unsuited and his powers inadequate, and a brilliant career ended almost in tragedy.' In support of a favourable view of Asquith's leadership up to August 1914 we may point not only to a solid legislative record but to the very fact of the government's continued survival, surmounting one crisis after another – the quarrels over naval expenditure, the Budget crisis of 1909, the battle with the House of Lords, the miners' strike of 1912, the Marconi affair, revolt in Ulster, and entry into the European war. It is true that the style and tactics of Asquith's pre-war leadership proved unsuitable for the peculiar conditions of war politics. But, if he was unsuccessful as a war premier, he is also open to criticism for his conduct in the earlier years of his stewardship. He overcame many crises. Perhaps, too, the crises were in part his own creation. As a sympathetic writer later admitted, 'friends began to wonder whether the highest statesmanship consisted in overcoming one crisis by creating another'.[131] Certainly the record of a Prime Minister under whom the nation goes to the brink of civil war must be subjected to the severest scrutiny. And, after sixty years, with almost all the relevant evidence now available, a new generation of scholars is attempting the searching examination of Asquith's career which has long been overdue. *

* I am grateful to a number of historians who have answered questions, allowed me to consult unpublished theses, and commented on the evidence and arguments presented in this survey. In particular, my thanks are offered to Dr John Brown, Dr Peter Clarke, Dr Michael Dockrill, Dr Nicholas d'Ombrain, Dr José Harris, Mr Roy Hay, Dr Ross McKibbin, Dr Kenneth Morgan, Dr Neil Summerton, Mr Philip Williams and Dr Keith Wilson.

This study was completed in 1969 and was first published in *The English Historical Review*, vol. LXXXV (July 1970). I have altered a few passages in the light of subsequent findings, and have revised the footnotes to take account of more recent publications; but no attempt has been made to incorporate major changes in the text. *Asquith*, by Stephen Koss (London 1976), though quoting from more private papers, adds little to the information and insights in earlier biographies.

Notes

1. H.H.Asquith to Sir Alfred Milner, 12 January 1898, quoted in Peter Stansky, *Ambitions and Strategies, The Struggle for the Leadership of the Liberal Party in the 1890s* (Oxford 1964), p. 234.

2. The King's private secretary complained that 'the machinery connected with the Office of Prime Minister has come to a complete standstill'. James Pope-Hennessy, *Lord Crewe 1858–1945, The Likeness of a Liberal* (London 1955), p. 63.

3. John Morley to Lord Minto, 12 March 1908, quoted in John, Viscount Morley, *Recollections* (2 vols, London 1917) ii, 248.

4. Winston S.Churchill to Walter Runciman, 30 December 1907, *Runciman MSS*. For permission to consult the Runciman MSS I am grateful to the Hon. Sir Steven Runciman and Lord Runciman. Quotations from the letters of Winston Churchill are made by kind permission of C. & T. Publications Ltd.

5. Asquith to Lord Ripon, 4 March 1908, *Ripon MSS*, B.M., Add. MS 43518, ff. 216–7. Asquith's letters are quoted by kind permission of the Hon. Mark Bonham Carter.

6. Asquith to James Bryce, 28 April 1908, *Bryce MSS*, Box H.

7. J.P.Alderson, *Mr Asquith* (London 1905), p. 268.

8. *Ibid.*

9. Lord Vansittart, *The Mist Procession* (London 1958), p. 77.

10. Ronald Hyam, *Elgin and Churchill at the Colonial Office 1905–1908, The Watershed of the Empire – Commonwealth* (London 1968), though a trifle indulgent, is the best discussion of Elgin's abilities.

11. Sir Almeric Fitzroy's Diary, 9 March 1908, quoted in his *Memoirs* (2 vols, London, n.d. [1923] i, 342.

12. Viscount Lee of Fareham, *A Good Innings, and a Great Partnership, being the Life Story of Arthur and Ruth Lee* (3 vols, privately printed, 1939) i, 314. I am grateful to Lord Clark and Mr William Hardcastle for access to the Lee MSS. Portsmouth was out of favour with the King; and, according to Lord Ripon, was no use at the War Office and unhelpful at the House of Lords. (Peter Rowland, *The Last Liberal Governments: The Promised Land, 1905–1910* [London 1968], pp. 145–6). According to Wilfrid Scawen Blunt, Portsmouth had also harmed himself by 'a foolish quarrel with one of his country tenants for shooting hares'. (Wilfrid Scawen Blunt, 13 April 1908, in *My Diaries, Being a Personal Narrative of Events, 1888–1914* [2 vols, London 1919–20] ii, 201.)

13. Lord Elgin to Lord Tweedmouth, 20 April 1908, Tweedmouth MSS, quoted

from a draft in the Elgin MSS, in Hyam, *op. cit.*, p. 511.

14. Lord Esher's Journal, 10 April 1908, *Esher MSS*; Oliver, Viscount Esher (ed.), *Journals and Letters of Reginald, Viscount Esher* (vols. iii, iv, London 1938), iii, p. 303; cf. Stephen E.Koss, *John Morley at the India Office 1905–1910* (New Haven 1969), p. 61

15. Esher's Journal, 14, 20 March 1908, *Esher MSS*, quoted by kind permission of Lord Esher. In 1921 Morley stated that Asquith had intended to appoint Haldane. 'I went to him and objected to such ascendancy of the old Liberal League and threatened to resign, whereupon Asquith said, "Then I'll send for Lloyd George".' (John H.Morgan, *John Viscount Morley, An Appreciation and some Reminiscences* [London 1924], p. 48.)

16. Herbert du Parq, *Life of David Lloyd George* (4 vols, London 1913) iii, p. 506.

17. Frank Elias, *The Right Hon. H.H.Asquith, MP, A Biography and an Appreciation* (London 1909), p. 208.

18. Herbert Gladstone to Henry Gladstone, 10 April 1908, *Henry Gladstone MSS*.

19. J.A.Pease's Diary, 7 April 1908, *Gainford MSS*, quoted by kind permission of Lord Gainford.

20. Asquith to the Hon. Venetia Stanley, 16 April 1915 and 10 August 1914, *Montagu MSS*. I am grateful to the late Mrs Milton Gendel for allowing me to consult Asquith's letters to her mother.

21. J.A.Spender, *The Public Life* (2 vols, London 1925) i, p. 110. Lloyd George told Sir George Riddell: 'It is unwise for a Prime Minister to have as his chief friend a member of his Cabinet. If he does, he creates jealousy. . . . Disraeli, Gladstone and Asquith all selected for their private friends men who were not in their Cabinet.' (Sir George Riddell's Diary, 8 February 1913, quoted in Lord Riddell, *More Pages from My Diary, 1908–1914* [London 1934], p. 121). Lloyd George was, in fact, wrong about Gladstone, whose private friends included Granville and Spencer.

22. Asquith to Runciman, 6 December 1908, *Runciman MSS*.

23. Reginald McKenna to Runciman, 2 October 1911, *Runciman MSS*.

24. Arthur J.Marder, *From the Dreadnought to Scapa Flow, The Royal Navy in the Fisher Era, 1904–1919*, vol. i, 'The Road to War, 1904–1914' (London 1961), pp. 248–51.

25. Lloyd George to Crewe, 13 February 1911, *Crewe MSS*. Lloyd George's letters are quoted by kind permission of the 1st Beaverbrook Foundation.

26. Grey to Runciman, 2 October 1911, *Runciman MSS*.

27. Grey to Lloyd George, 20 June 1913, *Lloyd George MSS*, C/4/14/9; Riddell's Diary, *op. cit.*, 9 July 1913, p. 168.

28. McKenna's Memorandum of a conversation with Asquith, 20 October 1911, quoted in Marder, *op. cit.*, p. 251.

29. It was Harcourt who received the 'somewhat sharp remonstrance' which

Asquith mentioned in his *Fifty Years of Parliament* (2 vols, London 1926), ii, p. 197. Churchill and Morley were the instigators of the rebuke. Harcourt's diary for this period is closed to scholars but a few of his Cabinet notes survive in the Harcourt MSS. Charles Hobhouse's diary, whose existence was only recently disclosed, has been edited by Edward David as *Inside Asquith's Cabinet* (London 1977).

30. Augustine Birrell, *Things Past Redress* (London 1933), pp. 250–7.

31. Sir Almeric Fitzroy's Diary, 17 January 1912, quoted in his *Memoirs*, ii, p. 475.

32. *Great Contemporaries* (London 1937), p. 140; for a parody of a Cabinet meeting in 1912, possibly written by Herbert Samuel, see *Samuel MSS*, A/155 (IV), ff. 97–100. See also the euphoric fantasies about the Asquith Cabinets purveyed in an anonymous review of Thomas Jones' *Whitehall Diary*, i, in *The Times Literary Supplement* (17 July 1969), no. 3516, pp. 775–6.

33. Lucy Masterman's Diary, 16 October 1908, quoted in her *C.F.G. Masterman, A Biography* (London 1939), p. 111.

34. Pease's Diary, 20, 25 January 1911, *Gainford MSS*; a list by Runciman, headed 'Cabinet Committees', 25 January 1911, *Runciman MSS*; Arthur Murray's Diary, 27 January 1911, *Elibank MSS*, 8814, ff. 3–5.

35. Morley to Minto, 9 November 1909, quoted in Morley, *op. cit.*, ii, p. 321; see also Marian Jack, 'The Purchase of the British Government's Shares in the British Petroleum Company 1912–1914', *Past and Present*, no. 39 (April 1968), p. 161; John Edward Kendle, *The Colonial and Imperial Conferences 1887–1911*, A Study in Imperial Organization (London 1967), pp. 148, 153–4, 158–63; H.J. Hanham (ed.), *The Nineteenth Century Constitution 1815–1914*, Documents and Commentary (Cambridge 1969), pp. 94–6.

36. Asquith to the King, 26 April 1909, *Asquith MSS*, 6, ff. 106–7; José Harris, *Unemployment and Politics: A study in English Social Policy 1886–1914* (London 1972), pp. 275, 325.

37. Pease's Diary, 20 January 1911, *Gainford MSS*; Lewis Harcourt's Cabinet note, 29 February 1912, *Harcourt MSS*.

38. Sir Edward Cook's Diary, 23 February 1912, *Cook MSS*, quoted by permission of Mr Douglas Duff.

39. J.P. Mackintosh, 'The Role of the Committee of Imperial Defence before 1914', *English Historical Review*, lxxvii (1962); Nicholas J. d'Ombrain, *The Military Departments and the Committee of Imperial Defence 1902–1914* (Oxford University DPhil thesis 1970) published in an abbreviated form as *War Machinery and High Policy: Defence Administration in Peacetime Britain, 1902–1914* (London 1973), Samuel R. Williamson Jr, *The Politics of Grand Strategy; Britain and France Prepare for War, 1906–1914* (Cambridge, Mass. 1969), Neil W. Summerton, *The Development of British Military Planning for a War Against Germany 1904–1914*

(London University PhD thesis 1970), John Gooch, *The Plans of War*: The General Staff and British Military Strategy *c.* 1900–1916 (London 1974).

40. Morley to Churchill, 2 July 1908, *Churchill MSS.*
41. Harcourt to Runciman, 26 August 1911, *Runciman MSS.*
42. Pease's Diary, 1, 15 November 1911, *Gainford MSS.*
43. Runciman to Harcourt, 24 August 1911 (copy), *Runciman MSS.*
44. Birrell, *op. cit.*, p. 250.
45. Vol. ii, p. 196.
46. Asquith to the King, 9 December 1908, *Asquith MSS*, 5, ff. 71–4; see also Bruce K.Murray, 'The Politics of the "People's Budget",' *The Historical Journal*, XVI, 3 (1973), p. 556.
47. H.V.Emy, 'The Land Campaign: Lloyd George as a Social Reformer, 1909–14' in A.J.P.Taylor (ed.), *Lloyd George: Twelve Essays* (London 1971), pp. 58–9.
48. Asquith to Margot Asquith, 20, 21 January 1914, quoted in J.A.Spender and Cyril Asquith, *Life of Herbert Henry Asquith, Lord Oxford and Asquith* (2 vols, London 1932) ii, 76.
49. Lloyd George to Asquith, 28 December 1912 (copy), *Lloyd George MSS*, C/6/11/12.
50. Grey to Runciman, 2 October 1911, *Runciman MSS*; Asquith to Crewe, 7 October 1911, *Crewe MSS.*
51. Alfred Emmott's Diary, 12 March 1911, *Emmott MSS*, quoted by kind permission of Mrs Brian Simon.
52. The fullest account is in G.R.Searle, *The Quest for National Efficiency* (Oxford 1971).
53. Runciman to McKenna, 27 March 1910, *McKenna MSS*; McKenna to Runciman, 28 March 1910, *Runciman MSS.*
54. J.A.Hobson, *The Crisis of Liberalism* (London 1909), p. xii.
55. Lloyd George to Churchill, 25 September 1910, *Churchill MSS.*
56. For some of the proposals on housing, land, health and low incomes which were being discussed and drafted in 1914, see Paul Wilding, 'Towards Exchequer Subsidies for Housing 1906–1914'. *Social and Economic Administration*, 6, No. 1, January 1972, pp. 15–16.
57. *The Daily Chronicle*, 8 December 1913.
58. Churchill to Lloyd George, 20 June 1909 (copy), *Churchill MSS.*
59. Asquith later said that his own Cabinets were too big. In 1920, he told a Select Committee on Ministerial Remuneration: 'I should make the Cabinet smaller. There are one or two offices, even among the old offices – and I am not speaking of any of these new creations – which I think might very easily be omitted normally from what is called Cabinet status.'

He had in mind the Presidency of the Council, the Privy Seal, and the Duchy of Lancaster. *Fifty Years of Parliament*, ii, pp. 203–4.

60. Sidney Low, *The Governance of England* (London 1925), introduction to 1914 edition, p. xxii.

61. Alfred Mond's (unpublished?) typescript article, 14 July 1910, *Melchett MSS*.

62. Lloyd George, memorandum on coalition, 17 August 1910, *Lloyd George MSS*, C/3/14/8. This candid paragraph is perhaps the best explanation of why Lloyd George's proposal was shown to so few members of the Asquith ministry.

63. Speech at the National Liberal Club, 31 January 1913, *The Manchester Guardian*, 1 February 1913.

64. Lloyd George to Crewe, 20 October 1910 (copy), *Lloyd George MSS*, C/4/I/1.

65. Crewe to Lloyd George, 21 October 1910, *Lloyd George MSS*, C/4/I/2.

66. On the 1910 elections, see Neal Blewett, *The Peers, The Parties, and the People: The General Elections of 1910* (London 1972); for a detailed and persuasive discussion of the vitality of the Liberal Party in Lancashire, see P.F.Clarke, *Lancashire and the New Liberalism* (Cambridge 1971).

67. Harold Begbie, 'A Gentleman With a Duster', *The Mirrors of Downing Street* (New York 1921), p. 41.

68. Countess of Oxford and Asquith, Preface to Earl of Oxford and Asquith, KG, *Memories and Reflections, 1852–1927* (2 vols, London 1928), i, p. xi.

69. Sir John A.R.Marriott, *English Political Institutions, An Introductory Study* (Oxford 1948), p. xxv; Lady Lloyd George testified that 'My recollection is that Mr Asquith had only employed one typist. We certainly needed more. Even the opening of L.G.'s mail was a lengthy process.' (Frances Lloyd George, *The Years that are Past* [London 1967], p. 99.)

70. Montagu's period as Asquith's PPS is documented in S.D.Waley, *Edwin Montagu, A Memoir and an Account of his Visits to India* (London 1964) ch. II, and in the Montagu MSS at Trinity College, Cambridge.

71. Lucy Masterman's Diary, March–April 1910, Lucy Masterman, *op. cit.*, p. 160.

72. Alexander Mackintosh, *From Gladstone to Lloyd George, Parliament in Peace and War* (London n.d. 1921?), p. 153. Mackintosh subsequently assisted Asquith in the preparation of his memoirs.

73. Addison recorded one such meeting on 21 July 1914 'to consider the present position of Irish affairs. ... We are determined, so far as Members can, to apply ginger to the Government. ... We are told that the Cabinet will be glad to have this declaration of our determination; it will help them at the Palace.' (*Four and a Half Years, A Personal Diary from June 1914 to January 1919* [2 vols, London 1934], i, p. 27.)

74. Asquith told Liberal MPs at the Reform Club on 30 April 1908: 'It has for

many years past been the custom of our party when through death or through retirement a change of leadership took place that the Liberal members in the House of Commons should meet together to declare their intentions as the succession.' He agreed with an earlier speaker who asserted that it was the prerogative of the Liberal MPs, inviolable even by the Sovereign, 'to determine who the Liberal leader shall be'. *The Liberal Magazine*, May 1908, p. 230.

75. Edith Gulland to Elsie Gulland Osborne, 2 February 1915, *Gulland MSS*; and see my book, *Politicians at War, July 1914 to May 1915*, A prologue to the triumph of Lloyd George (London 1971), pp. 128–34.

76. George Dangerfield, *The Strange Death of Liberal England* (New York 1961, [1st edn 1935]), p. 72.

77. A.J.Dorey, *Radical Liberal Criticism of British Foreign Policy 1906–1914* (unpublished Oxford DPhil thesis 1964), pp. 120–2.

78. Churchill to the King, 17 March 1910 (copy), *Churchill MSS*.

79. Dorey, *op. cit.*, p. 290.

80. Francis Hirst's phrase, in *The Economist*, 25 Novembr 1911, p. 1086.

81. Colleagues who wished to discuss foreign policy on the platform encountered as little sympathy from Grey as inquisitive back-benchers. Seely, asking, as Secretary of State for War, for some help over a speech, was advised 'the less you say the better at this moment about the foreign situation. The rule used to be that only the PM and Foreign Secretary dealt with Foreign Affairs in public' (Grey to Seely, 14 December 1912 [copy], *Grey MSS*, P.R.O. F.O. 800/102.)

82. Dorey, *op. cit. passim*, emphasizes this dilemma which weakened radical bargaining strength. See also A.J.Anthony Morris, *Radicalism Against War, 1906–1914, The Advocacy of Peace and Retrenchment* (London 1972).

83. *The Economist*, 28 October 1911, p. 862.

84. Richard Holt's Diary, 19 July 1914, *Holt MSS*. Miss Anne Holt has kindly permitted me to examine and quote from her father's papers.

85. *The Liberal Magazine* (December 1912), p. 657.

86. Riddell's Diary, *op. cit.*, 15–16 November 1912, p. 101.

87. Holt's Diary, 15 November 1912, *Holt MSS*.

88. Alexander MacCallum Scott's Diary, 11 November 1912, *MacCallum Scott MSS*. I am grateful to Mr John H.MacCallum Scott for generously making his father's diaries available to me.

89. Spender and Asquith, *op. cit.*, ii, p. 16.

90. *Fifty Years of Parliament*, ii, p. 152.

91. James William Lowther, Viscount Ullswater, *A Speaker's Commentaries* (2 vols., London 1925), ii, pp. 154–5; A.Lawrence Lowell, *The Government of England*

(2 vols, New York 1912), i, pp. 336–8, explains the contemporary usage.

92. Sidney Low, *op. cit.*, pp. 87–8.

93. *Report from the Select Committee on House of Commons (Procedure)*, 1915, pp. 150–1 (evidence of Asquith, 11 June 1914).

94. Austen Chamberlain to Joseph Chamberlain, 16 November 1912, quoted in Sir Austen Chamberlain, *Politics from Inside, An Epistolary Chronicle, 1906–1914* (London 1936), p. 493.

95. Obituary of Percy Illingworth in the *Western Morning News*, 4 January 1915; Autobiographical notes and correspondence of William Wedgwood Benn, Lord Stansgate, in the Stansgate MSS. I am indebted to Lady Stansgate for permission to make use of her late husband's papers.

96. Bernard Porter, *Critics of Empire, British Radical attitudes to colonialism in Africa, 1895–1914* (London 1968), p. 328 and *passim*.

97. L.M.Thompson, *The Unification of South Africa, 1902–1910* (Oxford 1960), pp. 430–1; Ronald Hyam, 'African Interests and the South Africa Act, 1908–1910,' *The Historical Journal*, XIII, 1 (1970), pp. 104–5.

98. Kenneth O.Morgan, *Wales in British Politics 1868–1922* (Cardiff 1963), pp. 268–9.

99. A.J.A.Morris (ed.), *Edwardian Radicalism 1900–1914: Some aspects of British Radicalism* (London and Boston 1974), especially the essays by Alan J.Lee and Howard Weinroth; Alfred F.Havighurst, *Radical Journalist: H.W.Massingham (1860–1924)* (Cambridge 1974); Stephen Koss, *Fleet Street Radical: A.G.Gardiner and the 'Daily News'* (London 1973).

100. John Gulland to Elsie Gulland Osborne, 27 February 1910, *Gulland MSS.* Herbert Gladstone told his brother that 'the Whips Dept. should have warned the Cabinet of the extraordinary & unexpected strength of feeling against the Lords in the north', Gladstone to Henry Gladstone, 1 February 1910, *Henry Gladstone MSS.*)

101. Runciman to McKenna, 27 March 1910, *Runciman MSS.* There is no evidence that Churchill and Lloyd George ever intended to make a bid for power. By May 1910, Alfred Emmott reported that they were at loggerheads as to pressing veto 'with Lloyd George taking the more moderate stand'. (Emmott's Diary, 20 May 1910, *Emmott MSS.*)

102. Lucy Masterman, *op. cit.*, p. 159.

103. Speech at Plymouth, April 1894, quoted in Alderson, *op. cit.*, p. 205.

104. Graham Wallas, *Human Nature in Politics* (2nd ed., London 1910), p. 87.

105. *Ibid.*, p. 95.

106. *Truth*, 16 April 1913, from Sir Henry Norman's press-cutting collection. For permission to consult the Norman MSS, I am indebted to Lady Burke.

107. *The Morning Post*, 18 September 1909.

108. Norman to Asquith, 20 November 1909 (copy), *Norman MSS.*

109. The minutes of the editorial conference, held on 9 July 1909, are in the Norman MSS. The League distributed copy to as many as 240 daily and weekly papers.

110. Norman to Asquith, 20 November 1909 (copy), *Norman MSS*. Transcripts of the recorded speeches were also issued as a leaflet and the record was available for sale to private customers.

111. By August 1913, Donald Maclean held £13,000 worth of shares in *The Westminster Gazette*, and £8,750 worth in the *Birmingham Gazette*, as the nominee of the Chief Whip. (See correspondence and papers in the Maclean MSS. Mr Alan Maclean kindly permitted me to make use of the papers of his father, Sir Donald Maclean.) All of the shareholders of *The Westminster Gazette* were prominent Liberals who had bought out Sir George Newnes in 1908. This purchase, and a subsequent increase in the capital in 1912, were organized by successive Liberal Chief Whips, J.A.Pease and the Master of Elibank. *Asquith MSS*, vols 144 and 148.

112. Ralph D.Blumenfeld, *RDB's Procession* (London 1935), pp. 121–3.

113. Pease's Diary, 25 January 1911, *Gainford MSS*. For another example of Asquith's political sensitivity to press criticism, see his letter to the Master of Elibank, 22 April 1912, *Elibank MSS* 8803, f. 45.

114. Montagu to Asquith (n.d. 19 June 1908?) copy, *Montagu MSS*.

115. Francis Hirst to Sir John Brunner, 15 July 1912, *Brunner MSS*; Hirst badgered Brunner for three years, with considerable success, to use the president of the NLF's 'enormous influence on behalf of principles which the party once in office is so apt to violate'. (Hirst to Brunner, 20 December 1911, *Brunner MSS*. I am grateful to Sir Felix Brunner, Bt, for allowing me to consult his grandfather's papers, and to Mr A.F.Thompson for permission to quote Hirst's letters.) For a fuller account of Brunner's activity, see Stephen E.Koss, *Sir John Brunner: Radical Plutocrat, 1842–1919* (Cambridge 1970).

116. J.A.Spender, *Sir Robert Hudson, A Memoir* (London 1930), p. 40.

117. Lloyd George to Asquith, 5 June 1914 (copy), *Lloyd George MSS*, C/6/11/15; Cecil Beck to Charles Masterman, 26 May 1914, *Lloyd George MSS*, C/5/15/5; Montagu to Asquith, 27 May 1914 (copy), *Montagu MSS*. See also the discussion in *Politicians at War*, pp. 128–34.

118. Mr Jenkins has deployed formidable arguments in favour of Asquith's unadventurous Irish policy (Jenkins, *op. cit.*, ch. XVII). But R.B.McCallum's verdict cannot be set lightly aside: 'As it was not morally possible to coerce either part of Ireland, there remained only the ruthless surgery of severing the six counties from the rest. A statesman who would have gone for this policy from the first might have met with reverses, but he would have had the judgement of posterity on his side.'

R.B.McCallum, *Asquith* [London 1936], p. 100.

119. McKenna's view, paraphrased by Sir George Riddell, was quoted in Riddell, *op. cit.*, p. 216. McKenna and Runciman had spoken to colleagues four years earlier of evidence that 'the PM is losing any faculty of decision he ever had'. Emmott's Diary, 20 May 1910, *Emmott MSS*.

120. Addison's Diary *op. cit.*, 20 July 1914, i, p. 27.

121. T.E.Harvey to A.M.Harvey, 28 March 1914, *Harvey MSS*. Mr Edward Milligan kindly allowed me to quote from the Harvey MSS.

122. Charles Trevelyan to Lady Trevelyan, 4 April 1914, *Trevelyan MSS*. I am grateful to Sir George Trevelyan Bt. and Mrs Pauline Dower, for kindly allowing me to quote from their father's papers.

123. Memorandum by Percy Illingworth, 6 May 1914, *Illingworth MSS*, cited by kind permission of Mr Henry Illingworth.

124. Asquith's wartime premiership is discussed at length in *Politicians at War* and in volumes in preparation on *The Crisis of Liberalism* and *The Triumph of Lloyd George*.

125. Runciman to Sir Robert Chalmers, 7 February 1915, *Runciman MSS*.

126. Maurice Hankey's Minute for the Prime Minister, 17 May 1915, quoted in Lord Hankey, *The Supreme Command, 1914–1918* (2 vols, London 1961), i, p. 326.

127. Lord Crewe's memorandum, 20 December 1916, quoted in Pope-Hennessy, *op. cit.*, p. 182.

128. Balfour to Asquith, 5 December 1916, quoted in Blanche E.C.Dugdale, *Arthur James Balfour, First Earl of Balfour* (2 vols, London 1939), ii, p. 128.

129. Trevor Wilson, *The Downfall of the Liberal Party 1914–1935* (London 1966), p. 97.

130. Lord Stamfordham's Report of a Conference held at Buckingham Palace, 6 December 1916, quoted in Harold Nicolson, *King George the Fifth, His Life and Reign* (London 1953), p. 291.

131. Stephen McKenna, *While I Remember* (London 1921), p. 107.

David Lloyd George

Kenneth O. Morgan

'The Power of the Man in the Saddle': this was the burden of the Liberal Chief Whip's advice to David Lloyd George in April 1918.[1] But the Prime Minister hardly needed any instruction in this theme: the uses and the limitations of power formed his absorbing passion. Even at the time many felt that his period as Prime Minister had marked a totally new departure in British politics. Some later commentators (such as Humphry Berkeley)[2] have even claimed to detect the dawn of a new political era between 1916 and 1922, one in which 'prime-ministerial government' gradually took the place of conventional Cabinet government. But, despite their certainty, the precise character of Lloyd George's premiership, like the man himself, is still shrouded in mystery. Was it rule by a dictator or by a democrat? Did any consistent principle animate the 'man in the saddle', or was it all opportunism gone berserk? Was Wales's Great Commoner really 'rooted in nothing', as Keynes was to allege? Not even Lloyd George's closest associates, Kerr and Riddell, felt able to say with any assurance. They were as baffled as the rest. Lloyd George was suddenly thrust from office in October 1922 with the issue still inconclusive. Ever since then, the debate about his premiership has been passionate and unremitting. Each observer seems to have seen a different Prime Minister, one created in his own image. Fifty biographies on, the essential Lloyd George remains as elusive as ever. He remains the most controversial and contradictory of political animals, 'the Big Beast', the rogue elephant of twentieth-century Prime Ministers.

To many critics then and later, his years of office had been a period of unalloyed dictatorship, one that invited frequent comparison with the presidency of the United States. Arthur Henderson, looking back in 1918 on his unhappy nine-months' membership of the government, claimed that 'L.G. was the War Cabinet and nobody else really counted'.[3] Northcliffe's *Times* took this critique much further. It alleged, in March 1921, that the personal ascendancy of the Prime Minister had undermined not only the collective responsibility of the Cabinet, not only the liberties of parliament, but the very balance of the constitution itself. Nostalgically, it recalled Dunning's resolution in the days of Lord North on the perils of an overmighty executive.[4] Shortly afterwards, Edwin Montagu wrote bitterly of the political demoralization which had resulted from the Prime Minister's personal rule.[5] When he was forced out of the government in March 1922, Montagu publicly renewed the charge of dictatorship, and denounced the discordant cadences of the one-man band.

And yet, during his premiership as throughout his entire career, Lloyd George was thought by many more to be uniquely identified with the mass democracy, more responsive than any previous premier to the popular will. A relatively poor man from a poor Welsh home, a Prime Minister who, as he himself wrote, had risen up from the ranks rather than through the staff college of a university, he had been elevated to power in a people's war. In war and in peace, no member of the government was more sensitive to the pressures of public opinion, whether in parliament or in the country. Whether policy dealt with trouble in the mines, arms to Poland, peace in Ireland or war in Turkey, it must reflect the general will in all its natural purity. With some justice, Sir Alfred Mond could appeal to Lloyd George during the 1922 election as 'the greatest democrat of the age',[6] still the champion of the dispossessed that he had always been.

From the outset of his career, Lloyd George had felt tension between his instinctive populism and his urge for power, between his loyalty to his radical roots in Wales and his commitment to a new political order. He had entered Campbell-Bannerman's government in 1905 as the voice of traditional radicalism, of provincial dissent and little Englandism, as the Welsh Baptist outsider thrusting his way through a patrician, Anglo-Saxon world. Down to 1914 he had been the living symbol of the union of the old Liberalism with the new, wreaking the people's vengeance on the bishop and the squire, the peer and the publican, and yet at the same time championing new concepts of social reform. He seemed the embodiment of the class passions of the new democratic age, John Bright and Joseph Chamberlain fused into one.

And yet this extreme radical could also operate through consensus rather than through conflict. Unlike other radicals, he could display a rare artistry in the uses of power. At the height of the church disestablishment campaign in Wales back in 1895, he had closeted himself with the Welsh bishops to try to obtain a self-governing church in a self-governing Wales.[7] During the fury of the 'People's Budget' campaign in 1910, he had tried to form an all-party coalition with his Unionist opponents, on behalf of a programme of social reform and military preparedness.[8] The 'cottage-bred boy', idolized by the chapels as the messiah of the underprivileged, felt deeply stirred by the vision of a higher synthesis of politics, presided over by a Theodore Roosevelt, a Louis Botha, perhaps a Joseph Chamberlain. A new age would dawn in which the petty partisanships of such mundane issues as free trade, the Lords' veto or Irish home rule would be swept away. When world war transformed the domestic scene in August 1914, none embraced more passionately than Lloyd George the cause of a national coalition to meet the crisis. He was to find the closest parallel to himself in the social imperialist Alfred Milner. 'He is a poor man and so am I. He does not represent the landed or capitalist classes any more than I do. He is keen on social reform and so am I. Asked by Riddell to define his political creed, he alighted on the ominous term, "Nationalist–Socialist".'[9] The state and the economy must be transformed to meet the challenge of total war. With the imminent collapse of Asquith's government in December 1916, only Lloyd George, a Cabinet minister for over a decade, yet in some curious way a new and untried figure, seemed to possess the charisma of leadership that could save the nation.

Lloyd George's strength as a wartime Prime Minister arose essentially from the circumstances that brought his government into being. The complex events of 1–7 December 1916 were brilliantly described years ago by Lord Beaverbrook;[10] a host of subsequent accounts have not totally altered the basic outlines of his story. Few can deny that Lloyd George's rise to power resulted from a manoeuvre to subordinate (though not to supplant) Asquith by means of a War Committee, with Carson, Bonar Law and Beaverbrook as the essential allies, and Northcliffe lending ambiguous assistance in the wings. Fewer still have explained what other means existed for transforming an incompetent government, which commanded little confidence, but whose failing leader clung tenaciously to power. Asquith's war leadership had been condemned not only in the press and on the back benches: military men such as Colonel Repington and even General Robertson were in the autumn of 1916 desperate for a new impulse of leadership.[11] By 11 December, days of tortuous negotiations had ensured an all-party basis for the new Lloyd George government. Even the national executive of the Labour Party decided by a majority of one, after Lloyd George had put on one of his most dexterous and persuasive performances for its benefit, to support the administration and to allow itself to be represented in it. After this, Lloyd George's transition to power was relatively smooth. The public yearned for new inspiration from the supreme command; as long as the war went on, Lloyd George alone seemed even remotely likely to meet this need. The American ambassador, Walter Hines Page, no friendly critic, thought him 'the one public man here who has an undoubted touch of genius'.[12] Throughout the course of the war, therefore, Lloyd George's position as premier, viewed from this general standpoint, became increasingly impregnable.

The immediate instrument of his ascendancy lay in his coordination of the War Cabinet, and hence of the whole vast nexus of central government. His newly created directorate of five – himself, Bonar Law, Curzon, Henderson (later succeeded by Barnes) and Milner (with Smuts, Austen Chamberlain and, briefly, Carson added later) could serve only to magnify the ascendancy of the man who led it. Meeting almost daily, it was less a fixed institution than a fluid morass of *ad hoc* or standing committees, with innumerable other ministers and advisers called in as the agenda required. In addition, several new ministries were created as satellites of the Cabinet – Shipping, Labour, Food and Pensions being formed almost at once, National Service and Reconstruction in 1917, and the Air Ministry at the start of 1918. Of Lloyd George's Cabinet colleagues, Curzon, Henderson and, especially, Milner were given roving assignments as coordinators or chairmen of inter-departmental committees. Only Bonar Law was essential in party terms: even he was increasingly by-passed as the war went on, especially on issues of strategy or foreign policy. Again, as Chancellor of the Exchequer, Bonar Law was the one member of the War Cabinet able to exert departmental pressure on the premier. He largely failed to do so, while in any case Treasury control of the traditional kind was meaningless in war-time. The other ministers, outside the Cabinet, were usually confined to departmental affairs of the most limited kind and played no part in supreme decision-making. Only the Foreign Office, perhaps, might have claimed an initiative of its own, but it was safely held in the pliant grasp of Balfour, whose support for Lloyd George had assisted in the fall of Asquith. For the rest, the very confusion and complexity of the War Cabinet system, with its varied and overlapping personnel, worked inevitably to elevate the position of the only conceivable supreme arbiter, the Prime Minister.[13]

In the light of this secure position, the grievances of discontented subordinates, excluded from the magic circle of the War Cabinet, was a small enough price to pay. Many of them – Maclay, Eric Geddes, Devonport, Rhondda – were industrialists content with running their departments. Sir Alfred Mond repeatedly complained that his talents were being ill-utilized, but he carried little weight.[14] More formidably, Churchill, brought into the government as Minister of Munitions in July 1917, delivered a constant barrage of criticism about the way the government was run. 'Under the present system, the War Cabinets alone have the power of decision and the right of regular and continuous consultation. Their burden cannot be shared by departmental ministers occasionally invited to express an opinion on particular subjects or phrases.' He deplored 'the new system wh. Carson invented of governing without a regular Cabinet', and worked off his resentment by interfering in the affairs of other departments, to the particular annoyance of Derby at the War Office and Sir Eric Geddes at the Admiralty.[15] But Lloyd George could bear these lengthy diatribes with equanimity. However potentially dangerous on the opposition benches, Churchill in office was largely muzzled. Indeed, Lloyd George would probably have agreed with some of Churchill's criticisms. For his authority over his own government lay less in the ordered simplicity of the system, as the *Official Report* ecstatically proclaimed in 1917, than in its complexity. Its improvement over the Asquith regime lay only partially in the machinery of government, far more in the man who governed.

Lloyd George's ascendancy over the War Cabinet was in essence a personal affair, a reflection of the imagination and the resource of its leader. However, it was notably underpinned by the one permanent institutional innovation of his premiership, the Cabinet secretariat. Under Sir Maurice Hankey and his omnipresent Welsh assistant, Thomas Jones, this body became a major instrument of power. It soon showed itself to be far more than simply an organization to draw up the agenda and to record and circulate the minutes of Cabinet meetings (all of these duties being novelties). In effect, it became an ancillary department attached to the Prime Minister which could permeate the entire fabric of central government. Its potentialities were summed up in Thomas Jones's incomparable description of his own role: 'a rather fluid person moving amongst people who matter'.[16] While the secretariat maintained the closest contact with every government department (assisted by *ad hoc* committees), it was answerable to the Prime Minister alone. It could arrange for the presence of appropriate non-governmental personnel at Cabinet meetings, at the private behest of Lloyd George. Perhaps most important of all, it gave him the exclusive power of determining the agenda and priority of Cabinet business – a function that assumed greater significance after the war when 'conferences of ministers' largely supplanted the official Cabinet. In time, the secretariat was to become a whipping-boy for wider assaults on the Prime Minister's power. In June 1922, after a singularly confused Commons debate, many speakers attacked the secretariat for alleged encroachments into the execution of policy, especially in foreign affairs.[17] Some of these criticisms were exaggerated and ill informed, but the secretariat would undoubtedly have strengthened the authority of a premier less commanding than Lloyd George. In the abnormal circumstances of wartime, staffed as it was in part by highly assertive men like Leopold Amery, Mark Sykes and other survivors of Milner's pre-war 'kinder-garten',[18] it provided an essential link between the all-encompassing control of the Prime Minister and the various branches of government at all levels. When unified command at home began to be transferred into something resembling allied unity at the front, after the creation of a Supreme War Council at Rapallo (5–7 November 1917), it was again the Cabinet secretariat, with the ubiquitous Hankey, which provided the British premier with his general staff.

Even more symptomatic of Lloyd George's personal methods was his own personal secretariat or 'Garden Suburb', originally housed in huts in the gardens of No. 10. Its proceedings were altogether more unorthodox and intimate than those of the Cabinet secretariat. At the same time, during the earlier years of Lloyd George's premiership the work of the two institutions so overlapped that the distinction between them became largely academic. Even as late as June 1922 Thomas Jones admitted that the Cabinet office was inextricably 'mixed up with the PM's personal secretaries and with Sir Edward Grigg in the Garden Suburb'.[19] The five founder members of the Garden Suburb were a bizarre mixture, all in their way characteristic advisers of Lloyd George. Two were millionaires, David Davies MP, grandson of Wales's railway king, and Waldorf Astor, owner of the *Observer* (whom the Tory Walter Long dismissed as 'a sentimental socialist').[20] Professor W.G.S.Adams was an All Souls' professor, Joseph Davies a commercial statistician. The most influential of them all, however, was Philip Kerr, editor of the *Round Table* and yet another of Milner's pre-war imperialist protégés, whose relationship with the Prime Minister was to be the closest of all. The original purposes of the Garden Suburb were to carry out special enquiries on behalf of the Prime Minister and to arrange weekly reports for him from the various government departments. (The use he made of this information was a different matter: Joseph Davies observed, 'He tends to treat statistics from a buoyant, not to say romantic angle.')[21] The work was shared out between the five secretaries. Adams dealt with Treasury affairs, labour and, above all, Ireland; David Davies (soon to be succeeded by Cecil Harmsworth) with war and munitions; Waldorf Astor with liquor control; Joseph Davies with commodities and shipping.[22] But from the outset the activities of the Garden Suburb reflected the Prime Minister's own intuitive and disorganized methods of work. As Thomas Jones commented in April 1917: 'Adams he rarely sees, Kerr much oftener, Astor sometimes. Kerr pumps things into him and he seems to agree and then goes and does the opposite. You hate and love him in turns, as Kerr put it to me today.'[23] One instance of the flexibility of the new body was the use of Joseph Davies early in 1917 to investigate the possible take-over of a strongly Asquithian newspaper, the *Westminster Gazette*.[24]

The potentialities of the Garden Suburb, however, were best exemplified in the work of Philip Kerr. His specialities lay in the fields of foreign and imperial policies, areas largely beyond Cabinet, let alone parliamentary, scrutiny. His inquiries on behalf of his master rapidly assumed formidable proportions.[25] They ranged from American reactions to the Irish conscription issue, to secret discussions about the Russian situation with Kerensky. Kerr was deeply implicated in the peace probes of December 1917, when he was sent on the first of two missions to Switzerland. On the second mission, in March 1918, he investigated the possibilities for separate peace negotiations with the Austrians and the Turks. His access to power could be exaggerated, and often was. For instance, he communicated with the Foreign Office only indirectly, through Sir Eric Drummond, Balfour's private secretary. Still, when the preliminaries to the Paris peace conference vastly inflated Kerr's status, there were frequent criticisms that Lloyd George had turned him into a kind of supernumerary Foreign Secretary, accountable only to himself, yet another agent for exalting the Prime Minister's personal rule.

The Cabinet secretariat and the Garden Suburb assisted Lloyd George in dominating his government from within. An additional body which he created was intended, if necessary, to outflank it from without. This was the Imperial War Cabinet, which first met under the Prime Minister's chairmanship in March 1917. A simultaneous series of 'conferences' of the various imperial premiers met under the somnolent presidency of Walter Long. Ardently advocated by a group of Empire-minded Unionist backbenchers led by W.A.S.Hewins,[26] with Amery as their voice within the administration, the Imperial Cabinet was used by Lloyd George as an alternative source of advice on foreign and colonial affairs. The imperial ministers were most actively used in the preliminaries to the post-war peace conferences in the autumn of 1918. The main legacy of this body, however, was a personal one – the drafting of General Smuts, the South African Minister of Defence, into the British War Cabinet. In practice, Smuts turned into a second Milner for the Prime Minister, another invaluable chairman of Cabinet committees; despite his unfortunate *penchant* towards the military mind, he could usually be relied on to back up the Prime Minister's view and to invest it with a suitable air of philosophical detachment.[27] The adherence of a man utterly removed from the British scene, who had turned down the suggestion that he should enter the House of Commons, served only to underline the way in which the Prime Minister seemed to ride roughshod over constitutional convention.

Armed with these weapons, Lloyd George's authority steadily mounted as the war went on. At home, his position was safe enough by July 1917 for him to reconstruct his Cabinet by his own methods. Sir Eric Geddes replaced Carson at the Admiralty, Edwin Montagu went to the India Office. Most controversial of all, Churchill entered the government as Minister of Munitions, an appointment that Lloyd George had previously lacked the authority to make. Derby, the Secretary of State for War, protested in vain at this *coup*. 'I never knew a word about it until I saw it in the papers ... but you can judge of my surprise when I found the War Cabinet had never been told. Lloyd George had acted on a prerogative which is undoubtedly his, to make any appointment he liked without consulting his colleagues, though I believe they did know about Carson leaving the Admiralty.' Derby, however, acknowledged the political advantages stemming from the adherence of Churchill and Montagu. '[Lloyd George] has removed from Asquith his two most powerful lieutenants and he has provided for himself two first-class platform speakers, and it is platform speakers we shall require to steady the country ...'.[28]

The most decisive test of prime-ministerial authority, however, lay in his ability to impose civilian control over the strategy of the war, on land and sea. Lloyd George won a major triumph over the Admiralty in April 1917 when the introduction of the convoy system was forced upon the reluctant First Sea Lord, Jellicoe, to combat the menace of the U-boat. He had already used private advisers like young Commander Kenworthy and Reginald Henderson to circumvent the Admiralty officials. Now centuries of protocol were shattered on 30 April as the Prime Minister visited the Admiralty to impose his will. Professor Marder has called this visit 'anti-climactic', but it seems difficult to dissociate the acceptance of the convoy principle by Admiral Duff and leading naval officials on 26–27 April from the prospect of the premier's impending visit, three days later.[29] By December, Jellicoe had gone, and Carson, his one intermittent advocate in the Cabinet, followed him soon afterwards. The army, however, was a far tougher adversary. Haig and Robertson were well supplied with political allies: Robertson, so Hankey complained in November 1917, was 'intriguing like the deuce'.³⁰ In July 1917, Lloyd George had set forth at great length before the Cabinet committee on war policy his doubts about the projected offensive in Flanders: he urged instead a peripheral 'eastern' strategy in Italy, the Balkans or the Levant, to 'knock the props out from under the enemy'. But his Cabinet colleagues were reluctant to veto Haig's insistent advice; while Lloyd George's authority on military matters had been gravely diminished by his passionate advocacy of the undeniably 'western' and ultimately disastrous offensive under General Nivelle, at the Calais conference in February. The Prime Minister was, for once, overruled, and the Passchendaele offensive thus approved.³¹ Its appalling results in loss of life further poisoned relations between Lloyd George and his generals.

By February 1918, Lloyd George had decided that, in order to enforce civilian supremacy, it was vital that Robertson, the Chief of Staff, be removed – and if possible Haig as well. After months of experiment, he fashioned for himself the mechanism for effecting a change – the new Supreme Allied Council established at Versailles the previous November. Robertson was faced with the hopeless dilemma of retaining his present post, almost certainly with reduced powers, or else moving to the unknown hazards of the council at Versailles as chief British military representative. It was a desperate moment for Lloyd George. He asked Philip Kerr: 'Have you packed up? We may be out next week.'³² But with his Cabinet behind him, Lloyd George was just able to force the issue. Derby was persuaded to withdraw his third resignation, even Haig stayed, and Robertson alone was sacrificed. In his place, the more congenial General Sir Henry Wilson followed as the new CIGS. Soon after, Lloyd George's ally, Milner, replaced Derby at the War Office. For much of the rest of the war, supreme strategy was essentially directed by the so-called 'X Committee', consisting of Lloyd George, Wilson and Milner, the last now a declining force. The Prime Minister's control of military policy, though still far from being complete, became increasingly secure.

The initiative in wider diplomatic policy rested even more firmly with the Prime Minister, assisted by unorthodox aides such as Kerr or the munitions agent Basil Zaharoff. A typical instance was the mediation of possible peace terms with Germany, with proposed territorial concessions at the expense of Soviet Russia, in the winter of 1917–18. This was very much the personal responsibility of Lloyd George, in 'pacifist' mood at this time. Equally characteristically, he tried to underpin his position at home with personal approaches to pressmen such as C.P.Scott of the *Manchester Guardian* and even to opposition leaders like Asquith and Grey. The moral of this episode was pointed out for Scott's benefit: 'The Cabinet as a whole is never informed and asks no questions; it takes its information simply on the authority of the Prime Minister.'[33]

At the level of central decision-making, therefore, Lloyd George's wartime supremacy became increasingly pronounced. But over the wider political front, his position was much more vulnerable. His control over parliament, for instance, was quite unpredictable. He had assumed leadership as an individual, not as party leader, as a result of a political manoeuvre conducted largely outside the House. Unlike Churchill in 1940, he had no reliable Commons majority. His immediate supporters were the Liberals (claimed to be 126 in number) marshalled by Addison and David Davies in the crisis of December 1916. In concert with them were the majority of Unionists and 'official Labour'. But there was always an opposition of fluctuating strength, the political truce notwithstanding. With Asquith on the opposition front bench, an alternative premier seemed always to hand. Lloyd George himself was constantly apprehensive, perhaps too much so, at the possible loss of ministerial control of the Commons. This largely accounted for the delay in bringing Churchill into the government, while at the height of the Robertson crisis in February 1918; it was here that he seemed most vulnerable. Even with Churchill and Montagu safely absorbed into the administration, there were always shifting groups of critics likely to crystallize behind Asquith, or perhaps Carson or discontented ex-ministers. The issue of a critical debate seemed hard to predict, while a dissolution of the House was unthinkable. The major parliamentary crisis of the later period of the war was the debate of 9 May 1918, following General Maurice's allegations in the press that Lloyd George had starved Haig of reinforcements on the western front.

The crisis may appear to have been negotiated fairly comfortably. In reality, despite a crushing speech by the Prime Minister, which apparently demolished Asquith's hesitant objections, still the formidable tally of 106 rebels (including 98 Liberals) voted against the government. Then and later, the Prime Minister without a party was in parliamentary terms always at risk.

Another sphere of uncertainty was the Prime Minister's influence over the organs of opinions. An extreme preoccupation with the power of the press had been a consistent theme in Lloyd George's career ever since his early connections with the Caernarfon newspaper, *Y Genedl Gymreig*, in the 1880s. In the parliamentary vacuum of the war years, it was the press that in large measure provided a political dialogue and an effective opposition. Lloyd George, therefore, devoted immense effort to this field. Press barons such as Rothermere and Beaverbrook were temporarily brought into the government. Other newspaper men, frequently nonconformists, were Lloyd George's close companions, George Riddell, C.P.Scott and W.Robertson Nicoll (of the *British Weekly*) being the most conspicuous. In the case of a persistently critical journal like the *Westminster Gazette*, Lloyd George attempted without success to obtain a majority shareholding or else to remove its editor, J.A.Spender. His most notable *coup* was the secret deal in September 1918 which resulted in a take-over of the Liberal *Daily Chronicle* (at a cost of £1.6 million) by a pro-Lloyd George syndicate. Its editor, Robert Donald, who had dared to offer General Maurice a position as the journal's military correspondent after his recent disclosures, was ruthlessly cast out.[34] More generally, William Sutherland, the premier's press secretary, and sometimes the ubiquitous Kerr, were active in withholding unfavourable military dispatches from the press, or else in supplying discreet leaks from 'a well-informed correspondent'. Yet, despite all his ingenuity, Lloyd George's control over the dissemination of news could only be partial. Indeed, his more notorious adventures with the press barons, especially the tragi-comic relationship with the 'grasshopper', Northcliffe, were becoming counter-productive, as Milner warned him.[35] Guest, the Coalition Liberal whip, urged that 'Bronco Bill' Sutherland ought to curtail his operations. As Guest delicately phrased it, 'there is some evidence available to the effect that he has subordinated the interests of your collegues in his intense loyalty to yourself'.[36] Guest proposed that the sources of information for distribution to the newspapers should again be vested in the whips' office, and in the course of 1918 this was partially effected.

Over the political public more generally, the Prime Minister's hold was still more uncertain. The mood he sought to evoke was that of national unity, the cause of 'the people' against 'the interests'. But this was difficult to sustain in a democratic country, so recently torn by class and party conflict. Labour, for instance, was always hard to keep in line, especially after Henderson's departure from the government over the Stockholm conference, in August 1917. Lloyd George himself was a rural rather than an urban radical: the class struggle in an industrial society was remote from his experience. He tried to distinguish between 'patriotic labour' (represented by Victor Fisher's British Workers' League or by C.B.Stanton, the Welsh Mussolini who had followed Keir Hardie as a member for Merthyr) and the 'Bolshevik and pacifist element' who followed MacDonald and the ILP. But this distinction became increasingly unreal, especially after the excitement of the revolution in Russia. Lloyd George's contacts with the world of labour were inevitably with the union leaders he had won over on 7–8 December 1916. Thomas Jones had brought him into close touch with his fellow Welshman, J.H.Thomas of the NUR. But, as movements such as the shop stewards or the Welsh miners' Unofficial Reform Committee indicated, it was a leadership that the rank and file frequently rejected. Lloyd George attempted to broaden his appeal by factory visits or by the occasional major public appearance such as his Caxton Hall speech to the trade unions on war aims on 5 January 1918. Even so, the reports of the commissions on industrial unrest in 1917 ought to have warned the Prime Minister how tenuous his authority could appear at the pithead or on the shop floor. There was to be a massive response to Bernard Shaw's appeal to the Labour Party conference in November 1918: 'Go back to Lloyd George and say "nothing doing".'

Ireland was even more alienated from the Prime Minister's *ersatz* coalition. He could try to bring together Redmond and Carson, when setting up a convention which could provide a negotiated compromise over home rule. Professor Adams urged on the premier the merits of a federal system of devolution. But in Ireland itself, newly inflamed by the rise of Sinn Fein and the ruthless suppression of the Dublin rising, any settlement imposed by the English government would have no validity. Even a moderate like John Dillon was now hopelessly alienated from the British government.[37] Lloyd George raged to H.A.L.Fisher against the Catholic priests who, he believed, were the force behind Sinn Fein. He claimed that 'English public opinion would applaud the violent enforcement of [Irish] conscription.'[38] But it had no effect: anyway, the Prime Minister had never been much of a Home Ruler even back in 1886. The Irish looked at his united front of patriotic constitutionalists, and rejected it out of hand.

Somehow, Lloyd George had to transform his ascendancy from a transient mood into a permanent movement. He recognized instinctively that the war had made the old pre-war politics, especially Liberal politics, out of date. He thought 'that it may come to a fight between him and Henderson and that all parties, including Labour, will be split and reconstituted'.[39] But what would he offer instead in this post-war world? His power rested on interlocking cadres of leaders – politicians, bankers, press lords, self-made industrialists, and similar 'responsive personalities'. But unless he could relate this to some form of mass political structure, he would head a post-war army overflowing with field marshals but lacking a rank and file.

From the start of his premiership, therefore, Lloyd George was most actively involved in constructing a new political base for himself. At times, he entertained the dream of a new Coalition party of patriots, but he saw that this lay very far off. In the short run he had to create a viable Coalition Liberal organization that would enable him to bargain with the Unionists on something like equal terms when peace drew near. This was a constant theme in his Wednesday breakfasts with Liberal colleagues in the government. In April 1917, he appointed the faithful Dr Addison, his Minister of Munitions, to head a committee on Liberal party organization, but this made little headway.[40] That December, he reviewed the position with Addison, Milner, Victor Fisher of the British Workers' League and Waldorf Astor, a remarkably odd foursome of advisers. They all agreed that 'L.G.'s chief weakness is that he has no organization.'[41] His main instrument here was Captain Frederick Guest, the Coalition Liberal Chief Whip from April 1917, a man of limited political insight but infinitely loyal. Lloyd George largely relied on Guest for information about backbench opinion on both sides of the House, and his influence could be considerable. In 1917 he warned Lloyd George against a premature challenge to Asquith's leadership of the party.[42] In February 1918 his warnings of the dangers of delay impelled the premier towards resolving the fate of Robertson.[43] After the Maurice debate, on 17 May, Guest and other Coalition Liberal ministers advanced an important stage towards turning themselves into a separate party organization.[44] Their programme was quite simply the perpetuation of Lloyd George as national leader. It served to give him a much stronger hand in the bargaining with the Unionists two months later. Without this rudimentary party machine, his ascendancy would surely have remained a wartime phenomenon. The rise of Coalition Liberalism, however fragile in the constituencies, offered a prospect of translating that ascendancy into something more durable.

This was put to the test in the 'coupon' general election of December 1918, the vital transition from the wartime into the peacetime premiership. Acting through Guest and the newly formed Coalition Liberal machine, Lloyd George conducted highly successful secret negotiations with the Unionists in July and August, which ensured his party's electoral future. At this time, it was assumed that the war would still be going on when the next election was held. Somewhat reluctantly, Bonar Law agreed to jointly sponsored Coalition candidatures, and in the event over 150 Coalition Liberal candidates received the 'coupon', an arrangement remarkably favourable for the weaker partner of the Coalition.[45] It was Lloyd George himself who insisted on the magic number of 150.[46] The Coalition's manifesto was in large measure the work of Lloyd George, with stylistic embellishments from the pen of H.A.L.Fisher. An agreed formula was devised over the most contentious issues – free trade, Ireland, the Welsh Church, Lords reform, the peace settlement. Bonar Law left most of the final details to Lloyd George himself.[47] With the Unionists now won over, Lloyd George turned to the less difficult task of ensuring Liberal participation. In a vital meeting with Montagu, Churchill, Fisher and other ministers on 6 November, their misgivings on anti-dumping legislation, on India and Ireland, were pacified. These ministerial Liberals had few illusions about what they had done. Montagu suspected that already a deal had been concluded with Tories, while Churchill told Fisher that he knew the Liberals would be divided henceforth. 'Here is a great split.'[48] Fisher's own perplexity of mind had dissolved by 12 November when he moved a resolution in support of the Coalition at a meeting of Liberal MPs. 'A thoroughly satisfactory meeting from the Liberal point of view,' he concluded.[49] Montagu's qualms were stilled by the thought that 'a change of Prime Minister would be fatal'.[50] In any case, he expected to get his own way about India.

Churchill was more belligerent. On 9 November, he wrote to Lloyd George in an agitated manner, demanding to know whether the War Cabinet would be retained and inquiring about the personnel of the post-election government. Lloyd George fiercely rebuked him. It was without precedent (so he claimed) to inquire how a subsequent government would be composed. 'The choice of the members of the Government must be left to the Prime Minister.' He claimed that the overriding emotion present throughout Churchill's letter was that of driving ambition. 'You will one day discover that the state of mind revealed in that letter is the reason why you do not win trust even when you command admiration. In every line of it, national interests are completely overshadowed by towering personal concern.' In the face of this onslaught, Churchill had no alternative but to submit.[51]

The course of the 'coupon election' reflected the mood of a nation unbalanced by the relief and the exaltation of victory. The campaign was generally free from the strident nationalism later alleged by Keynes. Nevertheless, demands for extreme reparations and for vengeance from the defeated Germans figured with increasing prominence, in the speeches of Asquithians and Labour leaders as in those of members of the government. Following Kerr's advice,[52] Lloyd George at first kept aloof from the party 'ding-dong' of the election. Like Franklin D.Roosevelt in 1936 and 1940, he sought to fight on a national rather than a party platform, demanding the return of certificated supporters of his government from whatever party. The result was that Liberal 'pacifists' and ILP 'Bolsheviks' were almost wiped out. Over 520 supporters of the Prime Minister were returned, a unique personal endorsement for the saviour of the nation. In the words of an admiring compatriot, the polls were 'a great ceremony of congratulation' for 'the greatest Welshman yet born'.[53] One conclusion was beyond dispute. Edwin Montagu gave it sycophantic expression. 'There has never been an election like this one in its one-man nature. Somebody said to me the other day that the only speeches in the papers were your speeches, that the only thing the country listened to was what you said.'[54] Lloyd George seemed to have climbed to a rare pinnacle of personal domination, 'the strongest man since Pitt', two Labour MPs later told Stamfordham.[55] It could apparently be said of Lloyd George now as William Allen White wrote of Roosevelt in 1934: 'he has been all but crowned by the people.'[56] Or, in Bonar Law's more prosaic words, 'he can be Prime Minister for life if he likes.'[57]

Lloyd George's semi-presidential stature during the war years had been in large measure an a-political phenomenon, isolated from party and parliament. Now he had to translate it into political terms, to give it stability and permanence. For almost a year, his intention seemed to be to perpetuate the political methods of the war years. Despite protests from Churchill, the War Cabinet was largely preserved intact until October 1919: even Austen Chamberlain, the Chancellor of the Exchequer, was almost excluded from it at first, much to his own disgust. While Lloyd George was away at the Paris peace conference, the Cabinet remained firmly under his direct control. Even a former ally like Milner was summarily dispatched from the War Office when he appeared to mishandle the demobilization of the armed forces. Lloyd George had become increasingly disenchanted by Milner's handling of his department since April. In full Cabinet, the Prime Minister now subjected him to 'vehement charges of dilatoriness and neglect'; poor Milner was forced to bewail in his diary that the proceedings were 'rather indecent'.[58] All major business was filtered through the Prime Minister before coming up in Cabinet. When Churchill, who had succeeded Milner at the War Office, stepped out of line, he was sternly rebuked. 'I have heard,' wrote Lloyd George, 'that you propose bringing before the Cabinet on Tuesday the question of continuing military service for an army of 1,700,000. I am surprised that you should think it right to submit such a scheme to my colleagues before talking it over at least before submitting it in the first instance to me. ... This is a question not of detail but of first class policy which may involve grave political consequences (it might even produce trouble in the Army) and I ought to have been consulted in the first instance.'[59] Churchill, reasonably enough, pointed out the difficulty of obtaining a decision while half the Cabinet was absent in Paris, but he forwarded his proposals to Lloyd George meekly enough.

While the peace conference continued at Paris until July, the Cabinet virtually conducted a holding operation for the Prime Minister. It seemed at times little more than a sounding-board for him to try out ideas about the peace terms. For instance, it had referred to it, in late March, his Fontainebleau Memorandum (largely drafted by Hankey and Kerr) which challenged the severity of the treatment of Germany over both frontiers and reparations.[60] For the rest, the Cabinet appeared to be largely a coordinating machine for a growing number of committees, of which the standing committees on Home Affairs (chaired by Fisher and set up at Bonar Law's insistence in February 1919) and on Finance, chaired by the Prime Minister, were the most important. Crucial issues of domestic policy Bonar Law referred direct to the Prime Minister in Paris: he was involved especially closely in the threatening situation in the coal-mining industry.[61] Very reluctantly, Lloyd George restored the large pre-war-style Cabinet in October 1919. He would have endorsed Milner's private comment on 27 October: 'It appears that the War Cabinet system is now coming to an end and that we shall again have a Cabinet of 22 members! Awful mistake!'[62]

Even so, the personal direction of policy by the Prime Minister continued inexorably, often to the irritation of colleagues. For instance, Sir Alfred Mond, a Welsh member, protested in July 1919 when the financial settlement with the disestablished Church in Wales was decided in private sessions between the Prime Minister and Bishop of St Asaph. 'With some others of my colleagues,' wrote Mond, 'I feel that the practice of continually being made responsible for policies, in which we have had no voice, and in most cases of which we have not even been informed, is most unsatisfactory and places one in a position of difficulty.'[63] Mond, however, was ignored: the Welsh Church Temporalities Bill was swept through in a fortnight. A few months later, Mond had a further disappointment to swallow when he was excluded from the reconstituted Cabinet.

Of course, governments would hardly be imperilled by the operations of the serpentine Bishop of St Asaph, and it might be argued that on Welsh affairs the Prime Minister had a unique expertise. But on issues of wider significance, he seemed to dominate the whole range of domestic policy, from the fixing of wheat prices to the import duty on fabric gloves. When he led the resistance to his own government's Safeguarding of Industries Bill in March 1921, Beaverbrook observed: 'He continues to lead Government and Opposition.'[64] In particular, Lloyd George turned himself into a kind of collateral Minister of Labour. He played a major personal role in the 'foiling of Labour' during the sequence of lengthy industrial disputes between 1919 and 1921, employing the whole formidable range of weapons in his political armoury – delay or coercion, summit diplomacy or personal charm. He could use supremely skilful delaying tactics, as in the frustrating of the miners in 1919 by the appointment of the Sankey Commission and subsequent disregard for its findings. He could occasionally contemplate simple coercion as in the threatened seizure of transport services in mining areas in March 1919 to starve the recalcitrant miners into submission, or again in the proposal for a Citizen Guard during the national railway strike that October. The Cabinet even considered forming battalions of loyal university-trained stockbrokers to overpower the Triple Alliance. Lloyd George dismissed with contempt the feebleness displayed by Sir Albert Stanley, the President of the Board of Trade, during the quasi-revolutionary disturbances in Glasgow in January 1919: 'Stanley, to put it quite bluntly, is a funk, and there is no room for funks in the modern world.'[65] Again, Lloyd George could apply the full resources of his personal diplomacy as when he negotiated with the deputation from the TUC Council of Action, led by Bevin, in August 1920, after trade unionists had threatened to use direct industrial action to prevent the shipment of British arms to Poland.[66] Alternatively, he could isolate and charm an individual labour leader into submission, as when poor Frank Hodges, secretary of the Miners' Federation, was beguiled into an unofficial acceptance of the government's terms over miners' wage rates, quite distinct from the issue of a national 'pool' for wages, on 'Black Friday' (15 April 1921). Usually, Lloyd George's diplomatic success in these difficult crises was astonishing; he served in effect as the roving chairman of a supreme court of conciliation. He virtually eliminated the threat of a general strike. But even his Cabinet entered a discreet protest when he brought a miners' strike to a close in October 1920. 'Comment was made on the great drain which these frequent and prolonged labour negotiations made on the time of the Prime Minister, and the difficulty which might be experienced in the future if there should be a Prime Minister less experienced and skilful in negotiations of this kind.'[67] Even the distilled prose of Hankey's minutes could not suppress the note of concern.

Even more striking in the immediate post-war period, however, was the Prime Minister's involvement in foreign policy. During the Paris peace conference, with its emphasis on summit diplomacy, this was inevitable. But over the next three years, with Wilson and Clemenceau removed from the scene, Lloyd George was left almost alone to shape the post-war world. He embraced the opportunity with avidity. Between Paris in January 1920 and Genoa in April 1922, he conducted over twenty major conferences with foreign heads of government. As long as Balfour was at the Foreign Office, all this provoked little friction: his abiding principle was 'a free hand for the little man'.[68] But the advent of Curzon in October 1919, a difficult enough colleague in more tranquil times, inevitably led to conflict. For the next three years, an intermittent stream of complaints came from the Foreign Office about its being excluded from diplomatic conferences or left in ignorance about policy decisions. Curzon also criticized the casual, disorganized way in which conferences were conducted. Relations with Eastern Europe caused a good deal of difficulty. Curzon protested in vain when a British ambassador was sent to Poland in July 1920 without his knowledge.[69] He resented negotiations with the Russians over a trade treaty in 1921 being conducted by the Board of Trade and by Lloyd George's personal adviser, E.F.Wise, rather than by himself.[70] H.A.L.Fisher, at the Board of Education, also frequently interfered in the conduct of foreign policy. By the following March, Derby (now ambassador in Paris) could report that 'Curzon has no weight whatsoever with Lloyd George in foreign affairs,' a view echoed by d'Abernon, the ambassador in Berlin. Edward Grigg of the Garden Suburb was said by Thomas Jones to 'do the PMs Foreign Office work', to the fury of the civil servants.[71] Lloyd George, for his part, did not spare Curzon when they came into conflict in the Cabinet. He flayed him mercilessly in 1920 for allegedly concluding an Anglo-Russian treaty behind his back.[72]

Yet it may be that too much has been made of the clashes between Lloyd George and Curzon. The flame of conflict blazed fiercely at the time but somehow flickered out. On wide areas of policy – questions of protocol apart – Curzon's principle equally seemed to be 'a free hand for the little man'. He endorsed readily the main lines of Lloyd George's policies on France and Germany. He also acquiesced in much of his policy towards Russia, for instance in the astonishing negotiations with Krassin in August 1920 about the war in Poland. The one persistent area of difficulty was the Near East, especially relations between the Greeks and the Turks in Asia Minor. Yet even here, on several occasions, Curzon threw his influence behind Lloyd George's passionately pro-Greek policy. They both defended in Cabinet discussions in January 1920 the decision to keep the Turkish Sultan out of Constantinople.[73] They were united in trying to implement the Sèvres settlement later in the year. Not until the Chanak crisis flared up in September 1922 did persistent tension seem to develop between the Foreign Office and No. 10 Downing Street. Otherwise, Lloyd George's foreign policy usually proceeded without serious challenge from his colleagues.

Most members of the Cabinet seemed content enough with all this. Griffith-Boscawen, Minister of Agriculture from 1921, was impressed by the harmony of the Cabinet and by the Prime Minister's tolerance in allowing debate to proceed without interruption.[74] Bonar Law had frequently echoed this view.[75] At times, Lloyd George was actually outvoted, as over the Constantinople issue in January 1920. Fisher admiringly commented, 'The PM took his defeat splendidly';[76] perhaps his thoughts were already turning towards by-passing it at the Sèvres conference. Sometimes, the premier had to bludgeon his colleagues – for instance, in the appointment of the Geddes Committee on public economies; more often they were beguiled, as in the starting of talks with the Sinn Fein leaders in August 1921. When necessary, Lloyd George could still 'charm a bird off a bough'. The major complaint, indeed, was not that the cabinet was being subjected to dictatorship, but rather that it was being made irrelevant. By mid-1920, it seemed almost to have dissolved into a series of 'conferences of ministers', committees or simply 'conversations', often with shrewdly chosen personnel. In February 1922, Mond protested that a major policy decision on India had been taken by only eight Cabinet members out of nineteen. 'It is very difficult for a member of the Cabinet to know at the present time whether questions are to be considered Cabinet questions or not. Sometimes questions are discussed and subsequently decisions come to us without the Cabinet being again consulted, as in the case of the recent Austrian loan. ... The principle of collective responsibility on these subjects becomes almost impossible to maintain.'[77] Montagu echoed this theme in the bitter speech that accompanied his resignation in March and some other ministers privately agreed with him. Churchill, another Liberal, pointed out that government legislation was being sent direct from the Cabinet Home Affairs Committee to the government whips, without the Cabinet proper being consulted at all: 'the Home Affairs Committee was practically converting itself into a Bill factory.'[78] The mounting stockpile of defunct measures indicated that government could no longer be run by the imperatives of the war years.

As peacetime politics gradually returned, the Cabinet saw the Prime Minister begin to descend from Olympus. The non-party men invaluable during the war were rapidly disappearing – Smuts home to South Africa, Auckland Geddes to Washington, Eric Geddes back to industry, Milner out of public life altogether. After the Versailles treaty, the Cabinet secretariat resembled more a piece of formal administrative machinery for recording and implementing decisions than a kind of prime-ministerial department. More significant still, the 'Garden Suburb', once so significant in reinforcing the premier's supervision of his departmental colleagues, was now disintegrating, amidst general approval. In March 1921, Philip Kerr left to manage the post-Donald *Daily Chronicle* on behalf of the Coalition Liberals. He advised Lloyd George to dissolve his personal secretariat entirely and to divide its functions between Hankey and J.T.Davies, his private secretary. 'The Cabinet Office is really your secretariat and has all the knowledge and experience I can supply. And the other work, now that you have drawn out of the active management of Foreign affairs, can I think be done by an intelligent Private Secretary. ...'[79] Edward Grigg, Kerr's successor, however, still managed to exert some influence over foreign policy. But over the whole range of central government, the Prime Minister was being forced slowly to accommodate himself to the varying pressures within the Coalition. After the departure of Bonar Law in March 1921, this became noticeably more difficult, as his successor, Austen Chamberlain, lacked Law's calm authority over the Unionist MPs. To shore up his position in the government, therefore, Lloyd George had somehow to manufacture his own area of support. Instead of confining his main attention to Liberal subordinates like Addison or Fisher, he found himself creating for himself a new 'inner Cabinet'. Emerging out of the fluidity of the negotiations with Sinn Fein in the autumn of 1921, a new cross-party triumvirate crystallized in Lloyd George, Churchill and Lord Birkenhead, with Chamberlain to manage the Commons, and Horne and Worthington-Evans as an outer penumbra of loyalists. It was this new formation of which Montagu complained in the months prior to his own resignation – the new ascendancy of Horne, Churchill and 'F.E.': 'The Cabinet is hardly ever called together and then only to register decisions.'[80] But his criticisms were no longer a comment on 'prime-ministerial government' as understood in 1919, but rather on the growing diffusion of power within the Cabinet, not on the Prime Minister's strength but on his growing weakness.

By March 1922, Lloyd George's authority over his own Cabinet ministers was increasingly strained. Grigg thought that three-quarters of them were now disloyal to him. He suffered a severe rebuff when his colleagues, led by Churchill, voted him down on the issue of the recognition of Soviet Russia at the forthcoming Genoa conference.[81] At Genoa, Lloyd George's overtures to the Russians went far beyond his brief, nevertheless, much to the alarm of Poincaré and The Times. But no longer could he employ the old weapons with the same certainty of success – or even of survival.

The beginnings of decline in his control of the Cabinet had already been mirrored in difficulties with parliament. For the first year after the 'coupon election', the House of Commons was taken for granted. The Prime Minister kept aloof, with an occasional triumphant return to flay the 'die-hards'. But his varied array of supporters could not be reined in for long. There was an ominous rebellion against the Aliens Bill in October 1919, when over a hundred right-wing Unionists voted against the government. Lloyd George responded in the most direct way, summoning the leaders of the revolt (Carson among them) before him for a personal rebuke.[82] But it was noticeable that his first appearance at Question Time for over three years followed shortly after, though he aroused comment by casually answering sixteen questions at once. With the premier absent at international conferences for much of 1920, his control over the Commons became less secure. There was a fierce 'die-hard' demonstration in support of General Dyer, of Amritsar notoriety. Lee of Fareham circulated a note in the Cabinet at this time to the effect that these Unionist backbench revolts were partly a demonstration against the Prime Minister's absences abroad. 'If you could attend at Questions only, say 2 days a week, it would put the Coalition members who are quite loyal in a much better temper.'[83] His constant intervention in labour disputes and unemployment policy in 1921 announced that the Prime Minister had clearly returned to the domestic scene. From now on, his preoccupation with the Commons was almost as exaggerated as had been his unconcern earlier. In debate after debate, it was the Prime Minister who led off for the government, often at immense length, usually with devastating effect.

But the signs were mounting that ministerial control of the Commons was beginning to slip. The furore that accompanied the troubles (and eventual dismissal) of Addison in June and July 1921 was one indication. Austen Chamberlain told Lloyd George that he could no longer restrain Unionist backbench rebels on the issue of Addison's salary. 'The only chance of averting defeat is that you should yourself undertake its defence and exert all your influence and authority.'[84] Younger, the Unionist party chairman, added another typical backbench grievance: 'far too many Jews have been placed in prominent positions by the present government.'[85] The conclusion of the Irish treaty in December 1921 imposed a whole series of new strains. Already the conduct of government business in the House was under fire; its substance was even more open to attack. There was little enough that Lloyd George could do. He now lacked the usual prime-ministerial controls over the rebels. The inducements of patronage were of little avail in a declining government: there was a humiliating delay in finding a successor to Montagu at the India Office in March 1922. Again, as the Liberal leader of a largely Unionist majority, Lloyd George lacked effective control through the whips. He relied on Chamberlain's ability to keep Younger in hand. But when Younger, almost single-handed, wrecked the premier's plans for an immediate election after the Cannes conference in January 1922 by revealing them to the newspapers, it was evident that Chamberlain could neither discipline Younger nor dismiss him.[86] Even the Coalition Liberal members were difficult to keep in hand now. They pressed strongly against the Safeguarding of Industries Bill, with its threat to free trade, and agitated for possible Liberal reunion.

Faced with these signs of parliamentary revolt, Lloyd George attempted to construct a new party political base for himself. He showed all his usual resource. Until mid-1920, much of his energy was apparently being devoted to forming a new Centre party. He tried to win over his Liberal colleagues in February 1920: 'Liberal labels lead nowhere; we must be prepared to burn them.' He outlined a possible programme for them – Irish home rule, temperance, security for the agricultural tenant. 'After these measures are passed there will have to be a period of administration.'[87] Previously, he had refused to be elected parliamentary leader of the Coalition Liberals, 'so as not to frighten the Tories who had acquiesced most loyally in his social programme'.[88] Birkenhead and Churchill backed him up in demanding a Liberal–Conservative 'fusion'. But these schemes got nowhere as Unionists felt their self-confidence returning. Liberals were equally suspicious. They now saw Lloyd George 'veering over to the Tory point of view',[89] rather than as a claimant for the moderate middle ground of politics. At two crucial meetings on 16 and 18 March 1920, first the Coalition Liberal ministers, then the backbenchers turned down Lloyd George's 'fusion' proposals. His use of the Black and Tans in Ireland, his violent rhetoric against 'the ludicrous creed of Bolshevism' made them wonder what had happened to his old radical ideals. The successive purging of Addison and Montagu from the government (in July 1921 and March 1922) over housing and Turkey respectively confirmed these fears.

Since a Centre party was still a chimera and reunion with the

Asquithians impracticable, the premier was forced to turn instead to building up the Coalition Liberal machine. It was notorious that in the country the Coalition Liberals were pathetically weak, by comparison with the 'Wee Free' organization. The Prime Minister himself had never taken any interest in the complexities of party organization. In 1920, therefore, Guest inaugurated moves to set up a nationwide Coalition Liberal party in every constituency in the land; but, by the time he was succeeded as Chief Whip by C.A.McCurdy in early 1921, little had been achieved.[90] Further, the electoral record of Coalition Liberal candidates in by-elections had been dismal in the extreme, despite occasional consultation with the Prime Minister on the selection of candidates. McCurdy's main strategy in 1921–2, therefore, was to conduct a holding operation, to build up Liberal strength to a point where meaningful bargains could again be struck with the Unionists, as in July 1918, to prolong the Coalition after the election. He summarized his leading principles in March 1922: '1. The situation will not improve until the Conservative majority has disappeared. 2. The situation cannot therefore improve until an election is held. 3. If an election is held on the lines I have suggested, the Coalition Liberals will be returned in the largest possible numbers.'[91] But, unfortunately, the main decisions in his optimistic strategy lay almost wholly with the dominant Unionists. In any case, the Prime Minister was almost wholly absorbed with trying to seduce the Unionist leaders from their party, on the pattern of the Peelites of the 1850s, and treated his own Liberals with contempt and neglect.[92]

In fact, Lloyd George's relations with the Unionist Party in the country were becoming increasingly difficult. Even with no more formidable a spokesman than Sir Henry Page Croft, the constituency parties' pressure on Lloyd George became more intense. It was this that made Younger, the Unionist party chairman, the 'cabin-boy' in Birkenhead's contemptuous phrase, such a decisive figure in the political manoeuvres of 1922. Churchill had given Lloyd George some sound advice during the Irish peace talks, on the dangers of underestimating the Unionist threat. 'The delusion that an alternative Government cannot be formed is perennial': he cited Balfour and Asquith as premiers who had suffered from it.[93] At least it could be said until early 1921 that no-one resembling a credible alternative Prime

Minister could be seen: the parliamentary Labour Party cut a poor figure, while Asquith was a spent force. But the return of Bonar Law to partial health in the autumn of 1921 transformed the situation. For the first time, Lloyd George had a serious, if undeclared, rival. After this, Unionist hostility became more serious. Younger's calculated disclosures to the press in January 1922 deprived the Prime Minister of his basic weapon, the right to dissolve parliament. Fisher commented to Lloyd George at this time that 'the cabin-boy and his following will not have us'.[94] Lloyd George actually offered his resignation on 27 February, but Chamberlain predictably refused the 'crown of thorns'.[95] Unionist pressure in the country also created difficulties for Lloyd George before he went off to the Genoa conference. He might rage about their (and Churchill's) 'obsession' with the menace of Bolshevism: they were impervious to argument. He could not even carry the Unionists in the Cabinet with him on this. Chamberlain insisted that the Cabinet could survive only on the assumption that *de jure* recognition of the Soviet government was unthinkable. He added, significantly, 'I ought to add that Bonar was restless about Genoa.'[96]

The Prime Minister's hold over the wider political public is far harder to assess. It was certainly more secure than a scurrilous press campaign against him might suggest. Northcliffe's violent abuse in *The Times* left Lloyd George – the 'cheerful pachyderm' in *Punch*'s eyes – largely unscathed. In the end, *The Times*'s campaign became counter-productive when Wickham Steed's virulently distorted accounts of the proceedings at Genoa backfired on their author.[97] Certainly, the attitude of the public became more and more disillusioned with the government in the light of the trade depression and other discontents. Throughout 1921 there was a severe industrial recession, with unemployment over a million and a half. The government's by-election record was appalling. But how far this bore on Lloyd George's position is less certain. His resilience and stamina were extraordinary. His policies seemed always to produce a new initiative, a new expedient. There was something for everybody – the Irish treaty and Genoa for Liberals; the Geddes axe for the die-hards; housing and employment reforms for Labour. Despite Northcliffe, the press was far from being universally hostile to the Prime Minister. Several London dailies – the *Daily Chronicle*, the *Daily Telegraph*, the *Daily Mirror* – were strongly sympathetic; the Rothermere and, more erratically, the Beaverbrook press gave general support.[98] Lloyd George made a more ambitious move for press backing. When Northcliffe retired in June 1922, a dying man, Lloyd George attempted through the mediation of Grigg and Rothermere to acquire *The Times*, perhaps even to become its editor. Another abortive scheme was for Rothermere to become editor, with Lloyd George gaining financial control. This fascinating plan ultimately foundered.[99] Even so, there was real justification for the Coalition Liberal council's report in 1920 that the Prime Minister's personal hold on the public in all parts of Britain was still immense, especially since he had ceased to be mainly preoccupied with foreign affairs. 'No alternative Premier can be suggested and with the possible exception of unemployment we see nothing that can unseat him.'[100] Sales of the *Lloyd George Liberal Magazine* (38,000 copies printed) mounted steadily. He invariably met·with an enthusiastic reception at public meetings or at ceremonies to receive the freedom of cities. His spectacular vacation at Gairloch in the Scottish highlands in September 1921 (during which a Cabinet meeting was held in Inverness town hall) was to attract immense publicity. The Prime Minister still seemed able to sustain a kind of 'direct contact' with the people, a personal communion over the heads of their elected representatives. As long as this continued, he would still continue to dictate the political future.

Somehow from the autumn of 1921 things seemed rapidly to go awry. Ironically, this arose in large measure from one of his greatest achievements, the Irish free state treaty of December 1921, which incensed the Unionists. Ireland continued to plague the government, culminating in Field Marshal Wilson's assassination. Thereafter the strains within the Coalition became more and more pronounced. 'The PM seemed to be losing his punch and grip.'[101] Two surrenders of the period were indicative of the general decline – on 'anti-waste' and the 'honours scandal'. The 'anti-waste' campaign saw Lloyd George forced into a retreat before a right-wing clamour of the most primitive kind: when the Geddes committee was appointed, Fisher commented: 'the point is the PM is dead tired and wants to throw a sop to Anti-Waste before the recess.'[102] The results were to be lamentable for education and the social services. The crusade against the sale of honours had a little more substance. Certainly Sir William Sutherland, 'Bronco Bill', had been notorious for 'hawking baronetcies in the Clubs'. Even so, the distribution or sale of peerages in return for political services rendered was a hallowed practice of Prime Ministers, while in any case the Unionists shared in the proceeds now. Perhaps it was the scale of Lloyd George's operations that made them seem less respectable. Perhaps the 'Lloyd George fund' gave them a more identifiable personal flavour. Perhaps his own Welsh contempt for the hereditary system rankled with the class-ridden English. Or perhaps it was that the Unionist whips were incensed by 'Freddy [Guest] nobbling our men'.[103] Whatever the cause, the sale of honours caused a considerable outcry in 1922. In July, the Lords, in all solemnity, devoted a debate to examining the quality of their newly-ennobled recruits, and in particular to the conferring of a peerage on Sir Joseph Robinson, a South African capitalist of appalling reputation. Lloyd George yielded and appointed a Commission of Inquiry. The furore then died away, though the glittering millions of the 'Lloyd George Fund' weighed the premier down for the rest of his career.

Still, in the late summer of 1922 there was little on the surface to suggest that the downfall of the government was at hand. The clamour over the honours system came and went: the Genoa conference, with all its disappointments, seemed already forgotten. The economy appeared marginally to improve following counter-cyclical public works schemes by the government, and the interminable strikes of the previous year died away. Northcliffe was in his grave, Horatio Bottomley in gaol. Repeated attempts to rally discontented Unionist backbenchers had collapsed one after the other. From Washington to the streets of Belfast there were signs of a world at peace. The one major crisis on the horizon was the simmering conflict between the Greeks and the Turks in Asia Minor, but hitherto it had received little popular attention.

Suddenly in late August, the Near Eastern crisis exploded. The Turks under Mustapha Kemal smashed through Greek resistance and started to advance across Asia Minor towards the British-held position at Chanak. From the outset, action in this theatre had borne the personal stamp of Lloyd Georgian foreign policy. He had been the major influence behind the abortive Sèvres treaty in August 1920 which had carved up the Turkish dominions. He had urged Venizelos and the Greeks to hazard their military fortunes against the Turks, for whom he had a fine Gladstonian contempt as an inferior race, unfitted to rule. He had fiercely rebuked Churchill in the Cabinet for suggesting that Smyrna be surrendered to the Turks, and had insisted that possession of the straits was vital to British interests.[104] Now Kemal's army threatened to advance across the Dardanelles and into Eastern Thrace, in Europe itself. On 15 September, an anxious Cabinet accepted the Prime Minister's insistence that Britain must resist, even though Curzon later demurred that he 'did not hold quite such strong views for the retention of Chanak as some of his colleagues' and pointed out that Gallipoli would be far more defensible a position.[105] Three days later, service chiefs were called in to discuss the defence of Chanak and for the next three weeks Britain and Turkey seemed perilously near to war.

The Chanak crisis came for Lloyd George in precisely the wrong area and at the wrong time. All at once, his weaknesses on every side were exposed. Abroad, he had largely lost the diplomatic initiative, since neither the French nor the Italians were prepared to join Britain in resisting the Turks: Poincaré, the French Prime Minister, was even prepared to cede Eastern Thrace to them. Lloyd George was left instead to pin his slender hopes of assistance on the Yugoslavs and Rumanians.[106] His appeal to the dominion premiers found response only from New Zealand. Most crucial of all, opinion in Britain was intensely hostile to any policy that might lead to war. Already, the mood of appeasement was widespread and Keynes's onslaughts on the Versailles treaty had had immense appeal. The press was overwhelmingly critical, even Rothermere's *Sunday Pictorial* and Garvin's *Observer*, hitherto loyal to the government. Labour was instinctively pacifist and, when Lloyd George saw trade union leaders on 21 September, there were murmurs of 'direct action'. Most serious of all, Unionist protests swelled into a mighty chorus. They were known to have sympathizers within the Cabinet, Griffith-Boscawen, Baldwin, perhaps even Curzon. After all, Conservatives were traditionally pro-Turk. Most telling of all was Bonar Law's letter to *The Times* on 7 October. While he generally endorsed the government's Turkish policy, his warnings against Britain's acting alone as 'policeman of the world' chimed in with the isolationist mood. The rebels had found a credible leader, and Beaverbrook was urging him on towards a final break with his old colleagues.[107]

Somehow, in this last crisis, Lloyd George seemed to lose his usual self-possession. Talking to Fisher on 4 October, he said that he regarded defeat as inevitable. He forecast an early election in which the Unionists would fight alone and win 300 seats, the Liberals' total slumping to a mere fifty.[108] Yet on 12 October he managed to get the Unionist members of the Cabinet, Baldwin and Boscawen alone dissenting, to agree to an immediate election, to forestall the coming conference of the National Union when a declaration of Unionist revolt was anticipated. In fact, thanks mainly to Curzon, the Chanak crisis was now over. The Treaty of Mudania, negotiated by General Harington with the backing of Curzon, had turned the armistice into an agreed territorial settlement with the Turks. The government could now claim to have maintained the freedom of the straits, to have repelled an aggressor, and to have helped protect the Greek Christian minorities, to have been faithful to Disraeli and to Gladstone at one and the same time. All that was needed was to maintain intact the alliance between the Prime Minister and the Unionists. In fact, he went out of his way to reject them. His speech at Manchester on 14 October, violently anti-Turkish in tone, was aggressively Liberal (even though it contained a memorable rebuke to Viscount Gladstone). It even opened the door to possible reunion with the 'Wee Frees'. The following day, the Unionist junior ministers virtually declared their independence; Baldwin threw in his lot with them on the 16th.[109] Now at the Carlton Club meeting of Unionist MPs that Austen Chamberlain had summoned for 19 October, a split seemed inevitable. All that the rebels needed for final triumph as the leadership of Bonar Law. In fact, on the night of 18 October, Beaverbrook's siren voice beguiled him into submission: he had already rejected a direct personal overture from Lloyd George.[110] At the Carlton Club meeting, Bonar Law's voice, pleading for party unity, had immense effect. Despite all the pleas of Chamberlain, Balfour and Birkenhead, the Unionists voted the Coalition down by 187 to 87. Lloyd George resigned the same day. His crushing defeat at the December general election confirmed that his career as a political figure of major consequence had abruptly ceased.

At the time, many felt that his fall marked the end of a distinct era. *The Times* found in his premiership 'the greatest experiment in political improvisation which Great Britain had ever known'.[111] Certainly, his wartime premiership was a unique exercise in instant leadership, which has found no subsequent parallel. Churchill's coalition government after May 1940 provided a counterpart in some respects; yet, in his concern for parliament and his insistence, on Chamberlain's retirement, that he be elected Conservative leader, Churchill's suggested some essential differences from Lloyd George's war premiership. It is, however, by the peacetime premiership of 1918–22 that the claim (implicit in the writings of R. H. S. Crossman, for instance) that Lloyd George inaugurated a new era of prime-ministerial government must be tested. There is little doubt that the evidence largely points the other way. Indeed, the years since 1922 could well be regarded as a reaction against Lloyd George's personal ascendancy rather than a continuation of it. Baldwin and MacDonald both traded on the reputation that they had positively no connection with Lloyd George. Thomas Jones even thought that Baldwin's later pre-occupation with the Welshman's dictatorial ways was obsessional.[112] Certainly Lloyd George left his successors a range of institutional aids, but of these only the Cabinet Office survived and with an increasingly modest role. The abolition of the Garden Suburb was confirmed by Bonar Law. Certainly, the powers of the central government were enormously expanded during these years, but its connection with the personal supremacy of any one Prime Minister is only intermittent and incidental. To perpetuate itself, Lloyd George's system needed a new political order, in which the parties would melt away, in which the Hankeys, Joneses and Kerrs would come into their own, and in which legislative and executive control would radiate uniquely from the presidential command of the man at the centre. In effect, Lloyd George's concept of premiership required Britain to turn itself into the United States in a period of strong presidency. Years later, in 1935, Lloyd George's 'Council of Action' was consciously modelled on Roosevelt's 'New Deal', brains trust and all. For four years after 1918, Lloyd George seemed to achieve an approximation of this system; but time soon showed that this was basically a result of the party vacuum after the war rather than a permanent transformation of the governmental

12. Page's Diary ? February 1917 (Harvard University, Houghton Library, b MS Am 1090.5 (2)).

13. For good general accounts, see J.Ehrman, *Cabinet Government and War, 1890–1940* (London 1958), ch. III; J.P.Mackintosh, *The British Cabinet* (London 1962), ch. 13; A.M.Gollin, *Proconsul in Politics* (London 1964), *passim*. Also see *The War Cabinet: Report for the Year, 1917* (Cd. 9005).

14. Mond to Lloyd George, 27 February 1917, *Ll.G. Papers*, F/36/6/12.

15. Churchill to Lloyd George, 2 May 1918, *ibid.*, F/8/2/19; Sir E.Geddes to Lloyd George, 16 August 1917, *ibid.*, F/17/6/7; Derby to Lloyd George, 15 August 1917, *ibid.*, F/14/4/63.

16. T.Jones to his wife, 12 December 1916, cited in Keith Middlemas (ed.), *Thomas Jones: Whitehall Diary. Vol. I. 1916–25* (Oxford 1969), p. 15. There is a full account of the formation of the secretariat in S.W.Roskill, *Hankey, Man of Secrets. Vol. I, 1877–1918* (London 1970), pp. 335–46.

17. Hansard, *Parl. Deb.*, 5th ser., vol. 155, pp. 213ff.

18. L.S.Amery, *My Political Life II, 1914–1929* (London 1953), p. 92; P.A.Lockwood, 'Milner's Entry into the War Cabinet, December 1916', *Historical Journal* VII, part I (1964), p. 133. Hankey had accepted Amery's appointment with great reluctance (Roskill, *op. cit.*, pp. 344–5).

19. *Thomas Jones: Whitehall Diary*, p. 202.

20. Walter Long to Bonar Law, 16 July 1918, *Ll.G. Papers*, F/30/2/38.

21. J.Davies, *The Prime Minister's Secretariat* (Newport 1953), p. 153.

22. Adams's memorandum *Ll.G. Papers*, F/74/10/4.

23. *Ibid.*, p. 31.

24. Joseph Davies, *op. cit.*, pp. 56–7.

25. See Ll.G. Papers, F/89/1–2 *passim*. J.R.M.Butler, *Lord Lothian* (London 1960) is disappointingly uninformative on these matters.

26. W.A.S.Hewins, *Apologia of an Imperialist* (London 1929) II, 132ff.

27. W.K.Hancock, *Smuts* (London 1962) I, pp. 489ff.

28. Lord Derby to Sir Philip Sassoon (n.d. 1917), quoted in Randolph Churchill, *Lord Derby, King of Lancashire* (London 1959), pp. 281–2.

29. Lloyd George, *op. cit.*, I, 1035; A.J.Marder, *From the Dreadnought to Scapa Flow* (London 1969), pp. 153–66.

30. Sir Maurice Hankey, *The Supreme Command, 1914–1918* (London 1961) II, p. 728; Roskill, *op. cit.*, p. 458.

31. Cabinet Committee on War Policy, 21 June 1917 *Milner Papers*, Bodleian Library, Box 125, 102–14.

32. Lord Riddell, *op. cit.*, pp. 313–14.

33. J.L.Hammond, *C.P.Scott of the Manchester Guardian* (London 1934), p. 225; War Cabinet Minutes, 3 January 1918 (W/C 313); see also Gollin, *op. cit.*, pp. 552ff.

34. H.A.Taylor, *op. cit.*, pp. 168–72.
35. Milner to Lloyd George, 27 February 1918, quoted in Lord Beaverbrook, *Men and Power, 1917–1918* (London 1956), pp. 284–5.
36. Guest to Lloyd George, 26 February 1918, *Ll.G. Papers* F/21/2/13.
37. F.S.L.Lyons, *John Dillon* (London 1968), pp. 435ff.
38. H.A.L.Fisher's diary, 24 April 1918, *Fisher Papers*, Bodleian Library, Box 8.
39. Riddell, *op. cit.*, p. 309.
40. C.Addison, *Four and a Half Years* (London 1934) II, 315, pp. 365–6.
41. *Ibid.*, pp. 458–59.
42. Guest's memorandum, *Ll.G. Papers*, F/168/2/3.
43. Guest to Lloyd George, 15 February 1918, *ibid.*, F/21/2/12; Milner's diary, 12 February 1918, *Milner papers*.
44. Guest to Lloyd George, 17 May 1918, *Ll.G. Papers*, F/21/2/22.
45. 'Draft of agreement to be signed by the Prime Minister and Mr Bonar Law', *ibid.*, F/21/2/28; cf. T.Wilson, 'The Coupon and the British General Election of 1918', *Journal of Modern History*, XXXVI (1964), especially pp. 35–9.
46. Sir George Younger to J.C.C.Davidson, 2 December 1918, *Bonar Law Papers*, Beaverbrook Library, 95/4.
47. R.Blake, *The Unknown Prime Minister: The Life and Times of Andrew Bonar Law, 1858–1923* (London 1955), pp. 383–5.
48. Waley *op. cit.*, pp. 184–5; Fisher's diary, 6 November 1918, *Fisher Papers*.
49. Fisher's diary, 12 November 1918, *Fisher Papers*.
50. Waley, *op. cit.*, p. 185.
51. Churchill to Lloyd George, 7 November 1918; Lloyd George to Churchill, 7 November 1918, *Ll.G. Papers*, F/8/2/37–8.
52. Kerr to Lloyd George, 20 November 1918, F/89/1/13.
53. *Welsh Outlook*, January 1919.
54. Montagu to Lloyd George, 16 November 1918, *Ll.G. Papers*, F/40/2/24.
55. Lord Stamfordham to Lloyd George 19 March 1921, quoted in Beaverbrook, *Men and Power*, p. 338.
56. Arthur M.Schlesinger Jr., *The Age of Roosevelt*: III *The Politics of Upheaval* (London 1961), p. 1.
57. Beaverbrook, *op. cit.*, p. 325.
58. Milner to Lloyd George, 7 December 1918, *Ll.G. Papers*, F/38/4/41; Milner's diary, 6 December 1918, *Milner Papers*. cf. *Thomas Jones: Whitehall Diary*, pp. 121–2.
59. Lloyd George to Churchill, 18 January 1919; Churchill to Lloyd George, 20 January 1919 (telegram) *Ll.G. Papers*, F/8/3/2–4.
60. Lloyd George to Bonar Law, 31 March 1919, *ibid.*, F/30/3/40.
61. There are many letters on this theme in *Ll.G. Papers*, F/30/3.
62. Milner's diary, 27 October 1919, *Milner Papers*.

63. Mond to Lloyd George, 15 July 1919, *Ll.G. Papers*, F/36/6/50.
64. Beaverbrook to Bonar Law, undated, quoted in Beaverbrook, *The Decline and Fall of Lloyd George* (London 1963), p. 260.
65. Lloyd George to Bonar Law, 29 January 1919, *Ll.G. Papers*, F/30/3/10; *Thomas Jones: Whitehall Diary*, p. 101.
66. L.J.Macfarlane, 'Hands off Russia in 1920', *Past and Present* (December 1967), p. 138.
67. Cabinet Minutes, 26 October 1920 (P.R.O., CAB 23/22); Fisher's diary, 26 October 1920, *Fisher papers*.
68. Blanche Dugdale, *Arthur James Balfour* (London 1936) II, p. 196.
69. Curzon to Lloyd George, 20 July 1920, *Ll.G. Papers*, F/13/1/1.
70. Curzon to Lloyd George, 5 August 1921, *ibid.*, F/13/2/38.
71. Randolph Churchill, *op. cit.*, pp. 428–9; cf. Lord Ronaldshay, *The Life of Lord Curzon* (London 1928) III, pp. 316–17; and Sir Valentine Chirol, 'Four Years of Lloyd Georgian Foreign Policy', *Edinburgh Review* (January 1923). Also see *Thomas Jones: Whitehall Diary*, p. 202.
72. Fisher's diary, 7 June 1920, *Fisher Papers*.
73. *Ibid.*, 6 January 1920.
74. A.S.D.Griffith-Boscawen, *Memories* (London 1925), pp. 230–2.
75. E.g. Fisher's diary, 22 March 1918, *Fisher Papers*.
76. *Ibid.*, 6 January 1920.
77. Mond to Lloyd George, 13 February 1922, *Ll.G. Papers*, F/37/2/3.
78. Churchill to Lloyd George, 6 July 1922, *ibid.*, F/10/3/15.
79. Kerr to Lloyd George, 19 January 1921, *ibid.*, F/90/1/36.
80. Montagu to Reading, 30 November 1921, quoted in Waley, *op. cit.*, p. 261.
81. *Thomas Jones: Whitehall Diary*, p. 197; P.R.O., CAB 23/29.
82. *The Times*, 25 October 1919.
83. Cabinet Note, undated, *Ll.G. Papers*, F/100.
84. Austen Chamberlain to Lloyd George, 9 June 1921, *ibid.*, F/7/4/5.
85. Younger to Chamberlain, 10 June 1921, *ibid.*, F/7/4/8. Churchill had also pressed the anti-semitic point (Churchill to Lloyd George, 26 December 1918, *ibid.*, F/8/2/49).
86. Lloyd George to Chamberlain, 10 January 1922, *ibid.*, F/7/5/3.
87. Fisher's Diary, 28 January and 4 February 1920 (*Fisher Papers*). On all this, see the present writer's chapter, 'Lloyd George's Stage Army: the Coalition Liberals, 1918–22' in A.J.P.Taylor (ed.), *Lloyd George: Twelve Essays* (London 1971). Also cf. Bentley B. Gilbert, *British Social Policy, 1914–1939* (London 1970), pp. 33–45, where the connection of the 'fusion' plans with social reform is emphasized.
88. *Ibid.*, 21 February 1919.

89. Riddell, *Diary of the Peace Conference and After, 1918–23* (London 1933), p. 179.

90. Guest to Lloyd George, 16 April 1920, *Ll.G. Papers*, F/22/1/30.

91. C.A.McCurdy to Lloyd George, ?March 1922, *ibid.*, F/35/1/37.

92. C.P.Scott's diary, 23 October 1922, *Scott Papers*, B.M. Add. MSS 50906, ff. 196–200.

93. Churchill to Lloyd George, 9 November 1921, *Ll.G. Papers*, F/10/1/40.

94. Fisher to Lloyd George, 20 March 1922, *ibid.*, F/16/7/84.

95. Lloyd George to Chamberlain, 27 February 1922, *ibid.*, F/7/5/6.

96. Chamberlain to Lloyd George, 23 March 1922, *ibid.*, F/7/5/22.

97. *History of the Times* (London 1952) IV, p. 66.

98. Guest to Lloyd George, 30 December 1919, *Ll.G. Papers*, F/21/4/34.

99. *History of the Times*, IV, pp. 683ff.

100. Annual Report of the Coalition Liberal Organization for 1920, *Ll.G. Papers*, F/168/2/16.

101. *Thomas Jones: Whitehall Diary*, p. 197.

102. Fisher's Diary, 2 August 1921, *Fisher Papers*.

103. Younger to Bonar Law, 2 January 1921, quoted in Beaverbrook, *op. cit.*, p. 243. He alleged that Guest was putting Unionists in the Liberal lists for peerages.

104. Minutes of conference of ministers, 18 February 1921 (CAB 23/38)

105. *Ibid.*, 27 September 1922 (CAB 23/39)

106. Lloyd George to Curzon, 15 September 1922, *Ll.G. Papers*, F/13/3/33. See David Walder, *The Chanak Affair* (London 1969), pp. 209–20. Mr Walder makes clear the way in which British commanders at Chanak tended to take matters into their own hands as a result of not having any clear or consistent directives from the Cabinet.

107. Beaverbrook, *op. cit.*, pp. 170ff.

108. Fisher's diary, 4 October 1922, *Fisher Papers*.

109. Harold Nicolson, *Curzon: the Last Phase* (London 1934), p. 277; Keith Middlemas and John Barnes, *Baldwin* (London 1969); p. 119.

110. Beaverbrook, *op. cit.*, pp. 176–8, 198–9.

111. *The Times*, 20 October 1922.

112. *Thomas Jones: Whitehall Diary*, pp. 243, 255–6. Baldwin and his wife were actually moved to deface an album photograph of Lloyd George. Jones commented: 'How they do hate him.'

113. In the years that have passed since this chapter was drafted, many major works have been published relating to Lloyd George's premiership. Among the more significant are: Maurice Cowling, *The Impact of Labour, 1920–1924* (Cambridge 1971); V.H.Rothwell, *British War Aims and Peace Diplomacy, 1914–1918* (Oxford 1971); A.J.P.Taylor, *Beaverbrook* (London 1972);

S.W.Roskill, Hankey, *Man of Secrets, Vol. II* (London 1972); D.G.Boyce, *Englishmen and Irish Troubles* (London 1972); Kenneth O.Morgan (ed.), *Lloyd George, Family Letters, 1885–1936* (Oxford and Cardiff 1973); Stephen Koss, *Fleet Street Radical* (London 1973); Michael Kinnear, *The Fall of Lloyd George* (London 1973); Richard H.Ullmann, *The Anglo-Soviet Accord* (Oxford 1973); G.W.Jones, 'The Prime Minister's Advisers' in *Political Studies* XXI (1973); Kenneth O.Morgan, *Lloyd George* (London 1974); Howard Elcock, *Portrait of a Decision* (London 1974); Alan J.Ward, 'Lloyd George and the 1918 Irish Conscription Crisis', *History Journal*, 17 (March 1974); Martin Gilbert, *Winston S.Churchill* IV (London 1975); Roger Adelson, *Mark Sykes: Portrait of an Amateur* (London 1975); Lord Blake, *The Office of Prime Minister* (Oxford 1975); Peter Lowe, 'Lloyd George' in Herbert van Thal (ed.), *The Prime Ministers* 2 (London 1975); John Stubbs, 'The Impact of the Great War on the Conservative Party', in G.Peele and C.Cook (eds), *The Politics of Reappraisal, 1918–1939* (London 1975); C.Wrigley, *Lloyd George and the British Labour Movement* (Brighton 1976); Peter Rowland, *Lloyd George* (London 1976); Stephen Koss, *Asquith* (London 1976); Charles Townsend *The British Campaign in Ireland, 1919–1921* (Oxford 1976); H.C.G.Matthew, R.I.McKibbin and J.A.Kay, 'The Franchise Factor in the rise of the Labour Party', *English History Review*, CCCLXI (October 1976).

James Ramsay MacDonald

Trevor Lloyd

James Ramsay MacDonald formed three governments, and on each occasion he faced unusual political circumstances. In 1924 he formed a government although his party was clearly not the largest in the House. In 1929 his government depended, like Asquith's after 1910, on the support of a minor party. In 1931 his government depended, like Lloyd George's in 1916, upon the support of his former opponents to uphold him against his former political friends. Thus he is, with Lloyd George, one of the two people in this book who never held the full power of a Prime Minister with a majority in the House made up of his own followers.

MacDonald's importance in political history depends quite as much on what he did for the creation and development of the Labour party as on anything he did as Prime Minister. Obviously a great many other people helped with the work, but nobody else did so much to produce a new party which replaced the Liberals and thus transformed the political scene between 1900 and 1924. In some ways his period of office as Prime Minister was an anti-climax.

MacDonald was born in 1866, the illegitimate son of a Scottish peasant girl. He benefited from the egalitarian Scottish educational system and his first jobs were as a clerk; although he came from lower in the social scale than any other British Prime Minister, he was never a member of the manual working class. In 1896 he married the daughter of a relatively wealthy scientist, and this made him fairly well-off: when the TUC, the Independent Labour party, the Social Democratic Federation and the Fabian Society formed the Labour Representation Committee, to establish a 'distinct Labour group' in the House of Commons, MacDonald was elected Secretary and could give much more time to the job than any of the other leaders could have afforded. Of course, he was not chosen simply for this reason; he had been a socialist for fifteen years, he had gained some political experience as secretary to a left-wing Liberal candidate for parliament and he had stood as ILP candidate for Southampton in 1895.

As Secretary MacDonald did a great deal for the LRC; in particular he negotiated the secret 1903 agreement with Herbert Gladstone, the Liberal Chief Whip, which gave the LRC about 30 winnable seats with no Liberal opponents at the 1906 general election, in return for a promise of tacit LRC support for Liberals in other seats. He convinced the Liberal leadership that the LRC commanded widespread support and could put forward candidates who would draw off a substantial body of working-class Liberal supporters. This distinctly overstated the strength of the LRC position, though Gladstone was probably more willing to accept the LRC case because of his personal conviction that more working-class MPs ought to be returned. If Liberal constituencies had been more willing to adopt trade unionists as candidates in the 1890s (as Gladstone wished), the TUC might not have taken so much interest in setting up a political party.

The success of MacDonald's negotiations meant that between 1906 and 1914 the Labour party, as it called itself in 1906, provided about forty MPs on the Liberal left – some of them described themselves as socialists, but most of them were trade unionists with fairly strong Liberal sympathies. MacDonald was elected to Parliament in 1906, and retained his post as Secretary of the party, which meant that he continued to work away at keeping up the interest of the trade unions in their party, and at the same time maintained the electoral agreement with the Liberals. Most of the Labour Members were mainly concerned with the legal position of trade unions; once the Trade Disputes Act of 1906 had reversed the Taff Vale judgement, which had done so much to encourage the political activity of the trade unions by limiting their legal rights, their political interests were rather limited. MacDonald was one of the few Labour Members who was ready and able to show that there was a distinct Labour point of view and that the Labour party was willing to put forward its opinions over the whole range of parliamentary activity. In particular he took much more interest in Indian and foreign affairs than any of his colleagues, with the possible exception of Keir Hardie.

In addition he wrote several books and pamphlets – Disraeli is the only other party leader who has spent as much time trying to explain in writing what his party stood for. Almost inevitably MacDonald's writing does not add much to political philosophy, but he approached the problem more seriously than anyone else who has risen to high office in this century. He needed to present a political theory that would persuade the Independent Labour party, which was his own base in the Labour party, that it should adopt a moderate (or revisionist) line; he had to show the trade unions that while the Labour party could be useful to them as a pressure group it could help them even more if it became a party capable of forming a government; and he had to convince people outside the ILP and the trade unions that the Labour party was a moderate and trustworthy force. At the same time he had to show that it did have features that made it distinct and different from the Liberals.

His main emphasis was on the spirit of humanity and consideration for the poor that inspired the Labour party, and he said rather less about definite policies to be followed. MacDonald had become a socialist at a time when it was perfectly possible to do so without laying much stress on nationalization, and it did not mean as much to him as it did to the next generation of socialists. His idea of socialism rested on a biologist's analogy: he believed that society was an organism evolving by more or less inevitable stages into a more interdependent and socially responsible form, and that the organism must not be damaged by sudden revolutionary changes. Just as Liberalism had been the appropriate political belief for the nineteenth century, socialism was the appropriate political belief for the twentieth century. From this point of view socialism looked rather like the Fabian Society belief in the 'inevitability of gradualness', and MacDonald and the Fabians could agree about the details of domestic policy. The spirit was very different; their dull and thorough analysis of problems had very little in common with MacDonald's broad and sweeping approach.

The Chairmanship of the parliamentary Labour party was at first a post held on a rotating basis for a one or two-year period. But when MacDonald became Chairman in 1911, he occupied the position on what seemed a more permanent basis. He exchanged the secretaryship of the party for the less time-consuming post of Treasurer, which had been held by Arthur Henderson. His main difficulty in the next few years was in maintaining the electoral agreement between Labour and the Liberals, because the two parties opposed each other at by-elections, which was likely to lead to difficulties at the next general election. In 1914 all this ended abruptly: on 3 August MacDonald put the Labour party's arguments against the policy of British involvement in Continental war that Grey had indicated, but immediately afterwards the German ultimatum to Belgium was announced and the Labour party began to change its position. By 6 August the party was committed to the war and MacDonald, who still opposed Continental involvement, had to resign from the leadership.

The Labour party adjusted itself to the situation rather well, guided by Arthur Henderson who became the new Leader. The pro-war majority did not purge the anti-war minority, and MacDonald remained the party Treasurer. In less accommodating socialist parties the anti-war minority was usually driven out, and often became the nucleus of the post-war Communist party. MacDonald was not a pacifist who said that all war was wrong. His argument was that England had entered the war unnecessarily and mainly because Sir Edward Grey had deserted the principles of Gladstonian Liberalism; a good Gladstonian would have avoided entangling alliances like Grey's secret agreements with France. In 1914 all this seemed irrelevant in the blaze of patriotism; nobody was convinced and some of MacDonald's meetings were broken up by the more bellicose supporters of the war. But MacDonald maintained his position, though not in so heroic a way as some of the fervent pacifists. He organized, in cooperation with some Liberals who disapproved of Grey's policy, the Union for Democratic Control (of foreign policy), a step which helped draw some Liberals towards the Labour party. By 1916 and 1917 his opposition began to look much more sensible; supporters of a negotiated peace were beginning to appear, several politicians agreed that secret diplomacy had had a lot to do with the outbreak of the war and the Labour party was beginning to move away from its earlier unconditional approval of government policy. By 1918, when the Labour party organized itself for the first time to fight on a national scale instead of in chosen seats, MacDonald was re-established in the Labour party, and he and Henderson and Sidney Webb were the three men who worked out the party's new political platform, *Labour and the new Social Order*.

By the end of the war it was clear that the Liberal party was in difficulties. There were three distinct problems: some of the more active Liberal politicians felt that the Labour party best represented Liberal principles, especially in foreign policy; Asquith and Lloyd George had divided the party in two as a result of their struggle for power in December 1916; and the 1918 expansion of the electorate had, quite apart from enfranchising women, given the vote to the bottom third of the adult male population, who had not previously possessed it. The Liberals might very easily have managed to deal with this third problem and win the support of the newly enfranchised, if their capacity for organization had not been almost completely destroyed by the first two problems. When the newly enfranchised acquired the habit of using their votes, most of them supported the Labour party and a sizable minority supported the Conservatives; very few of them voted Liberal.

The Labour party did not benefit much from this in the 1918 election. Most of the old pre-war trade unionists were re-elected, but the men like MacDonald who had opposed the war were defeated. This knocked most of the brains out of the parliamentary party: it was so short of talent that people suggested that MacDonald should be available to advise it although he was not an MP. This proposal was turned down by the parliamentary party.

MacDonald got back into the House in the 1922 election, and promptly stood for the leadership against J.R.Clynes, who had held the post for the last year of the old Parliament. MacDonald was elected by 63 votes to 58. Much of the credit for this choice is often given to the dozen or so newly elected left-wingers from the Clydeside, who decided to support MacDonald as a group and thus could claim to have provided the margin of victory. In years to come, as MacDonald looked more and more right wing, the choice seemed odd, but at the time it was the natural result of MacDonald's position during the war – Clynes had held office under Lloyd George. But the Clydesiders' votes would not by themselves have been enough for success, and anybody who was concerned about widening the Labour party's appeal beyond the solid ranks of the industrial classes would have chosen MacDonald over Clynes. MacDonald was a skilled House of Commons man and a great orator. He possessed the power to make men see visions of the future and to convince them that he was leading them forward to daring and sweeping objectives when in fact he was not committing himself to anything very definite. An orator of this sort can be a great asset to a party, though there is a danger that he will become so involved in his own speeches that he becomes incapable of making the sharp decisions needed for effective government. Gladstone possessed the gift for arousing enthusiasm while always hedging his position very carefully, but he could give a precise answer when forced to face a precise question; MacDonald was not always able to do this, perhaps because (unlike Gladstone) he had no opportunity to grow accustomed to the work of administration in a departmental post.

He was probably the only person who thought the leadership of the Labour party in 1922 would lead on to the premiership, but even he cannot have imagined how soon the opportunity to form a government would come. In October 1923 Baldwin dissolved parliament because he wanted a mandate to impose protective tariffs. He did not get his mandate: although the Conservatives with 258 seats remained the largest party in the House the Labour party with 191 seats and the Liberals with 158 made up a free trade majority.

This situation, in which the House of Commons came closer to having three evenly balanced parties than at any other time in its history, was made more complicated by the prejudice against the Labour party. Before people accepted the fact that the Conservatives could not stay in office, because their policy had been rejected, and that MacDonald as Leader of the second largest party should be asked to try to form a government, some very odd proposals had been made. Supporters of Churchill's view that 'Labour is not fit to govern' suggested that a government under another Conservative Leader, or a Liberal government with Conservative help, or a government of National Trustees, pledged not to have an election for two years, would be preferable; presumably the idea of a government of National Trustees was inspired by the government that Mussolini had recently set up in Italy in time of crisis.

MacDonald denounced these attempts to 'wangle the constitution' and Asquith agreed that a Labour minority government was the natural solution.[1] The Conservatives decided to stay in office until they were defeated in parliament, so there was more time than usual to think about the problems of forming a Cabinet. The other Labour leaders agreed with Sidney Webb's advice to let MacDonald have a free hand, and in broad outline his Cabinet made good sense, with representation for the trade unions, the intellectuals of the party, the relatively recent converts from Liberalism, all garnished with the obligatory representation in the House of Lords.

The Labour leaders had to decide whether their government should do its best to stay in office or should present a socialist programme which would be defeated in the Commons and would then be the central issue in a general election. The most deeply committed opponents of the Labour party were afraid that MacDonald would follow the latter course, because they believed a socialist programme would win a lot of votes for the Labour party, but the Labour leaders decided without much argument that they would follow the former course, partly because they believed they could carry out some useful short-term measures, partly because they wanted to gain experience in office, and partly because they believed the electorate would think the Labour party was irresponsible if it forced another election almost immediately.

Because of this decision (and the similar decision taken in 1929 in similar circumstances) it is unusually difficult to tell what MacDonald's long-term goals in domestic policy were. Undoubtedly he wanted to follow Gladstonian anti-imperialist principles in external affairs, and he was able to do a certain amount in this direction in the next ten years. As a party leader he wanted to establish the Labour party as one of the two major parties and to make sure that it did not remain the pressure group for the industrial working class that it had originally been. He never had the chance to show what he would have done once Labour had got a parliamentary majority; his speeches combine references to day-by-day tactical problems with allusions to eternal principles, but say very little about the policy that he would have followed if he had had a free hand.

The Labour government did unexpectedly well during its nine months in office. The domestic successes, with which MacDonald was not directly involved, showed that a policy of not alienating the Liberals need not lead to sterility. Snowden's Budget took a distinct step towards free trade by removing the McKenna duties imposed during the war and reducing some of the 'breakfast-table duties' on sugar, tea, coffee and cocoa. Wheatley's Housing Act brought the government, the building contractors and the building trade unions together to their mutual advantage: the government offered loans and a small subsidy for a long-term programme of building houses for rent, the trade unions relaxed their rules of admission because they believed there would be adequate jobs in the future and the contractors undertook to build without letting their prices go up. The Wheatley programme, which was meant to run for twenty years, was brought to an end after eight but worked very well while it lasted. Snowden was a rigorous economizer but he was willing to finance the scheme, because the immediate burden would not be very great and the Treasury would get most of its money back over the course of time.

The Electricity Bill which was planned for the next session of Parliament was very similar in spirit. It would have provided a unified national grid which would allow the dozens of municipal and private electricity companies to draw on one another's supplies instead of having to keep up a high reserve capacity of their own. The Treasury was again willing to finance the scheme as it would be productive in the long run. The Bill would not have been particularly controversial and in the end it was passed into law by the succeeding Conservative government. The Labour government might have gone on for some time, producing legislation which, while not specifically socialist, demonstrated the advantages of government intervention.

MacDonald's own attention was focused on foreign affairs. When forming his Cabinet he combined the office of Foreign Secretary with the Premiership, apparently because he had an unreasonably low opinion of the ministerial talent at his disposal and, in particular, of Henderson. During the war Henderson had restrained the pro-war group from driving MacDonald from the party treasurership, he had a dominant position in the party machine and among trade unionists, and he had the capacity to be a good Foreign Secretary, as he showed between 1929 and 1931. Considering MacDonald's lamentations about the shortage of talent, it is astonishing that he tried to exclude from his Cabinet the only long-established member of the Labour party who had had Cabinet experience.[2] Henderson would not put up with this, and became Home Secretary after a quite unnecessary amount of discussion. MacDonald took up his self-imposed double burden.

Inevitably he was overworked, and could not do all the work of a normal Prime Minister; for instance, he served on very few Cabinet committees. But quite apart from his own long-established interest in foreign affairs this was the important issue in the minds of the people who said Labour was not fit to govern, and MacDonald was determined to prove them wrong. On the other hand there are plenty of examples such as Asquith and Grey, Attlee and Bevin, Churchill and Eden, and to some extent MacDonald and Henderson from 1929 to 1931, to show that a Prime Minister who is interested in foreign policy can play an important role in it while working with a talented Foreign Secretary.

Whatever problems it caused in the general running of the government, MacDonald's tenure of the Foreign Office was very successful, and it did help convince people that Labour was fit to govern. 'Mr MacDonald wished to re-establish relations of confidence and cooperation with France and Italy; to break the deadlock over reparations; to secure a French evacuation of the Rhineland; and to reintroduce Germany into the community of nations. He wished to further the cause of general disarmament by strengthening the machinery of international arbitration; and to bridge the gulf that, both politically and financially, sundered Great Britain from Soviet Russia. Within the space of eight months he was able either to attain or to promote all these seven objects.'[3]

By 1924 France had found her previous policy of rigorous enforcement of the Treaty of Versailles would not work, and was now looking for a new approach. MacDonald, and the Labour party in general, did not think the Treaty was either just or sensible, but he could hardly stress this point in discussion with the French, who were still basically strongly pro-Treaty. When French troops moved into the Ruhr in 1923, the Conservative government had protested and then sulked, without making any impression on Poincaré. MacDonald came to office at a time when it was probably easier to deal with the French, because occupation clearly had not solved the problem of getting the Germans to pay reparations.

He began the policy of reconciliation with a friendly letter to Poincaré – it was undoubtedly useful that he wrote as one Prime

Minister to another. He followed this up, a little later, by inviting Poincaré to Chequers and, when Poincaré was defeated in the 1924 election before his visit, his successor Herriot was invited. Herriot's visit increased the general desire to reach agreement; a conference was held in London, at which the Germans accepted the Dawes Plan for the payment of reparations and the French agreed to begin withdrawing their army of occupation. This was a distinct success for the Labour view that international tensions should be eased so that armaments could be reduced and trade flow freely, though it did not carry into effect any of the more radical criticisms of the Treaty of Versailles. MacDonald was widely praised for his chairmanship of the conference; no doubt the participants wanted to reach agreement, but his tact and skill steered them through the negotiations and made sure that they did not lose their desire for reconcilation.

While the conference was on, the British government was also negotiating a treaty with the Soviet Union. The Labour government recognized the Soviet government very quickly, in accordance with its election promises; it hoped that this would lead to agreements which might increase exports and reduce unemployment. As MacDonald was too busy to negotiate the Russian treaties, the work was mainly left to Ponsonby, the Under-Secretary at the Foreign Office – at one point a group of backbenchers intervened and saved the discussions from breaking down. The commercial treaty was perfectly orthodox but the general treaty regularizing diplomatic relations included a provision that, when the Russians had arranged a settlement of their pre-Revolution debts to British private investors, the British government would guarantee a Russian loan on the London money market. Countries which defaulted on loans usually did get a new loan when they acknowledged the old debts, but they did not usually get a government guarantee to help them.

The Liberals seized the issue and determined to defeat the government. But before they could do so a much smaller question came up; the government had decided not to pursue a prosecution for sedition that the Director of Public Prosecutions had launched against J.R.Campbell, a Communist newspaper editor, and the Conservatives moved a vote of censure on the grounds that this decision had been taken to placate the left wing of the Labour party.[4] The Liberals proposed a Select Committee instead, and they even offered to give up their seats on the Committee if the government would accept the proposal. The government could hardly accept this offer and in any case MacDonald had no intention of having a committee. When the Liberal motion was passed, MacDonald asked for a dissolution; it was granted, though the King did feel that in the circumstances it was not a matter of an automatic right.

The difficulties of combining the premiership and the foreign secretaryship were underlined during the election campaign. While MacDonald was on his speaking tour the Foreign Office asked him what should be done about a letter, apparently written by Zinoviev, President of the Communist International, plotting revolution and subversion in England. MacDonald suspected (correctly, as became known forty years later) that the letter was a forgery; he suggested a draft reply but told the Foreign Office not to publish anything until they could prove its authenticity. As the officials were afraid that the *Daily Mail* was about to print a copy of the letter, they disobeyed his instructions and published the letter and reply. MacDonald never said that they had done it deliberately to embarrass him, but he was a little surprised that they had done it without consulting him by telephone. [5]

The episode could not do the Labour party any good; its foreign policy seemed to have been shown to rest on establishing good relations with a country which was plotting revolution. On the other hand it does not seem to have caused the party much direct harm. [6] The by-elections had shown that the Conservatives were gaining ground, the Liberals were losing heavily and the Labour party was holding its own or perhaps gaining slightly, and this was reflected in the result of the general election, which gave the Conservatives a large majority. The Labour party was a little disappointed after the defeat, and it was suggested that the party should not form a minority government again. This idea was rejected at the 1925 party conference, and in his own speech to the conference MacDonald swept away any grumbling there had been about his leadership.

MacDonald's position as Leader was made much stronger by his easy command over party conferences. He seemed to have a very clear understanding of what needed to be said, and he knew what would move his audiences – at Llandudno in 1930, when Maxton of the ILP was taking part in a challenge to his leadership, MacDonald made a speech so moving that Maxton was reduced to tears, though as he wept he muttered 'the bastard'. MacDonald's dominance of conferences did not mean that he conceded any close control over policy to them; he explained on a number of occasions that, when there was a Labour government, ministers would have to apply the party programme in the light of the situation existing at the time. This was reasonable enough, but MacDonald sometimes went further than this in asking for a free hand in politics; on one occasion he denounced as 'easie-ozzie asses' the supporters of a resolution which seemed to him to be asking for more than could reasonably be provided in the foreseeable future by the Labour party. These people were launching no challenge to his leadership, and were not asking for anything that did not fit into the basic programme of *Labour and the new Social Order*; MacDonald did not suffer fools gladly, which is a natural enough reaction but not perhaps one that a party leader can indulge very often. MacDonald's own position as Leader in the 1920s was unusually secure; a challenge to his position could only be launched if it possessed the support of Henderson, and Henderson was completely convinced that MacDonald was the best leader the Labour party could have. Because of this, the grumbling and desire for a change could be ignored much more confidently than is usually the case for Leaders of the Opposition just after losing a general election.

The criticisms in Beatrice Webb's *Diary*, and her complaints about MacDonald as Prime Minister, deserve some attention, if only because her husband was one of the best-informed political theorists in the Cabinet. Although it is never made explicit, her line of argument suggests that (private life apart) Lloyd George was her ideal of what a Prime Minister should be. She wanted a Prime Minister who was interested in new ideas, accessible to his followers, insatiable in his willingness to talk to his ministers about politics and ready to use his Cabinet as a central clearing mechanism for forming policy.[7] But this is not the way Prime Ministers usually behave: MacDonald, like Asquith and Baldwin, liked to relax from politics, and he found that books, art and long walks in the country were sometimes more attractive than discussion about Bills and elections. The Cabinet is in normal times the rather untidy group of heads of departments which Beatrice Webb deplored; an attempt at more rigorous control might, except under the unifying conditions of wartime crisis, turn out to be a recipe for resignations and party disharmony.

Beatrice Webb also complained that MacDonald's refusal to use the Cabinet as a centre for discussion of policy had put too much power into the hands of the Prime Minister. As she gave no examples, it is not easy to see what she had in mind: MacDonald did not push forward policies of his own in the way that Baldwin had thrust Protection on his colleagues and his party in 1923. The type of Prime Minister that Beatrice Webb praised was almost bound to become a dominant figure in the way that Lloyd George had been dominant. One attraction for the Webbs about the Lloyd George style of government was that it offered to men like Sidney Webb the opportunity to catch the ear of a Prime Minister who listened to suggestions and then sometimes used his political power to put them into effect. MacDonald neither listened nor intervened; he left his ministers to devise their own policies and carry them out. Partly because he always had relatively detailed problems of his own to look after, he did not hold the position of a detached arbiter that Asquith had occupied, listening to a variety of proposals and then sorting them out into a programme. MacDonald, like Baldwin, fitted into the pattern of reaction against a very strong Prime Minister that had been noticeable in the last years of Lloyd George's tenure of office. With Baldwin this was a matter of laziness; with MacDonald it may have been more a matter of never having time to spare.

Haldane, who never served under Lloyd George, said MacDonald ran his Cabinet better than Campbell-Bannerman or Asquith had done, though he added that some of the credit must go to Hankey and the post-1916 way of doing things.[8] Like Beatrice Webb he said MacDonald was inaccessible, which he attributed partly to the burden of combining the Foreign Office with the premiership and partly to the attractions of country weekends at Chequers, away from political discussion. Asquith's ministers might have made just the same complaints about inaccessibility, and Baldwin's ministers undoubtedly did.

When Lord Salisbury combined the Foreign Office with the premiership, the parliamentary party was left to the Leader of the

House of Commons. MacDonald could not ignore the parliamentary party in this way, but because of the pressures of work he could not keep in touch with his backbenchers. This was bound to lead to irritation on both sides; the backbenchers were not as easy to satisfy as Lord Salisbury's had been, because they had definite policies they wanted to see carried out, and MacDonald felt that their eagerness to thrust their ideas on him meant that they did not trust him. Fenner Brockway came, as secretary of the ILP parliamentary group, to see MacDonald, and found him dressed for a banquet. 'Well, Brockway,' he snapped, 'what commands have you brought me today?'[9] Brockway may not have been the most emollient person to put forward the views of the ILP, and MacDonald may have had other things on his mind, but a Prime Minister has to take care not to be so busy that he cannot talk to his followers. MacDonald was in any case not good at arranging his work or delegating responsibility; he had the reputation of looking up railway timetables for his secretaries.[10]

It has also been suggested that MacDonald mishandled his party's relations with the Liberals, and that the two anti-Conservative parties could have returned to the harmonious partnership of 1906–14 if he had been reasonable. The trouble was that in the 1920s neither party could afford to be on particularly good terms with the other. The Liberal party was unwilling to support anything that might look like socialism; the Labour party was afraid of looking like the left wing of the Liberal party. The 1924 minority government had to work with the Liberals; but neither the Labour party nor the Liberal party could afford to make this clear.

In his speech declaring that he would not support Baldwin, Asquith said, 'it is we, if we really understand our business, who control the situation.'[11] This exaggerated the strength of the Liberal position, and did so in an unconciliatory way. A few days after Parliament had opened, Wheatley annulled the special Order which had restricted the expenditure of the Poplar Borough Council, a purely symbolic act because the Ministry of Health retained all its normal powers to restrain over-expenditure. Asquith denounced the move, and the Liberals seemed to be on the point of defeating the government when they realized what difficulties this would cause, and eventually they had to vote against their own motion. Both parties had been trying to score points; the Labour party emerged as the more skilful and the more resolute, but the incident showed the difficulties of cooperation.

While Asquith and Lloyd George thought they were more progressive than Baldwin, the Labour party did not forget that, during their premierships, socialists had been put in prison as conscientious objectors or as strike leaders. This helped explain why the Labour party could not see much difference between the Liberals and the Conservatives. The Labour party could work with the Liberals on free trade, but MacDonald was not himself very interested in the issue, and his ideas about the organic nature of society made him find left-wing Conservatives like Baldwin more sympathetic than the Liberals. He expressed the view that 'He could get on with the Tories. They differed at times openly then forgot about it and shook hands. They were gentlemen, but the Liberals were cads.'[12] This is surprisingly like Beatrice Webb's comment on the attack on Wheatley's annulment of the Poplar order that 'it is gross impertinence. ... Baldwin ... comes out in opposition as an English gentleman.'[13] The hostility to the Russian Treaty again shows that, even with good will, cooperation would have been difficult: the Labour party thought the treaty offered sound prospects of an increase in trade and employment and gave the bondholders as good a chance as any of getting their money back, but the Liberals regarded it as so bad that they were prepared to fight a general election on the issue, even though they knew the Conservatives were much more effective at banging on the anti-Communist drum.

Some of these problems of Liberal-Labour cooperation re-emerged in 1929. Baldwin's 1924 government achieved a decent record of social reform, but it was very dull and showed no signs of having any large-scale plans to deal with unemployment. In 1929 Labour won 288 seats, the Conservatives won 261 and the Liberals held the balance with 59 seats. The second Labour government came to office pledged to do something about unemployment, which had been the major issue in the election, and subsequently the major issue in the minds of historians studying the period. The government may not have seen things in quite the same light; unemployment was a difficult long-term problem to which there was no known solution, but there were several problems in foreign affairs and Commonwealth affairs which might with an effort be settled reasonably satisfactorily. MacDonald took the Gladstonian view that peace would help lead people back to prosperity, and was quite sure that the best thing he could do for trade and employment was to reduce international tension. The disastrous effects of international distrust and lack of cooperation in the early 1930s show that there was a great deal of truth in this.

Could the government reasonably have been expected to do better in facing the problem of unemployment? Gladstonian finance was not quite so completely taken for granted as in the past. In the 1929 election the Liberals had said the economy should be stimulated with a £250 million loan for road-building. In the first few months of the new administration Sir Oswald Mosley, as one of a group of four ministers in charge of the unemployment problem, argued that a policy of tariffs and public works would provide more jobs. In May 1930 he resigned from the government to campaign for this with greater freedom, and almost won a majority of the party conference to his side, though he later destroyed his influence by leaving the Labour party.

MacDonald wanted to find out about the problem, and certainly took more trouble about it than Baldwin. He created an Economic Advisory Council which gave him an opportunity of hearing different points of view. A committee of economists wrote reports for the EAC; the majority report (Hubert Henderson, Keynes, Pigou and Josiah Stamp) faced the combined problems with as much insight as could be found at the time. At the present day anyone can say that the British government should have devalued and budgeted for a deficit; these four economists, who were certainly not fettered by orthodoxy, did not go so far. Their report pointed to the stimulating effect on the economy of public works, and praised the government for what had already been done. The committee members did not like the idea of devaluation, but Keynes and Stamp asked for almost the same thing – they wanted a tariff of 10 % on all imports, combined with a subsidy of 10 % on all exports.[14] When the report was discussed at the Economic Advisory Council, Cole and Bevin went a step further and suggested that Britain should go off the Gold Standard.[15]

These proposals concentrated on Britain's problems in isolation, which cannot have appealed to MacDonald. Late in 1929 J.H.Thomas, the leading minister in charge of unemployment policy, submitted a report so barren of ideas and of hope that he might prudently have been moved to another post, but its last paragraphs argued, in just the terms MacDonald might have used, that successful foreign policies which reduced world tension and increased cooperation would solve the unemployment problem.[16] MacDonald's internationalism would have been wounded by devaluation or, worse still, going off the Gold Standard. A minority report to the Economic Advisory Council by Robbins ran on the same lines as Thomas's report; it denounced the majority report with some very high-minded internationalism, but had nothing to suggest.

At the beginning of the 1930s nobody deliberately advocated a Budget deficit. A large loan for public works, as proposed by the Liberals, would have had the same effect, but possibly not even Keynes at that time saw why. The government took up Lloyd George's suggestion of road-building; in 1930 a Liberal pamphlet called 'How to Tackle Unemployment' said that the government programme was exactly what the Liberals had suggested in the 1929 election except that the government expected to take five years and the Liberals thought it could be done in two. But the Liberals did not really understand deficit budgeting: their 1930 pamphlet recommended a 10% cut on current account, which would have wiped out some of the good effect of the loan for road-building. In 1931 the Budget deficit was rising to a level which, on the basis of Keynes' estimate that 5s. saved put a man out of work for a day,[17] was just about big enough to cure unemployment in England. But the Liberals showed no signs of approval; they wanted to turn the government out if it did not balance the Budget. And as an unbalanced Budget would have made devaluation inevitable, MacDonald would not have liked it either. The ideas for fighting unemployment were lying around in a fragmentary and disjointed form: a politician of great financial insight might have gathered them together, but nobody had seen the complete answer to the problem and it is only labouring the obvious to point out that MacDonald's talents did not lie in the field of economics.

He took more interest in economic affairs between 1929 and 1931 than in 1924, but questions of external policy continued to concern him. When forming the Cabinet MacDonald wanted Thomas as Foreign Secretary and wanted Henderson to lead the ministerial group on unemployment. Henderson insisted on being Foreign Secretary where he did well, though perhaps it would have been more to the point if he had accepted responsibility for unemployment instead of leaving it to Thomas, who did so badly that, after Mosley's resignation, sixty MPs asked MacDonald to get rid of him; as a result he was moved to the Dominions Office.

MacDonald and Henderson had very good conference manners, unlike Snowden, who was effective but unconciliatory at the Hague conference, and Thomas, who was neither effective nor conciliatory at the Imperial Economic Conference in 1930. During the first months of the new government, Henderson was fully occupied with the Young Plan for German reparations, relations with Egypt, and recognition of Russia, which took all his time in the summer of 1929; MacDonald retained control of the negotiations with the United States which were intended to lead to a naval agreement. His visit to America was a great popular success, but he did not possess the capacity for detail required in disarmament negotiations. Lord Thomson told the Webbs that the British and American admiralties were being allowed far more than they had expected, and Snowden wrote an angry letter for a Cabinet meeting that he could not attend in person, in which he said that the effect of the scrapping-and-rebuilding clauses was that more money would have to be spent on the navy than before.[18] Sidney Webb tried to make the best of it by saying that good relations with the United States were the really essential point, but this was all that the negotiations achieved; the 1930 naval conference in London, at which MacDonald presided, consolidated these good relations but did not make much further progress. For the rest of the Labour government's term of office foreign affairs were left almost exclusively to Henderson, who was becoming more and more interested in them – when he was invited to preside over the great Disarmament Conference which was being planned for 1932, the Cabinet said they would prefer him not to accept but would let him decide. Henderson accepted the post, and in the fullness of time received a Nobel Peace Prize for his work.

A good deal of MacDonald's time was taken up with Indian affairs. The Cabinet decided, after discussion with the viceroy, Lord Irwin (later Halifax), to announce that Dominion status for India was the ultimate objective of British policy. Irwin made the initial commitment to Dominion status, partly to give MacDonald an opportunity to argue the case for the change after hearing the first objections.[19] After this the government had to bring together the predominantly Hindu Congress party, the Moslems, the Indian princes, the Untouchable castes and the English military, civil service and trading interests in India, while remembering that a step as large as Dominion status would ideally be taken only when all three British political parties were in agreement. MacDonald arranged a Round Table conference for all the groups concerned, and presided over it with his usual charm and concern to bring people together. He had always been interested in Indian affairs, and the conference gave him an opportunity to help a constructive policy forward.

In the House of Commons there was much less that could be done, though it is not clear that the government had much legislation in mind which it would have introduced even if it had had a clear majority. Neither MacDonald nor the Labour leadership really seem to have been worried because they could not nationalize the mines, and they had very little else to suggest. Because the government could not rely on the Liberals for closure votes and control of parliamentary time, the Cabinet constantly worried about finding time for its measures, and was embarrassed by the need to consider Private Members' Bills seriously. On the other hand, when MacDonald asked whether the 1929–30 session should run on until the legislative programme had been cleared up, even if this meant sitting into September, or should end in early August as usual, the Cabinet chose the less strenuous path and gave up a certain amount of legislation.[20]

One effect of the government's relative lack of interest in legislation was that the backbenchers had very little to do. Parliamentary discipline became very weak; almost half the party voted against the government on one occasion or another. The most spectacular revolt was Mosley's creation of the New party, and the one that struck most deeply at the original foundations of the Labour party was the decision of the Independent Labour party to turn itself into a part separate from the parliamentary organization of the Labour party, but there were others, such as the revolt led by John Scurr which forced the government to accept a committment to increase financial aid to Catholic schools.

By this stage MacDonald had drifted into something like the same relationship with his party that Sir Robert Peel reached in the 1840s. He was, to an even greater extent than Peel, the architect of his party; perhaps because of this he seemed to assume that his party owed him unquestioning obedience. There may have been some Prime Ministers who were able to ignore their backbenchers without damaging their own position, but the lesson of Peel might have served to show that a Leader who is not careful to cultivate good relations with his parliamentary party is less able to manoeuvre and change his policy in moments in stress. Of course, it can still be said that a Prime Minister ought to be obeyed unquestioningly by his followers; all that can be said from the experience of Peel and of MacDonald is that in fact backbenchers who feel neglected and ignored by their leaders will not always obey them. MacDonald need not have surrendered control over policy to his backbenchers to remain on good terms with them; the geniality and amiability with which Disraeli or Baldwin courted their backbenchers was not accompanied by any particular willingness to let them dictate to the government.

But MacDonald felt no desire to be on good terms with his backbenchers, and showed even less concern about parliamentary morale than in 1924. He told a few friends at Chequers in 1931 that, if God offered him the choice between being Prime Minister or a simple country gentleman, he would reply 'Please, God, a simple country gentleman.'[21] This was not the frame of mind for keeping on good terms with his party; it is possible that nobody in this mood can retain the vitality needed for the exacting task that the premiership has become in this century.

MacDonald was able to do more of the general work of government than in 1924, and to take the chair of several Cabinet committees. He conducted the naval negotiations with the United States as Chairman of the Armed Forces committee, and after Mosley's resignation and Thomas's transfer he formed a panel of ministers concerned with the problems of unemployment and took the chairmanship of it himself. He also led a small committee to choose the next viceroy of India, led a very powerful committee investigating ways to deal with the issue of imperial preference without causing offence to the dominions, and in general was more active in Cabinet business than in 1924.

The unemployment situation grew worse in 1931, mainly because world trade was breaking down after the American economy had collapsed in 1929 and 1930. The Budget was clearly not going to balance. The government set up a committee of seven, two people nominated by each party leader with Sir George May, the ex-secretary of the Prudential Insurance, as chairman, to examine the Budget deficit and Snowden announced that he would not change taxes until the committee had reported. In July financial collapse spread through Austria and Germany; at the end of the month the May Committee presented its report, just as Parliament began its summer recess. Five members anticipated a Budget deficit of £120 million, and they recommended a small increase in taxation and a heavy cut in spending in order to meet it. Their attention was focused on unemployment payments, which they wanted to reduce by £66 million. MacDonald's own nominees saw things rather differently. They stated 'the present financial difficulties of the country and industry do not arise from any pursuit of wasteful public expenditure or lack of public control of such but are much more closely related to the policy of deflation followed since the war and confirmed by the return to the gold standard',[22] which was more or less what Lloyd George had said in 1929; however, Lloyd George's nominees on the committee stuck to the old orthodoxies.

So did MacDonald, and for the next four weeks he worked, skilfully and with regard for the demands of honour, to carry out the financial policy which he believed – almost certainly incorrectly – to be in the best interests of the nation. MacDonald, Snowden, Henderson, Thomas and Graham formed a Cabinet committee to work out possible economies in expenditure. Snowden convinced the committee that the true Budget deficit was likely to be about £170 million, and they decided to raise about half by additional taxation, which was left entirely in Snowden's hands, and half by cutting expenditure. After a couple of weeks' work the committee drew up a list of just over £78 million of cuts, though Henderson and Graham were less committed to this programme than the others.

The Cabinet reassembled on 19 August, and began discussing the proposals of the Economy Committee. MacDonald and Snowden discussed the situation with the Leaders of the Liberal and Conservative parties, because they needed the support of one, but preferably both, to pass an agreed set of proposals quickly. They also met the General Council of the TUC, which in effect stood by the minority report of the May Committee, and thus strengthened the opponents of the cuts in the Cabinet. On the 21st it seemed that no more than £56 million of the Economy Committee's proposed £78 million of cuts would be accepted.

On 22 August MacDonald told the Cabinet that the Liberals and Conservatives would defeat the government if it offered only the £56 million. Snowden then warned the Cabinet of the risk of 'reducing the standard of living of the workmen by 50 per cent, which would be the effect of departing from the Gold Standard'. This alarming prediction – for which no rational basis can be found – led MacDonald to make a fresh effort; he suggested that, in addition to the agreed £56 million, the Cabinet should make another £20 million of cuts, of which about £12½ million would come from a reduction in the standard rate of unemployment benefit. When this was rejected, Snowden and Thomas were so deeply disturbed that they asked that their disagreement with the decision should be recorded in the minutes, which meant that they were on the verge of resignation.[23] MacDonald tried, a few months later, to end the practice of recording disagreements in the minutes, on the grounds that it led to disunity; this suggests that he had felt Snowden and Thomas were going too far.[24]

At the moment he returned to the struggle, and suggested that he should be allowed to put this rejected proposal to the Liberal and Conservative leaders to test their reactions, and later in the day MacDonald obtained the Cabinet's permission to put the proposals, again without making any Cabinet commitment, to the bankers who would be asked for short-term loans to cover the period until the cuts were put into effect. The opposition leaders and, in the evening of the 23rd, the bankers expressed distinct interest in the proposals. The Cabinet had now to face the issue a second time; MacDonald declared that if there were any resignations the government could not go on. At least eight, perhaps nine, ministers offered their resignations. The government was at an end. MacDonald announced that he had arranged to meet the King and the Liberal and Conservative leaders next morning, and that he would then see the Cabinet again.

The King had already, with MacDonald's consent, asked Baldwin and Samuel (who represented the Liberals because Lloyd George was ill) what they advised – during the crisis, the King followed the advice of the three party leaders, and did not make any decisions without advice, let alone 'unconstitutional' decisions. The three party leaders gave advice which pointed in the direction of setting up the strongest available ministry in the Commons, which is what the sovereign ought always to help to bring about. Samuel advised the King that a coalition under MacDonald would be the best way to deal with the situation that would arise if the Labour government fell. This was obviously attractive to the Liberals: a coalition under a Conservative leader would clearly be only a short step away from Protection, but a coalition under the existing Prime Minister presented no such problems. Baldwin could accept the choice of MacDonald, because it solved the problem of what to do about the Liberals. The King accepted the advice given by Samuel and Baldwin, and persuaded MacDonald to accept it as well.

While the King was undoubtedly justified in following the advice of Baldwin and Samuel, and trying to persuade MacDonald, it is much less certain that MacDonald was right to let himself be persuaded. He was aware of the problem; he told the Cabinet on the 23rd 'it must be admitted that the proposals as a whole represented the negative of everything that the Labour Party stood for, and yet he was absolutely satisfied that it was necessary in the national interest to implement them.'[25] After this remark, MacDonald had no reason to be surprised if he was denounced as a traitor by members of the Labour party who were not convinced the measures were necessary. Without using such strong language, it does seem that there ought to be some relationship between what a Prime Minister says at one time and what he does at another. MacDonald may have thought that Baldwin and Samuel could not form a government except under his leadership, and that he was indispensable for this reason. But although MacDonald was a very convenient leader for a coalition it has never been established that no government could have been formed if he had retired from the premiership on the grounds that his previous commitments were not consistent with retaining office. The economy measures themselves might have been accepted more readily if they had been put forward by a Baldwin–Samuel government, with MacDonald as leader of the opposition to restrain Labour resistance – this, it may be remembered, was the position that Peel wanted to adopt over the Corn Laws, though it turned out in the conditions of December 1845 that he was indispensable.[26]

The Cabinet of his National government had four Conservatives, two Liberals and three other Labour ministers. He did not make any serious effort to encourage the Labour party to support the new government; he seems to have felt tired of the parliamentary Labour party, though he may have hoped to return to it when the crisis was over, in something like the way he had done in the later years of the war. But although he had been a good parliamentary leader inside the debating chamber, and a good party leader for rallying and rousing the mass following that the party had to have outside Parliament, he never appeared entirely at ease with the parliamentary party, and this had grown worse since 1929.

The new government was at first intended merely to pass the cuts in government expenditure through parliament. Snowden produced a balanced Budget but after a few days it was clear that people were still uneasy about the external value of the pound, and were moving their money out of London. The Cabinet did not discuss this, and seems not to have realized that, if the Gold Standard were important, something should be done to defend it. On 17 September the Bank was determined that the rate should be held, and the Cabinet thought that a general election, to produce a National government with a national policy, might be a good idea. The ministers then went away for the weekend, and when they got back on Monday the 20th MacDonald explained to them that over the weekend he had had to allow the Bank of England to go off the Gold Standard.[27] Undoubtedly the old rate of $4.86 to £1 could no longer be defended, but it is not clear why the Bank departed from the Gold Standard altogether; MacDonald probably did not understand what was happening, and so could not do much about it.

For the next two weeks the leaders of the new government argued over whether to have a general election. They had been able to agree without much difficulty about the measures needed to balance the Budget, but after they had failed to save the Gold Standard, they had no agreed objective in mind. At the beginning of October, under increasing Conservative pressure, they agreed to have an election, with Baldwin and Snowden issuing election manifestos as party leaders and MacDonald issuing an appeal as Prime Minister asking the electorate to give the government what was called 'a doctor's mandate'; as MacDonald put it in his election manifesto, 'the government must be free to consider every proposal likely to help, such as tariffs. ...' MacDonald showed his failure to understand the economic situation by appearing on election platforms waving billion-mark notes from the great German inflation of 1923; this event seems to have been the only economic parallel that came to anybody's mind in England in 1931, and it was quite misleading. There was very little prospect of inflation, and in any case nothing would have done the British economy more good than a sudden belief that inflation was at hand and that everybody should give up saving money and should go out and buy.

The National government won an immense victory. MacDonald united the free trade Liberal vote and the protectionist Conservative vote, and the Labour party's share of the poll dropped from 37% in 1929 to 30% in 1931. The National government had over 550 seats – 473 Conservatives, 68 Liberals and a dozen National Labour followers of MacDonald. Free trade supporters of the government were in a difficult position, because the vast Conservative majority naturally intended to press for tariffs and imperial preference. MacDonald's own position was relatively unembarrassed. He had no firm commitment to free trade, as he had shown during the Cabinet discussions of the previous year or two. He was not strongly committed to nationalization, though he thought the government ought to step in when it could do something to help, and the National government in the 1930s showed much more willingness to intervene in the economy than any previous peacetime government had done. The National government accepted a liberal attitude to Indian nationalism; the creation of the new government considerably strengthened Baldwin's position against defenders of the status quo like Churchill. MacDonald was committed to trying to solve international problems by discussion and sweet reasonableness, and the National government accepted this attitude.

The division of the Prime Minister's normal duties between Baldwin and MacDonald must have pleased both men: Baldwin looked after the backbenchers, and MacDonald handled the questions of international policy. Undoubtedly his contribution to Indian policy was useful, and he took more trouble over defence and foreign policy than Baldwin would have done, but his position was not comparable to that of a normal Prime Minister, because he did not show any readiness to appeal to public opinion and he had no party of his own to educate.

Economic affairs were left to Chamberlain, with a little help from Baldwin, and almost none from MacDonald; it was probably a great relief to the Prime Minister that the economic problems that had taken up so much of the attention of the Labour government now occupied less and less of the Cabinet agenda. One issue had to be settled: when the election was over, the pressure for tariffs began. Snowden and the Liberals in the Cabinet resisted this pressure, and offered their resignations. MacDonald felt that this would weaken the government's claim to be National, and that it would undermine his own position as a Prime Minister who could bring the political parties together. He persuaded the Free Traders to stay in the Cabinet by allowing them to speak and vote against tariff measures, while accepting Cabinet solidarity on other issues. This was a very odd way for the Free Traders to behave; presumably a Prime Minister chiefly wants to see his own policy applied without any of the embarrassments that resignations may cause, and MacDonald was succeeding in this, but the Free Traders merely made themselves look silly by staying inside a government which was attacking a principle that they were supposed to take seriously. This could not go on indefinitely, and when the Ottawa conference in the summer of 1932 established a system of imperial preference on the basis of treaties which would run for a number of years, Snowden and the Liberals resigned.

MacDonald did not like rearranging his government. He never dismissed a minister, and he only once moved a Cabinet minister to a different post, when Thomas had to be transferred. He once reshuffled some under-secretaries, at the end of 1929. Some changes were forced on him. Three of his ministers died in office, Hartshorn and Lord Thomson in the second Labour government, and Maclean shortly before the Free Traders resigned. Trevelyan resigned from the Cabinet, and Mosley from outside the Cabinet, during the second Labour government. Deaths and resignations were followed by shuffles of ministers, but MacDonald did not like parting with ministerial colleagues. The departure of the Free Traders was accordingly something of a shock, and it left MacDonald in an exposed position. His Conservative colleagues in the Cabinet were respectful and helpful; they found themselves much closer in their way of thinking to him than to their own backbenchers, and Baldwin was not the man to complain if MacDonald was at times vague and woolly in expressing himself.

MacDonald's style had never been precise, and in the early thirties it deteriorated to a point where his speeches in the Commons were sometimes incomprehensible. Some people have written as though he was slipping into senility in this period. His physical health was bad. He had trouble with his eyesight in 1932, and in 1934 he had to take a three-months' holiday. In his first Cabinet he had dominated the political scene; in his second Labour government he had been clearly established as Leader; during the National government his position became steadily weaker because he was neither the most forceful man in the government nor the man who commanded support in the parliamentary party or among the electorate. Even Baldwin began to feel the need for a change, and he told Thomas Jones in April 1934 that the Prime Minister couldn't make a decision about resigning,[28] which was presumably the closest that so amiable a man could go to saying that the sooner the Prime Minister went the better. Perhaps the best suggestion for a change was the idea, put forward when the Free Traders resigned, that MacDonald should become Foreign Secretary and Baldwin become Prime Minister. MacDonald was in a state of deep depression during his three or four years as Prime Minister, and John Buchan the novelist, who was a Conservative MP at the time, used to call on him early in the morning to try to cheer him up.[29]

The National government found itself confronted by international conferences to discuss reparations at Lausanne, disarmament at Geneva and imperial preference at Ottawa. MacDonald went to the Lausanne conference for the opening meetings and he made several visits to Geneva as the situation, not very cheerful at the beginning, grew worse and worse because the German desire for equality and the French desire for security were clearly not going to be reconciled.

MacDonald and Henderson, who had worked together so often despite their inability to establish any close relationship, found themselves together again at Geneva, Henderson as president of the conference and MacDonald as leader of the British delegation. At first the British delegation listened to the proposals of the other countries and tried to bring them closer together by mediation. It became clear by the beginning of 1933 that this would not bring any results, and the government decided to produce a scheme of its own, which was more useful than the earlier suggestions because it did offer definite figures to which military strengths should be reduced. MacDonald introduced it in March in a speech in which he said that 'we can hear civilisation creaking'. He was right, but no progress was made and in October Germany left the conference and Europe was on the road that led to war.

MacDonald has been accused of liking conferences too much and of suggesting meetings when nothing definite was likely to emerge from them, but the 1933 World Economic Conference in London happened almost by accident; apparently the United States thought there was going to be a conference, and expressed some interest in it, and the British government thought it would be useful to encourage this sign of interest in world problems.[30] The United States was inevitably involved in the last act of the struggle over reparations and war debts; reparations had been scaled down almost to nothing at Lausanne, and the British government was determined not to pay more to the United States than it received from its various debtors. MacDonald went to Washington to see Roosevelt in April 1933; though the discussion made the eventual British repudiation of war debts a little more amicable than might have been the case, the prospects for the Economic Conference were not good. The conference was designed to bring about stabilization but Roosevelt said during his talks with MacDonald that the solution to America's problems lay in inflation.[31] At the beginning of the conference it sounded as though Cordell Hull had persuaded Roosevelt of the case for stabilization and international cooperation, but after a little discussion Roosevelt repudiated Hull's policy; he was accused of torpedoing the conference, but he was in fact merely adopting the position which he had explained to MacDonald in April. In any case, the other countries at the conference probably could not have reached agreement among themselves, even if the United States had promised in advance to accept any conclusions that were reached. The French were still convinced of the virtues of the Gold Standard and the British government does not seem even to have considered the prospect of returning to it.

MacDonald presided over the conference and gave some eloquent speeches, but he did not convince people that he knew what should be done. At his other international conferences his charm and his oratory did rest upon some idea of the nature of the problems; even reparations was a political rather than an economic question, at least in the years when MacDonald was concerned with it, and his other conferences concentrated on foreign policy. It was his misfortune that, except for the brief interlude in 1924, he held office in a period when economic problems which he had never claimed to understand were of primary importance; if he had held power in the 1920s when the desire for peace and reconciliation was strong, he might have been able to do something about the Treaty of Versailles before all concessions appeared to be weakness in the face of Hitler, and if he had been in his prime in the 1930s he might have taken a more useful approach to problems than his successor did.

After the conference it was less and less clear what MacDonald was doing as Prime Minister. Baldwin, the obvious successor, was not an active man; between them, the two leaders had about enough energy for one normal Prime Minister. After his holiday in 1934 MacDonald did become more active; he was worried by the more aggressive policy that Germany was adopting under Hitler, and at the beginning of 1935 the Defence White Paper which committed Britain to rearmament appeared over his initials. In April he went with the Foreign Secretary to the Stresa Conference with France and Italy; though it seemed that an alliance had been formed which could hold Hitler in check, the agreements contained a flaw: Mussolini had made it as clear as international decency allowed that his price for standing in opposition to Hitler was acceptance of the old Italian claim to Abyssinia. The British representatives may not have realized what Mussolini was saying or may have thought that British opinion would accept his proposal, but in any case this led naturally enough to Hoare's speech at Geneva in September and to confusion over sanctions in the months that followed. By then MacDonald had left the premiership; he changed places with Baldwin, taking the presidency of the Council with special responsibility for rearmament – a curious end to the career of a man who had opposed both the Boer and the 1914–18 Wars.

During the last phase, from around the time that the National government shed its Free Traders, MacDonald had been in a weak position, and sometimes in a position that was not really relevant to what was going on. Over India, for example, MacDonald could do a certain amount to soothe the different groups there, but the struggle which was really dangerous to his government was that between the Conservative leadership and the Churchillian die-hards, and in this MacDonald could do very little.

In a way it is unfair to judge MacDonald politically by his work as Prime Minister. His 1929–35 period of office can be compared with Lloyd George's position between 1916 and 1922 in terms of parliamentary circumstances. But Lloyd George never let himself be dominated by circumstances; MacDonald in office was always letting himself be so dominated. Most of his life had been devoted to building the Labour party on a moderate non-Marxist basis, but in office he behaved just like a pessimistic Marxist who believes that the time for action has not yet arrived and that therefore nothing can be done. When MacDonald did nothing, it was not a matter of inertia, as it probably was with Baldwin. It was partly just that he never had a parliamentary majority committed to his own view of the world, but also and probably more important he never worked out a way to translate his long-term vision of the future into political activity for next day or next week. In his books he spoke of society growing slowly like a plant; the metaphor is a comfortable one and excludes any idea of revolution, but in its way it implies a doctrine of inevitability as complete as the Marxist's and rather less heroic. Gladstone once used a metaphor of a plant in a way that illustrated his dynamic idea of the premiership: perhaps with a memory of his own outdoor activities, he spoke of cutting down the upas tree. MacDonald's political ideals were more constructive than this, but it was never clear how he intended to express them in a policy of reform.

Notes

1. *The Times*, 18 and 24 December 1923.
2. P.Snowden, *An Autobiography* (London 1934), p. 596.
3. H.Nicolson, *George V* (London 1953), p. 393.
4. MacDonald denied that he had been consulted or had given an opinion about dropping this prosecution. It is clear that he had been present when the subject had been discussed in Cabinet (T.Jones, *Whitehall Diary*, ed. K.Middlemas (Oxford 1969) I, pp. 287–90), though it may be noted how discursive the Cabinet discussion was, and how little the recorded conclusion follows from what had been said.
5. R.W.Lyman, *The First Labour Government* (London 1957), p. 288.
6. *The Times*, 29 October 1924, had an advertisement of Selfridges, giving the latest news of their straw vote. It will be noted that it was more pro-Conservative than the country at large, less ready to support the Liberals and that it had shifted its opinion less, a few days before polling, than the country did on election day. This sample is not reliable, but it does suggest that Zinoviev helped the Conservatives and hurt the Liberals.

| | 1923 | | 1924 | |
	Selfridges	*actual*	*Selfridges*	*actual*
Con	50.74	38.1	55.94	48.1
Lib	21.26	29.6	15.50	17.6
Lab	27.57	30.5	28.39	33.0

411,000 people answered in 1924.

7. B.Webb, *Diaries 1924–32* (London 1956), pp. 13 and 20.
8. R.B.Haldane, *An Autobiography* (London 1929), pp. 231–2 and 348.
9. A.F.Brockway, *Inside the Left* (London 1942), p. 152.
10. T.Jones, *A Diary with Letters* (Oxford 1954), XXIX.
11. R.W.Lyman, *op. cit.*, p. 86.
12. T.Wilson, *The Downfall of the Liberal Party* (London 1966), p. 264.
13. B.Webb, *op. cit.*, pp. 9–10.
14. P.R.O.Cab. 24 C.P. 363 (30).
15. P.R.O. Cab. 24 C.P. 389 (30).
16. P.R.O. Cab. 24 C.P. 287 (29).
17. J.M.Keynes, *Essays in Persuasion* (London 1931), p. 152.
18. B.Webb, *op. cit.*, p. 220; P.R.O. Cab. 23/63, 14 January 1930.
19. P.R.O. Cab. 23/61, 25 September 1929.
20. Cab. 23/63, 15 January 1930.
21. H.Nicolson, *Diaries* (London 1966), I, p. 57.
22. Parl. Papers, Cmd. 3920.

23. P.R.O. Cab. 23/63, 22 August 1931.
24. P.R.O. Cab. 23/69,.25 November 1931.
25. P.R.O. Cab. 23/67, 23 August 1931.
26. Baldwin and Samuel together could command a majority; Russell in 1845 could not have had a majority without help from Peel.
27. P.R.O. Cab. 23/68, 20 September 1931.
28. T.Jones, *op. cit.*, p. 128.
29. J.A.Smith, *John Buchan* (London 1965), pp. 329–33.
30. P.R.O. Cab. 23/71, 1 June 1932.
31. P.R.O. Cab. 23/75, 5 May 1933.

Stanley Baldwin

John Campbell

Stanley Baldwin is one of the very few Prime Ministers who can be said to have had their greatness thrust upon them. As he himself wrote, 'The position of leader came to me when I was inexperienced, before I was really fitted for it, by a succession of curious chances that could not have been foreseen. I had never expected it: I was in no way trained for it.'[1] Nevertheless when his opportunity came he was not reluctant to grasp it, nor was he in any hurry to lay down the burden once taken up. He formed three administrations, and held the supreme office for a total of eight years between 1923 and 1937; on top of which he was also the dominant figure in the 'National' government nominally headed by Ramsay MacDonald between 1931 and 1935. In fifteen years Baldwin was out of Downing Street for only three. Yet he never set out deliberately to climb the greasy pole. That fact sets Baldwin apart from nearly all the other subjects of this book. From it flow both the unique qualities and the serious disqualifications that characterize his triple tenure of the office.

It was filial loyalty rather than personal ambition that first drew him into politics. At Cambridge he flirted briefly with the Church; the more feminine side of his nature was attracted by the literary and artistic world of his mother's family, his Kipling and Burne-Jones cousins; with a better degree he might have chosen an academic career. But a lazy Third, and his father's unconcealed disappointment – 'I hope you won't get a Third in Life'[2] – closed his options and condemned him to the Baldwin family ironworks in Worcestershire. The first twenty years of his adult life were spent dutifully working in his father's shadow at a business for which he had little love. He had no interest whatever in galvanized steel sheeting; but he did enjoy the management of men and the sense of occupying a certain position in the locality. Politics were an extension of that aspect of business. In 1892

Alfred Baldwin became the Unionist member for Bewdley; his son served as a Justice of the Peace, was chairman of the local school board, and sat for several years on the Worcestershire County Council. In 1906, in an attempt to expand the family's holding, he stood for the neighbouring parliamentary seat of Kidderminster. He lost. The same year he was proposed and rejected as candidate for Worcester City – 'turned down in my own county town in favour of a stranger'.[3] At the age of thirty-nine, with no general election due for seven years, Baldwin's political career seemed to be finished before it had begun. But within a year of this discouraging debut, he was in Parliament. At his father's sudden death he inherited his seat at Westminster as naturally as he inherited a directorship of Baldwin's Ltd.; his unopposed election was declared less than two weeks after the funeral. Thereafter, until he went to the House of Lords as Earl Baldwin of Bewdley in 1937, he never had to face a serious challenge in his constituency.

Recent biographers have been able to show that Baldwin's career up to 1921 was not quite so obscure as used to be thought. Close reading of Hansard reveals that in the turbulent years before 1914 he was already sounding with distinctive elegance the themes of industrial conciliation and trust between masters and men that later, as Prime Minister, he was to make his own; yet these speeches were very rare and went largely unnoticed. At a time when the Conservative benches were unusually short of talent, Baldwin made no effort to thrust himself into prominence. On his own limited range of subjects – industrial relations, wages, employment, the case for tariffs – his experience and reputation as a model employer earned respect. He served on several House and party committees. By March 1916 he carried enough weight in the counsels of his party to play host to some seventy Tory members meeting to coordinate support for Asquith's tottering coalition. Nevertheless this was by no stretch of the imagination the career of a rising star. As late as 1921, when he had been a junior minister for four years and was only two years off the premiership, his prospects still appeared so modest that his name was mentioned as a possible Speaker; nor was he certain that he would have refused a firm offer. Five years earlier, feeling that he was getting nowhere, he had been tempted to resign his seat and return to the narrower but familiar local stage, where he might hope to make a more satisfying contribution to the war (in which he was too old to fight) than seemed likely to be offered to him at Westminster; it was his wife who persuaded him to give national politics a few more years. Did she foresee that in wartime his age could be a positive asset? So it proved. In December 1916, when Lloyd George superseded Asquith, and Bonar Law, the Tory leader, became Chancellor of the Exchequer and needed a new parliamentary private secretary, Law's friend and private secretary J.C.C.Davidson suggested Baldwin, 'an older man who would not be likely to be taken for military service, and who could give his full time to the job, and above all keep his mouth shut.'[4] On this inglorious recommendation Baldwin received his first promotion.

One job led quickly to another. Law's nominal number two, Sir Hardman Lever, was frequently in the United States; Baldwin had to deputize, and was soon made joint Financial Secretary to the Treasury in his own right. First under Law, then after the war under Austen Chamberlain, he filled this exacting post for four years. His business training stood him in good stead; he was efficient and quietly impressive, noticeably courteous to a House of Commons that felt itself treated with scant respect by too many of Lloyd George's ministers. Then in April 1921 Bonar Law was forced to retire from the government on grounds of failing health; in the ensuing reshuffle Sir Robert Horne replaced Chamberlain at the Treasury and Baldwin was offered Horne's place at the Board of Trade which, after some characteristic hesitation, he accepted. It was almost certainly Law who pressed this appointment on Lloyd George, who had no reason to demur; to a Prime Minister concerned only to maintain the party balance of his Cabinet, Baldwin must have seemed a safe and suitable choice – like Lepidus in *Julius Caesar*, 'a slight unmeritable man meet to be sent on errands'. Indeed, a man less likely than Baldwin to make trouble for his leader could scarcely be imagined. But Baldwin still regarded Law, not Lloyd George, as his leader, which was why he hesitated before accepting his promotion. He was hardly closer to his new party leader, Austen Chamberlain, than he was to Lloyd George; so that, although a Cabinet minister, he did not feel himself after 1921 an integral member of the government, but rather as an inside observer of it. His year in Lloyd George's Cabinet was the critical year for Baldwin's political education. He worked conscientiously and unobtrusively in his own department, carrying the Safeguarding of Industries Bill successfully through Parliament despite his own reservations about it; but he took almost no part in Cabinet. He was content to spend his time silently studying the Prime Minister, 'that strange little genius who presides over us'.[5] Lloyd George fascinated Baldwin as he fascinated almost everyone who worked closely with him; but in Baldwin 'the Goat' excited, instead of admiration, an appalled fascination which grew into a profound antipathy. This obsession (Thomas Jones's word)[6] was the force which lifted and sustained Baldwin's career. He took great delight, around this time, in repeating a sly proverb, supposedly Afghan: 'He who lies in the bosom of the goat spends his remaining years plucking out the fleas.'[7]

The very atmosphere of Lloyd George's Cabinet repelled Baldwin. His sense of propriety was shocked by the evident enjoyment with which the Prime Minister and his principal colleagues, Winston Churchill and Lord Birkenhead, wielded power. Brought up in the language of 'duty' and 'service', he was deceived by Lloyd George's irreverence and habitual levity into doubting his sincerity and true seriousness of purpose. He had no quarrel with any particular policy, at least until the Chanak crisis – he supported the Irish Treaty which offended so many Conservatives – but from his ringside seat he came to share the growing conviction of most of the Tory party outside the Cabinet that Lloyd George's Government was both corrupt and corrupting. There was not only the scandal of his Chief Whip's too free and undiscriminating use of the established system of 'selling' honours in return for donations to party funds; the more fundamental criticism concerned Lloyd George's appearance of governing with little regard for either his Cabinet as formally constituted or the House of Commons, relying on two or three favoured ministers and his large and powerful private secretariat, interfering restlessly in the work of every department and conducting personal diplomacy behind the back of the Foreign Office. The autocratic style of government that had won the war was widely felt, three years after the armistice, to threaten the balance of the constitution in whose name the war had been fought. Baldwin, in the Cabinet but not of it, still at heart a shire backbencher, felt personally soiled by his participation in the government. From this unhappy experience he derived the principles that governed his own administrations. He now had before him a clear model, which he never forgot, of how not to run a government.

He could still, in the middle of 1922, have had no possible expectation that he himself would ever have the opportunity to put those principles into effect. But the succession of 'curious chances' that raised him to the premiership was under way. When he resolved on 10 October to resign from the government rather than fight another general election under Lloyd George, he expected only to salve his conscience at the cost of ending his modest career. He was at that stage the only Conservative Cabinet minister opposed to the continuation of the coalition on which the party leaders – Chamberlain, Birkenhead, Horne, Lord Balfour and, so it still appeared, Lord Curzon – were united. But it rapidly became clear that the leadership was totally isolated: not only were the party in the country, the party organization and a large number of Tory MPs increasingly insistent that the party should reassert its independence, but now most of the junior ministers and under-secretaries (whose prospects of promotion were blocked by the coalition) were ready to defy their seniors in a manner unprecedented in party history. Baldwin suddenly found himself at the centre of a cabal of like-minded rebels – Leopold Amery, Edward Wood and Philip Lloyd-Greame from the lower ranks of the Government, Sir Arthur Griffith-Boscawen (the Minister of Agriculture), another recruit from the Cabinet, and from the back benches Sir Samuel Hoare. But still the rebels had no leader of sufficient standing to give them credibility as an alternative government until Bonar Law was prevailed upon, against his inclinations and his better judgement, to emerge from his retirement. At the famous meeting at the Carlton Club on 19 October at which the party rejected Austen Chamberlain's advice, Baldwin's brief and deadly denunciation of Lloyd George – 'A dynamic force is a very terrible thing; it may crush you but it is not necessarily right'[8] – made the deepest oratorical impression; but it was Law's attendance which ensured the success of the revolt.

It was Bonar Law who made Baldwin's career. It was Law who first promoted him, Law who thrust him into Lloyd George's Cabinet, Law who by-passed Chamberlain and Birkenhead to overthrow Lloyd

George in 1922, making Baldwin Chancellor of the Exchequer. Seven months later his health broke again and he again retired, having returned to office for just long enough to leave Baldwin as his heir. Law's brief premiership was the narrow bridge by which Baldwin made his improbable crossing from obscurity to power, while Lloyd George was cast out into the wilderness.

There is some question whether Baldwin was actually Law's first choice for Chancellor; Law was certainly doubtful of the calibre of the ministerial talent available to him, and the post was offered to the Liberal Reginald McKenna (Asquith's last Chancellor); but this may have been a self-effacing suggestion by Baldwin after he himself had declined it. When McKenna too declined, however, Baldwin (who knew the Treasury from his period as Financial Secretary) was the obvious and only possible candidate. He was the new Prime Minister's natural first lieutenant; communication between Nos 10 and 11 Downing Street was particularly close; and in the general election campaign that followed immediately on the new government's taking office, he played a leading role as a more biting critic of the Coalition and its record than Law, as one of its architects, decently could be. It was at this election that Baldwin first unfolded before the national audience his impersonation of the honest Englishman; he contrasted his rustic simplicity so effectively with the 'first-class brains' of the coalitionists that he contrived to make conspicuous talent seem a liability. A couple of months later his own simplicity appeared a liability; returning in January 1923 from negotiations in the United States over Britain's war debt, his inexperience led him into unguarded revelations to the press which committed the government to a higher settlement than Bonar Law was prepared to contemplate, and nearly led to the Prime Minister's resignation. (Eventually Law contented himself with criticizing his own government anonymously in *The Times*.) In February, however, Baldwin made up for this gaffe with a notable speech in the House of Commons which added further depth to the appealing self-portrait he had drawn at the time of the election. Replying to Labour censure of the government, he expressed his robust contempt for 'that pentasyllabic French derivative "proletariat"', preaching instead from a text composed of four English monosyllables, 'faith', 'hope', 'love' and 'work':

No Government in this country today that has not faith in the people, hope in the future, love for its fellow-men, and which will not work, and work and work, will ever bring this country through into better days and better times.[9]

This speech, so characteristic of the homespun style and philosophy of the new Chancellor, struck a chord far beyond the chamber of the House of Commons. Here, it seemed to many, was a national leader, newly arisen with a message to inspire a distracted people. With this speech Baldwin emerged as a potential Prime Minister.

Even so, had Bonar Law's health held up for another year, it is probable that the feelings aroused by the ending of the Coalition would have cooled sufficiently for him to have reunited the Tory party before leaving office, by inviting Chamberlain and his coalitionist colleagues to join his government; Chamberlain would then have been the natural candidate to recover the leadership on Law's second retirement. As it was, however, Chamberlain was still in the wilderness when Law, had to resign in May 1923. Baldwin's only rival was then Curzon who, on Lloyd George's defeat, had retained the Foreign Office by throwing in his lot with Bonar Law. Too much has been made of the difficulty of the choice with which King George V was faced; of the manipulation by Law's secretaries, Davidson and Waterhouse, of Law's evasion of his duty to make a recommendation; and of the personal tragedy of Curzon's rejection. In truth there was scarcely anyone in the political world who actively wanted (or indeed could seriously imagine) Curzon as Prime Minister. On paper he might appear a powerful contender, a former viceroy of India whose long and distinguished public career would be suitably crowned by the premiership. Many people felt, reluctantly, that his claim could not be passed over. But few really liked or trusted him: his timely change of allegiance the previous year had gained him little respect on either side, while even genuine admiration of his qualities tended to be tinged with ribaldry – he was an anachronism. The idea of his receiving trade unionists with his customary hauteur was alarming to more modern Conservatives. Balfour's advice, or the Waterhouse memorandum, may have helped to sway the King's mind; it is more likely that they only confirmed his own judgement. The ostensible ground for preferring Baldwin was the impossibility, in the third decade of the twentieth century, of having a Prime Minister in the House of Lords – particularly since Labour, now the official opposition, was virtually unrepresented there. But it was fortunate that there was this plausible excuse to hand, otherwise Curzon would probably have been still more bitterly hurt; for he was rejected for good personal and political reasons, scarcely at all for constitutional ones.

Baldwin's qualities scarcely entered into the question; he had won just sufficient reputation to make him, despite his relative inexperience, a possible alternative. But he became Prime Minister more by default than in recognition of his own merits – still less, which was important, by his own efforts. Baldwin thus moved into No. 10 Downing Street with a real sense of humility, but at the same time a sense that providence – indeed the Almighty, for he was the most simply Christian of Prime Ministers – had ordained the almost miraculous chain of accidents by which he had emerged. This sense of having a divine mission – to clean up British politics after Lloyd George, and to bind the wounds of the British people after the turmoil of the war – gave him, in his exceptionally testing situation, a deep self-confidence. At first the humility prevailed. Baldwin knew that he must maintain continuity with Law's administration. He therefore made few changes in the Cabinet. Curzon magnanimously consented to stay on as Foreign Secretary, and Baldwin left all Law's other ministers where they were, only promoting two of his own supporters, Hoare and Sir William Joynson-Hicks, to the Cabinet, and bringing in Lord Robert Cecil as Lord Privy Seal (a move probably intended to appease Lord Salisbury, Curzon's only influential champion). McKenna now agreed to take the Treasury, but was temporarily unwell, so Baldwin himself retained the office; in fact McKenna was unable to find a seat in the House of Commons, and in August Baldwin appointed Neville Chamberlain, on whose efficiency he had quickly learned to rely. To Neville's half-brother Austen, Baldwin offered only half-promises for the future, dependent on his good behaviour, by which Austen was deeply insulted; at this interview, Baldwin's skill in handling men was not apparent. He did succeed in breaking the united front of the coalitionists, however, by inducing Sir Laming Worthington-Evans to accept office as Postmaster-General.

The policy of 'tranquillity' on which Bonar Law had won the 1922 general election suited the temperament of his successor admirably, and Baldwin was able to ease himself unobtrusively into his new office over the summer. Despite the continued disgruntlement of Curzon and some signs of disaffection on the part of Lords Derby and Salisbury, Baldwin quickly won the loyalty and appreciation of the less exalted members of his Cabinet, so that by the autumn the future of the government appeared secure for years ahead. But almost immediately its term was cut short, and interest in its life is overshadowed by controversy surrounding its demise. For Baldwin quite suddenly gambled on another general election and lost his majority. This recklessness has always seemed strangely out of character, and the most devious calculations have been advanced to account for it. The simplest explanation, however, is surely the very natural desire of a new leader who has attained office by succession rather than by election to win for himself the imprimatur of the electorate. It was under the same impulsion (but with more success) that Sir Anthony Eden went immediately to the country on succeeding Sir Winston Churchill in 1955, eighteen months before he need have done.

The ground on which Baldwin called a general election in December 1923 was his personal conviction, announced at Plymouth in October, that the government could do nothing to reduce the high rate of industrial unemployment unless it were empowered to impose protective tariffs – a course against which Bonar Law had specifically pledged himself in 1922. There is no reason to doubt the sincerity of Baldwin's conversion to a policy to which all his early political experience naturally inclined him: he had first entered the House of Commons as an avowed follower of Joseph Chamberlain. Yet his enthusiasm for the cause had noticeably diminished in recent years, and it would have been quite possible to extend considerably the application of the existing Safeguarding Act without substantially infringing Law's pledge. Again, there was no necessity to hold the election so quickly, even after the decision on tariffs had been taken: more time could and – in view of the electorate's well-tried resistance to tariff propaganda – surely should have been allowed for educating the public to support the new policy. It was Baldwin himself who pressed the issue to an early election. Conviction alone does not explain his precipitancy.

He himself explained it, years later, by affirming the extraordinary (and quite unfounded) rumour that Lloyd George was planning a protectionist package of his own, which the government had to move swiftly to pre-empt.[10] When his reputation for shrewd far-sightedness was established, the legend grew up that Baldwin had ridden deliberately for a fall in 1923, courting defeat so as to allow Labour a brief spell in office after which the Conservatives would return united to power. The first explanation may indeed contain some element of truth: Baldwin had no difficulty in believing anything of Lloyd George. But the second is utterly refuted by Baldwin's confidence at the time that he would win his election. It was certainly part of his purpose to reunite the Tory party; and he undoubtedly saw the purely political advantage to be gained from reviving the old tariff controversy which could be guaranteed to restore the old party divisions and lay the ghost of the Coalition, drawing Chamberlain and Birkenhead irresistibly back to the Tory standard while forcing Lloyd George back into the unwelcoming arms of Asquith. But the primary purpose of holding an election was to win it, and so establish himself firmly as the leader of the party, and of the nation, in his own right. Baldwin's concern was to free himself, not simply from Law's pledge against tariffs, but from all trace of obligation to his predecessor. His growing self-confidence could no longer stand in Law's shadow.

The calling of the 1923 election is certainly remarkable evidence of the power of the modern Prime Minister. Within six months of succeeding to the leadership, Baldwin was able to push through his Cabinet, without resignations, a policy contrary to the principles of half its members, and to insist on a dissolution of Parliament against the recommendation of Conservative Central Office and the advice of the King. This was not dictatorship, for Baldwin had the solid support and encouragement of that younger group of his ministers who were not exactly his creatures, but had risen with him and backed him loyally since the time of the Carlton Club revolt – Amery, Bridgeman, Hoare, Sanders, Lloyd-Greame and Neville Chamberlain. Yet these were, in Curzon's contemptuous phrase, 'the whipper-snappers of the Cabinet'.[11] Baldwin sprang his new policy virtually without warning on the senior members of his government who were likely to be hostile to it – Lords Curzon, Salisbury, Derby, Devonshire, Cave, Novar and Robert Cecil; and he got away with it. The rejection of Curzon in May was not the only defeat suffered by the House of Lords in 1923; in the heavily titled Cabinet which Baldwin inherited from Bonar Law, their lordships' influence counted for almost nothing.

Still more remarkable, perhaps, is the fact that Baldwin retained his leadership after his electoral defeat. Strictly speaking, of course, he was not defeated: the Conservatives actually won slightly more votes than in 1922, a million more votes and 67 more seats than Labour. But Labour (191) and the Liberals (159) – the free trade parties – together had a majority in the new parliament of nearly a hundred seats: protection had been decisively defeated. It was clear that Baldwin must resign. What was not at all clear was who should succeed him in office The three-way division of seats had produced a result of unprecedented constitutional uncertainty. The most obvious course was for Ramsay MacDonald, as leader of the second party, to form a minority Labour government. But the Tories were still substantially the largest party: it was arguable that only Baldwin himself and those of his ministers most closely associated with the rejected policy need resign: the party could remain in office under another leader, perhaps in coalition with the Liberals, dropping protection from its programme. There were many voices, alarmed by the prospect of a Labour government, urging this solution. The timing of Baldwin's resignation became critical. His first instinct was to resign at once. But he soon saw that to do so would, by creating a vacuum, play into the hands of those who were trying to do some deal to keep Labour out. He himself was convinced that Labour must not be cheated of its due, and determined to prevent the formation of any new coalition. Knowing MacDonald, he judged socialism to be a less imminent danger to society than the restoration of Lloyd Georgism. So he resolved to remain in office until defeated in Parliament, as nineteenth-century governments had done. By that time, the panic had passed away and the alternatives had collapsed. The Liberals found that they had no choice but to join with Labour to turn out the Tories and then support MacDonald, who duly took office as the first Labour Prime Minister in January 1924. This was an ironic outcome of Baldwin's attempt to consolidate his own position; but having failed in that major objective, it was a matter for some self-congratulation that he had ensured MacDonald's succession. For, quite apart from the dangerous constitutional injustice that any attempt to deny Labour would have involved, MacDonald's succession saved Baldwin's own leadership.

He still faced considerable discontent within the party; his electoral miscalculation seemed to have fully vindicated those who had doubted his judgement. But he still had no acceptable rival; and the violence of some of the attacks on him in the Rothermere and Beaverbrook newspapers helped to swing sympathy behind him. The parliamentary situation was anyway too delicate for another change of leadership. As soon as he had recovered from the shock of his defeat, Baldwin set about preparing the party for another election, which was not likely to be long delayed. He set in motion the reorganization of Central Office; he established for the first time a formal Shadow Cabinet, to which Austen Chamberlain and Birkenhead were now invited; Neville Chamberlain drafted a new manifesto; and Baldwin himself made a series of speeches elaborating his personal view of Tory democracy. By the time the Liberals tired of the thankless task of sustaining MacDonald's government and were driven to defeat it, the Tory party was ready – with the help of the Zinoviev Letter – to win a famous victory. Baldwin was returned to office in November 1924 with an overwhelming majority of 223.

It is on the record of his second administration that Baldwin must be judged. Between 1924 and 1929 he enjoyed four and a half years of single-party rule, in peacetime, with a secure majority. It is here that his style of government can be seen most clearly. In 1923 he had taken over an existing administration and had scarcely time to put his own stamp upon it before he was turned out. In 1935 he again took over a going concern, this time a coalition; admittedly MacDonald's National government was a Tory government in all but name and Baldwin was already its effective leader, but still he was under some constraints. He was also a much older man. In 1924 he was in his political prime and under no obligation to anyone. He started out with an impressive mandate and a clean slate. This was his government.

Baldwin's conception of the job of Prime Minister was essentially different from that of any other modern holder of the office. Probably because he had not fought his way up the hard way, but had been so suddenly lifted into the top place, he had an unusually static conception of his task – more conservative in the literal sense of the word than that of any other Conservative premier. Baldwin came to the job with no positive ambition that could be formulated in legislation; he had very little interest in legislation. He felt himself, more vaguely, to have been entrusted with the sacred responsibility of protecting and preserving the British Constitution. It was the central article of Baldwin's political faith that the Constitution, as it had matured over the centuries, represented the most perfect expression of the English genius. The proper working of the Constitution depended on the correct balance between several concentric rings of power: the monarchy, the Prime Minister, the Cabinet, parliament and the country, with the Empire beyond. The exigencies of the war and the improvisations of Lloyd George's government after the war had been allowed to upset this delicate balance. It was Baldwin's mission to restore it. This overriding purpose informed his every action as Prime Minister. His first achievement was to restore the parties as the spokes which held the constitutional wheel together. Then the two major crises of his rule – the General Strike and the abdication of Edward VIII – both involved, or could be represented as involving, threats to the whole structure of the Constitution. But he was constantly meticulous in his care for each individual part. Long before 1936 Baldwin was notably punctilious in keeping the King in his place. For himself, he was very conscious of the dignity of his office. His interpretation of the Constitution equally explains his loose control of his Cabinet, and his unusual regard for the feelings and moods of the House of Commons, where he spent a great deal of time; it explains the particular trouble he took to befriend the Labour members – a potential threat whom he was anxious to assimilate peacefully within the Constitution. Finally it explains his exceptional desire to reach out to the country, to speak directly *to* the nation and sympathetically *for* the nation, in order to keep the hub of the wheel in touch with the circumference. Baldwin's conception of the job of Prime Minister was not simply that he should lead the government, but rather that he should embody the government to the country – even that he should in some mystical sense embody the spirit of the country.

His first practical task in 1924 was to select his team of ministers. This was not – it never is – simply a matter of picking the best-qualified man for each job. The problem was to find places for the reconciled coalitionists – not only Austen Chamberlain, whom Baldwin definitely wanted, but also Birkenhead and Horne, whom he personally disliked but felt obliged to include, and possibly Churchill, who had been gravitating back to the Conservative party over the last year – without upsetting too seriously those who had supported himself and Law since 1922. It was King George V who suggested that Austen Chamberlain should go to the Foreign Office; it is a measure of Baldwin's increased authority that he felt able thus further to disappoint Curzon, who had to be content with the largely honorific post of Lord President. Baldwin was not prepared, however, to deny Cave the Woolsack in order to allow Birkenhead to resume the seat he had filled with such distinction under Lloyd George; fortunately Birkenhead accepted the India Office. A similar dilemma over the Treasury was not so easily resolved. Rather than Horne, who had held the office with some success during the last year of the Coalition, it was perhaps natural that Baldwin should have wished to reappoint Neville Chamberlain to the office he had occupied so briefly in 1923. But he neglected to secure Chamberlain's agreement before offering Horne the Ministry of Labour. By the time he learned that Chamberlain, for his own good reasons, preferred to return to the Ministry of Health, Horne had indignantly declared himself unable to take office. In this impasse, Baldwin made his most astonishing appointment: he offered the second job in the government to the renegade Churchill – a Liberal for the past twenty years, still a convinced Free Trader and a close associate of Lloyd George. The latter disqualification was actually the reason for his appointment. Still thoroughly distrusting him, Baldwin and Neville Chamberlain together calculated that there was no point in giving Churchill a middle-ranking post; the best way to bind him firmly to his new allegiance was to give him a job that placed him heavily in the Prime Minister's debt and would demand his fullest energies. The fact that Churchill was utterly ignorant of finance was, if anything, an advantage. The important thing was to detach him from Lloyd George, thus isolating 'the Goat' from the last of his potentially dangerous colleagues. On this purely political calculation Baldwin appointed the Chancellor of the Exchequer to whom he would leave the economic direction of his Government.

Once the main positions had been filled, the lesser ministries gave Baldwin no great difficulty. Two of the most trusted of his 1923 colleagues returned to their former offices: Hoare to the Air Ministry and Lloyd-Greame (now Cunliffe-Lister) to the Board of Trade. Others – Bridgeman, Amery, Wood, Worthington-Evans – were switched around between jobs of similar status. Five of the men of 1922–3 – including Derby and Devonshire – were quietly dropped to make way for the three returning prodigals and four new faces, bringing the number of the new Cabinet up to twenty-one (among whom there were still six peers). Some eyebrows were raised at the promotion of the diehard Joynson-Hicks to be Home Secretary; Edward Wood (the future Lord Halifax) was an inappropriate choice for Agriculture, in which he was candidly uninterested; while Baldwin himself quickly regretted the hasty selection (on Horne's refusal) of the academic Sir Arthur Steel-Maitland to Labour, a ministry to which one might have expected him to send one of his closest colleagues. Nevertheless the government was generally acknowledged as a strong team. With its formation, Baldwin accomplished the outward reunion of the Tory party; during the next five years he succeeded in making that reunion a reality. There remained at first considerable mistrust between the old factions. Baldwin's most zealous partisans never ceased to suspect Birkenhead, Churchill and even Austen Chamberlain of nursing disloyal leanings towards Lloyd George. But on his resignation from the government (for business reasons) in 1928, Birkenhead was able to write to Baldwin without exaggeration, 'Your own personality has converted a Cabinet, which assembled upon the crater of some bitter and recent memories, into a band of brothers'[12] This was a considerable achievement.

His secret was a relaxed style of leadership, trusting his ministers and not imposing on them, in line with his doctrine of the Constitution. He acted on the belief that 'Ministers are not servants of the Prime Minister. They are responsible Cabinet ministers'[13] – with the emphasis on the word 'responsible'. 'His Majesty's Ministers,' he once told the House of Commons, 'are co-equal.'[14] Inevitably he confided more closely in some of his colleagues than in others – politically in Neville Chamberlain, more personally in William Bridgeman. But he had no regular 'inner Cabinet'; he made a point of being equally accessible, and in some respects equally aloof, to all his ministers. So far from being excluded, as they might have been, from the most critical discussions, Churchill and Birkenhead were often the very ministers on whom he placed the most responsibility – notably during and after the General Strike. But even Baldwin did not work entirely through his appointed Cabinet. Like all good party managers, he had a close understanding with his Chief Whip, Sir Bolton Eyres-Monsell. He also liked to talk over his problems with the Governor of the Bank of England, Montagu Norman (a close friend) and the Editor of *The Times*, Geoffrey Dawson. He had an exceptionally .discreet working relationship with his private secretaries, whose influence on him is for that reason unusually difficult to assess. But his two most trusted confidants were, without question, J.C.C.Davidson and Thomas Jones. These two very different men – alike only in their preference for working in the shadows of politics rather than in the public eye – were the central props of Baldwin's political personality. Each made an essential contribution to his style of government.

John Davidson was an earnest young civil servant who was Bonar Law's private secretary from 1915 to 1920, then entered parliament and became Baldwin's parliamentary private secretary at the Board of Trade. On succeeding to the premiership in 1923 Baldwin made him Chancellor of the Duchy of Lancaster (outside the Cabinet) and entrusted him with the sensitive task of formulating the government's contingency plans against the threat of a general strike. On Baldwin's return to office in 1924 he became Financial Secretary to the Admiralty, under Bridgeman, until in 1926 he was appointed Chairman of the Conservative Party. He was by now Baldwin's closest personal friend: the Davidsons' house in Barton Street, two minutes from the House of Commons, was the Prime Minister's second home, a haven to which he could always escape for peace and solace. But Davidson's role was more positive than that: while refreshing his spirit, he was continually reinforcing Baldwin's sense of mission, feeding his preoccupation with the machinations of Lloyd George, Beaverbrook and other bogeys, and bolstering, by contrast, his sense of his own righteousness in opposing them. Davidson's suspicious mind invariably ascribed the worst of corrupt motives to all opponents; he was a faithful political watchdog who saw conspirators against his master everywhere and pursued them fiercely. He acted, in fact, as Baldwin's hatchet-man, wielding behind the scenes the hard political cutting edge of Baldwinism that was rarely seen in public. As party chairman he took care of the seamier side of party politics – the discreet arrangement of peerages, the silencing of Maundy Gregory, the 'Watergate' activities of Conservative Central Office – allowing Baldwin to keep his hands clean. By relieving him, indeed, of many of the more tedious chores of the Tory leadership, Davidson played a vital role in enabling Baldwin to present himself plausibly as the custodian of the common heritage of the nation, transcending the petty divisions of mere party. Davidson represented the dark side of Baldwin's public face.

Tom Jones's function, on the other hand, was to polish up the image. Jones was a Welsh-speaking former professor of economics, of humble origin, whom Lloyd George had brought into his new Cabinet secretariat in 1916. As Deputy Secretary to the Cabinet he survived Bonar Law's purge of the Downing Street establishment in 1922 and stayed on until 1930 to serve Baldwin in particular in an unofficial capacity of extraordinary informality and trust, quite unlike the strictly official relationship observed by his superior, Sir Maurice Hankey. MacDonald mistrusted him, but Baldwin drew him closely into his personal household, despite the fact that he never concealed either his unshaken admiration for Lloyd George or his political sympathy with the Labour party. On both counts Baldwin found him useful as a devil's advocate. He felt that Jones gave him a valuable insight into the Welsh mind, and into the mind of Labour. Jones was a sounding-board by which he could test non-Conservative opinion. Yet at the same time Jones helped him with his speeches: if he did not actually write them, he shaped them and was responsible for many of those apt quotations and touching turns of phrase for which Baldwin's speeches were so much admired. His position in Baldwin's entourage was thus highly ambiguous. Significantly, his contact with Davidson was slight; the two of them ministered to quite separate needs. Davidson, as a good party man, probably regarded Jones as a doubtful asset. So, for different reasons, must the historian. As a corrective to Establishment thinking, Jones was so tame as to be useless. While remaining privately critical of Baldwin's lack of executive energy, Jones soothed his social conscience and flattered his complacent illusion that he could appeal equally to all classes of the nation. Unfortunately, Jones was a thoroughly untypical Labour voter, and more of a toady than a candid friend.

Jones's diaries do, however, contain an unrivalled picture of Baldwin's methods of working. For a businessman he was remarkably unbusinesslike. Where other Prime Ministers filled their engagement books with appointments, Baldwin 'liked a blank pad for the casual caller and the digressive friend'.[15] This again reflected his conception of the office. It was the job of his ministers to manage the routine business of the departments; he, having no routine, could hold himself free to see anyone at any time to sort out particular problems. Some ministers found him more helpful in this respect than others; his technique was usually to listen quietly while the minister clarified his own thinking, then promise his support. He rarely gave a decision, but would throw the responsibility back on to the minister concerned. His conduct of government was essentially permissive. The Cabinet under his chairmanship was less a committee, more a forum for real discussion, than under any other modern Prime Minister. Most of his colleagues agreed that it was 'nevertheless, from first to last, unmistakably a Baldwin Cabinet'[16] (Lord Eustace Percy); that Baldwin was always 'quietly but definitely in control'[17] (Cunliffe-Lister). But what this meant was that no decision was forced. Keeping the atmosphere friendly, Baldwin allowed disputants to talk themselves out without pressing for a conclusion, unless agreement was obviously near. His Cabinet was rent by only one major crisis, and that (in 1925) involved the traditional conflict between the Treasury and the Admiralty over the naval building programme: Churchill, who had fought for the Admiralty against Lloyd George at the Treasury in 1912, was now in the opposite corner demanding economies from Bridgeman. Both took up rigid positions and threatened resignation; the majority of the Cabinet was with Churchill; Baldwin himself was torn between his Chancellor and his friend; eventually he had to assert himself and did so, enforcing compromise on Bridgeman. But this was a rare storm of a sort that he usually managed to avoid.

Baldwin's quiet authority was by now unquestioned, but he did not often have to exert it. To a remarkable degree, the Government ran itself. The initiative was supplied almost entirely by the two Chamberlains. Austen Chamberlain was allowed almost complete freedom in foreign policy. This was no more than traditional, however, and in view of Baldwin's confessed lack of interest or expertise in foreign affairs, perfectly sensible: his only attempt at personal diplomacy, a meeting with Poincaré in 1923, was not a success. Chamberlain, on the other hand, achieved a personal triumph in 1927 as one of the architects of the Locarno Treaty, which appeared to have laid the foundation for lasting peace in Europe. What is more remarkable is the hegemony of Neville Chamberlain in domestic policy. Chamberlain himself emerged as a great social reformer whose network of interlinked Acts extending National Insurance, replacing the old Poor Law and reorganizing local government to administer the whole range of public services, ranks with the more spectacular achievements of Lloyd George before the First World War (on which he built) and Bevan after the Second (for whom he prepared the ground). Neville Chamberlain's was the only enduring monument left by Baldwin's second government. Some of the credit must be given to Baldwin for appointing and supporting him; but it must also be remembered that Chamberlain virtually appointed himself, declining the Treasury in favour of the Ministry of Health for which he already had his plans drawn up – he presented his famous schedule of twenty-five Bills only two weeks after taking office. Chamberlain's determination and success in carrying through his purposes merely underlines Baldwin's failure to lay down similarly clear objectives for the government as a whole.

Nowhere is this failure more striking than in those areas in which he was himself avowedly interested – industrial relations and unemployment. As regards unemployment, which remained steady at around 1,200,000 throughout the life of his government, Baldwin had the alibi that his proposed remedy had been rejected by the electorate. But the government made little effort to diagnose the root of the problem or to evolve other means to bring the figure down. Baldwin accepted the disease with placid fatalism, and had only scorn for those – principally Lloyd George – who sought a radical cure. His economic policy was to wait for the good times to come back, meanwhile doing his best by soothing speeches to reconcile people to the bad; he was deaf to the suggestion that there had developed in the British economy a serious imbalance which might be corrected only by positive action by the government and should at least be seriously studied. This shoulder-shrugging attitude is most apparent in regard to the coal-mines, about the nature of whose difficulties there was pretty broad agreement by the time he took office for the second time in 1924. Neither Baldwin himself, nor Cunliffe-Lister, nor the Secretary for the Mines, Lane-Fox, took any steps to encourage, let alone oblige, the coal-owners to reorganize their inefficient industry. The Prime Minister did not question the need to reduce wages; indeed by acceding to the insistence of Montagu Norman that the pound be returned to the Gold Standard at its unreal pre-war parity with the dollar, he and Churchill made reductions inevitable; but anticipating resistance from the miners, he was very concerned to ensure the government's readiness to meet it. When a strike threatened before the government was ready, he appointed another Royal Commission to investigate, meanwhile maintaining the status quo with a temporary government subsidy. The Samuel Commission reported, predictably and uncontroversially, in line with the existing liberal consensus: wage cuts, but also the amalgamation of pits, improved pithead facilities, and the nationalization of the mineral royalties. Still the government would not act, using the refusal of the miners to accept cuts as an excuse to ignore the other recommendations. The defeat of the General Strike in 1926 is often held to be Baldwin's political masterpiece; certainly his isolation of the constitutional question, on which he was unbending, from the industrial, on which he seemed ready to be conciliatory, was immensely skilful, detaching the TUC leaders from the miners' leaders and enabling the former to drop a weapon which they had never wielded with much conviction. But this success was essentially meretricious, since the strike need never have been allowed to happen at all had the government not shown in the preceding eighteen months a wilful refusal to tackle the overdue rationalization of the mining industry.

The true depth of Baldwin's vaunted commitment to industrial equity is still more sharply called in question by the aftermath of the General Strike. By defeating the strike he had won for himself a position of immense moral authority, not least by the personal appeal for peace which he broadcast at its height, concluding: 'Cannot you trust me to ensure a square deal to secure even justice between man and man?'[18] The TUC leaders did trust Baldwin. Yet after the General Strike was ended, the miners' strike was allowed to drag on for another six months, until the men were forced back to work on lower pay in an unreformed industry. Certainly the government, through Churchill in particular, tried hard to get a compromise settlement. But Baldwin would not use his authority to compel the coal-owners, although without some measure of coercion no square deal could possibly be ensured. It has been suggested that he suffered some sort of nervous collapse in the wake of the crisis; whatever the reason, his inertia can only be described as the betrayal of a solemn pledge. The following year, exploiting its victory, the government passed a new Trade Disputes Act declaring sympathetic strikes illegal and obliging trade unionists to 'contract in' to paying the political levy instead of 'contracting out' – thus implementing the very proposal against which Baldwin himself had intervened decisively in the House of Commons in 1925 with one of his most eloquent speeches, that speech which was supposed to set the conciliatory tone of his administration and which ended: 'Give peace in our time, O Lord.'[19] What did his government do to give effect to this pious and undoubtedly heartfelt prayer? Nothing at all. Perhaps Baldwin thought that the national reconciliation of which he spoke was a divine gift which it was beyond the power of any government to hasten. In that case, what did he mean in 1923 when he declared that no government which would not 'work and work and work' would ever bring the country through to better days? Baldwin 'distrusted all orators as dishonest';[20] he believed himself simple, direct and, above all things, honest. Yet it is difficult to resist the conclusion that he was as much a rhetorician as Lloyd George himself, without the will to translate rhetoric into action. Baldwin loved language, and loved shaping it into affecting patterns. But when he had found the right words for a problem, he was easily inclined to think that he had solved it. He tried, in fact, to govern by the word alone. No other Prime Minister has invested so much time and nervous energy in speeches – particularly in non-political speeches. They won him a great reputation: collections of them sold by the thousand. But those volumes on the shelves of second-hand bookshops now constitute the principal legacy of his premiership.

It may be said, on the contrary, that his words had their intended effect; that it was due to Baldwin that the inter-war decades of unavoidable depression passed off peacefully in Britain, that parliamentary democracy survived a revolutionary challenge in the 1920s and could laugh at Mosley's blackshirts in the 1930s; that by successfully stamping the period with his own comfortable personality, Baldwin damped down dangerous passions and ensured cautious but steady social progress where there might have been only continuing confrontation leading to chaos. It is argued, moreover, that Baldwin gave the British people what they wanted, and that by the skilful use of the new medium of the wireless he established a unique hold on the trust and affection of the public, thereby achieving a degree of national unity unsurpassed by any politician before or since. The first claim regards the constitutional threat of 1926 more seriously than it warrants and still leaves unanswered the charge that, having safely turned that corner, Baldwin failed completely to build on his victory. The second can be tested, in the absence of opinion polls, only by election results. These show that Baldwin was as vulnerable to the swing of the electoral pendulum as any other Prime Minister. The three-party politics of the 1920s make comparison with later years misleading, since the Tories always remained the largest party for reasons not attributable to the personality of their leader. The landslide victories of 1924, 1931 and 1935 are very largely explained by the divisions and weakness of the opposition parties. Between 1924 and 1929, however, the Conservative share of the poll fell heavily – from 48% back to 38%, precisely its level in 1918, 1922 and 1923. By-elections after 1926 ran consistently against the government, at a time when this was not taken for granted. With both the Labour and Liberal parties (the latter making their last great effort under Lloyd George) both apparently offering more dynamic alternatives, the great majority of the electorate was not, in 1929, enthusiastic for another dose of 'Safety First'.

Baldwin liked to believe that he was more than a mere party leader; he projected the goodwill of individual trade unionists and Labour MPs, who could not help liking him, on to the whole nation. 'My worst enemy,' he once claimed, with an arrogance which he was the first to ridicule in Lord Rothermere, 'could not say that I do not understand the people of England.'[21] This absurd belief was temporarily shaken by his defeat in 1929, which he took characteristically as a personal rejection, and again by the outcry over the Hoare-Laval pact in 1935. But it never had much foundation. For as he himself revealed, 'To me England is the country and the country is England.'[22] It was always rural England – the Worcestershire of his youth – that he apotheosized in his speeches evoking the national character; when he spoke of industry, he had in mind the small, paternalistic rural industries such as Baldwin's had still been in 1900; he had slight experience of modern industry, very little interest in the cities and suburbs of England, and still less in Scotland, Wales and the Empire. (He was fond of quoting his cousin Kipling; he might have done well to remember the line, 'What should they know of England who only England know?')[23] Of course his poetic appeals to an idealized Olde England struck a responsive chord in the imagination of many town-dwellers; but it was an utterly false – indeed escapist – vision for a Prime Minister to lay before an industrialized nation suffering from heavy unemployment. It was not even a realistic vision of the contemporary state of agriculture. The audience for this sort of nostalgia was surely much more limited than Baldwin imagined. His England was an essentially Tory England, of squires, parsons and deferential ploughmen, and the bodies to which he delivered his most famous homilies were different manifestations of the Tory party at leisure – the Classical Association, Harrow School, the Royal Society of St George. His appeal was not universal, but firmly rooted in the Conservative party. (Tom Jones noted with some impatience his reluctance to read any but the Conservative newspapers.)[24] When he declared that he sometimes wished he were the leader of the people who belonged to no party, he was expressing no more than the desire of every party leader to win the votes of the uncommitted. He could believe himself to be above party only because he believed the Tory party itself to be somehow – because more essentially English than the other parties – above party. With Davidson and Neville Chamberlain behind him to bear the more specifically party burdens, this was as effective a style of leadership as many. Baldwin was a better party man, in his own way, than perhaps he himself realized.

His capacity as party leader was again tested by the inevitable unrest that followed the 1929 defeat. He had to bow to pressure for Davidson's resignation from Central Office, but replaced him with Neville Chamberlain, thus cleverly sidetracking his only serious rival for the leadership. He survived the renewed challenge of Beaverbrook and Rothermere by crushing use of the same device by which he surmounted every crisis of his career – by emphasizing the constitutional aspect of their demands, denouncing the press lords' pursuit of 'power without responsibility'.[25] This period in opposition was in some ways Baldwin's finest hour, for he further risked his position by courageously committing the Tory party against the will of its imperialist wing to support of the Labour Government's policy of steady progress towards Dominion status for India. For all his habitually liberal stance, this was the only important issue on which Baldwin ever acted in defiance of his right wing. He was not in opposition for long, however. His part in the formation of the National government in August 1931 was somewhat marginal; he was on holiday while MacDonald's Labour government floundered towards dissolution, and as the destroyer of one coalition he was in no hurry to bail Labour out of its difficulties by forming another. But once it had been formed – supposedly as a temporary expedient – he was quick to seize the opportunity of an immediate general election to capitalize simultaneously on Labour's disarray and the fortuitous absence through illness of Lloyd George (who, as Liberal leader, would otherwise have had to be included). The overwhelming victory of the National government established in office under MacDonald's leadership all those Conservatives and Asquithian Liberals (Sir John Simon, Walter Runciman) who for the past decade had been most single-minded in their opposition to Lloyd George. This new coalition of the former anti-coalitionists was the ultimate, ironic consummation of the Carlton Club revolt of 1922.

Baldwin, as Lord President of the Council, was from the start the controlling figure in the National government; MacDonald, though Prime Minister, was increasingly obviously a 'pirated trademark'[26] to lend the appearance of national unity to a predominantly Tory government. Baldwin was perfectly content with this arrangement, which involved him in less departmental routine than ever. But by the summer of 1935 MacDonald's unfitness had become embarrassingly apparent; he was persuaded to exchange offices with Baldwin who thus became Prime Minister for the third time, at the age of 68. He made few changes in either the personnel or the direction of the government, despite very considerable unrest among the younger Conservative ministers at the endurance and lack of initiative of some of the 'old gang'. As a gesture to youth, Anthony Eden and Malcolm MacDonald were brought into the Cabinet, but the latter was promoted mainly to please his father, who would neither retire himself nor permit the dismissal of his old colleague J.H.Thomas, who was also patently unfit to retain office. Similarly, Simon was removed from the Foreign Office only to be compensated with the Home Office. There was some pressure on Baldwin to invite Lloyd George out of the wilderness to join the government – though now an old man, he was still an energetic one; Baldwin made a show of willingness to consider the idea, but he was quite safe, for Neville Chamberlain was still adamant against it. Lloyd George's proposals for a programme of national reconstruction were rebutted by a government White Paper as contemptuously as they had been in 1929, although by this time a wide band of Conservative opinion, including even *The Times*, had taken up the cry for some form of direct government action to mitigate the continuing depression. The policy of the government after Baldwin's takeover, however, remained as negative as it had been before: the economy must be allowed to recover naturally, in its own time – the government's role was limited to maintaining the availability of cheap money for investment; assistance for the 'special areas' of chronic unemployment remained minimal. The intellectual conviction behind this policy came from Neville Chamberlain, now as orthodox as Chancellor of the Exchequer as he had formerly been bold as Minister of Health. The temperamental conviction, however, that nothing much could be done and that therefore nothing 'showy' should be attempted, was Baldwin's. His conception of his job had not altered since 1929: it was still his only ambition to keep the ship of state safely afloat until he could hand over to a new captain, and a new king.

Admittedly the safety of the ship did concern him; as the European situation grew more menacing, Baldwin took an increasingly personal responsibility for the national defences. There is little credit left in

Churchill's famous allegation that he put party before country at the 1935 general election. It is true that Baldwin scarcely recognized the possibility of a conflict of interest between the two, but far from ignoring the need for rearmament for fear of losing the election, he fought quite openly to defeat the blinkered pacifism of the Labour party, making a point of stressing that the maintenance of peace by the League of Nations might involve the possession, if not the use, of military force. He timed the election shrewdly to gain the maximum advantage from the glow of patriotic celebration aroused by King George v's silver jubilee; and on this platform won another majority, not quite so inflated as in 1931 but still very large. The real crime of Baldwin's last administration was committed after the election. The revelation of a backstairs deal between the British Foreign Minister, Hoare, and the French Prime Minister, Laval, to partition Abyssinia for the benefit of Mussolini, concluded within weeks of Baldwin's public pledges to support the League of Nations and resist aggression, exposed the government and Baldwin himself to the charge of utter cynicism. Here was nemesis for his habit of trusting his Foreign Secretary to cover his own indifference to foreign affairs. Baldwin was at first honourably inclined to stand by his friend and colleague; but the government could only save its face by disowning Hoare, and Baldwin was obliged by his Cabinet to accept Hoare's resignation. He felt humiliated by this incident; the public outcry may have been less widespread than the press contrived to make it appear, but he had seriously and visibly affronted that section of the public whose confidence he was so proud of having earned over the previous thirteen years. It was probably the only major blunder in all those years for which he blamed himself.

The abdication crisis the following year, however, enabled Baldwin to redeem his reputation and retire in a blaze of public congratulation. For this kind of constitutional crisis he was the perfect premier: though he professed to find it distasteful, 'the King's matter' stirred his sense of history and roused him to decisive action as economic problems never could. He had certainly been worried about Edward for some time before his accession; but there is no ground for the suspicion that he deliberately used the question of his marriage to drive him from his throne. On the contrary he tried tactfully – perhaps too tactfully – to get Edward off the hook; only when he saw that Edward was determined to impale himself did he force the issue to a quick and irreversible conclusion. Any other Prime Minister (even Churchill) would probably have had to do the same – if there was an element of humbug in the case, it was national humbug; in the circumstances there can only be admiration for the deftly avuncular touch with which Baldwin dispatched the business. He stayed on as Prime Minister until the coronation of George vi in May 1937, and then made way at last for Neville Chamberlain.

Baldwin retired with his reputation high: within three years it was in ruins as he was blamed, unfairly, for the disaster of Dunkirk. More significant was the rapid shift of political opinion after 1940 which expressed itself at the 1945 general election; the new consensus that emerged, accepted by the Conservative party as much as by Labour, represented a far more fundamental rejection of Baldwinism. It revealed what a tide, not of revolution but of constructive social amelioration, Baldwin had been holding back, for most of what was planned and enacted by the Churchill and Attlee governments during and after the war had been urged vainly on Conservative, Labour and National governments by various party and non-party pressure groups for years before. Though it may not have been enough, Baldwin did his best, in the prevailing climate, to prepare the country militarily for war. But the possibility of economic management simply did not figure in his conception of his task. It is this lingering belief in *laissez-faire* that makes Baldwin's achievement peculiarly difficult to assess; for it is arguable that he must be judged according to the goals he set himself, which were not at all those of his immediate predecessors or successors – not economic or (in the legislative sense) social, but above all moral. His claim to be a great Prime Minister is that he restored the standards of public life, preserved the Constitution from a variety of threats, reconciled the Labour party to working within it (thus earning a share of the credit for its coming of age in 1945), gave the country valuable breathing-space after the upheaval of 1914–18, healed its social divisions and left it united to face the trials of 1939–45. These are all very abstract achievements, none the less valuable for that, perhaps, if they could be substantiated, but all in fact very questionable, depending as they do on a highly coloured view, first of the iniquities of the Lloyd George coalition, then of the revolutionary potential of British society in the early twenties. Even if Baldwin's success in quieting these demons is granted, however, a doubt still remains whether this constitutes a sufficient or even an appropriate achievement for a Prime Minister.

Baldwin's view of the role of the Prime Minister in the British Constitution is in some ways a very attractive one – a fatherly amalgam of prophet, priest and president. But it does leave a gap at the head of the government. In modern conditions – that is, since the First World War – the day-to-day running of a government is a full-time job in itself. That primary function of his office Baldwin neglected. Reacting against Lloyd George – whose interventionist style of government was only partly a reflection of his own temperament, partly also the only appropriate response to the new demands on government in a democratic world – Baldwin tried to revert to an older model, stepping back to a merely supervisory role and leaving the development of policy initiatives to his heads of department. In his major administration he was fortunate to have one departmental minister with the necessary self-confidence to use this freedom. But one Chamberlain (or even two) does not make a Government. Baldwin failed to provide the drive, stimulation and coordinating sense of direction that only a Prime Minister can provide. (He might have been perfectly placed as Lord President in 1931–5, if only MacDonald had been a clear-sighted Prime Minister.) This is not to say that a Prime Minister must be a dictator: Baldwin's respect for his colleagues undoubtedly created a more united Cabinet than did Lloyd George's methods. But Attlee and Asquith (in his peacetime administration) may be taken as models of Prime Ministers as mild as Baldwin who nevertheless gave their Cabinets of talented individuals very positive leadership. Baldwin exercised effective control over neither of the two most critical areas of policy, the economy and foreign affairs, nor did he compensate for this omission in those other fields in which he did claim a personal interest – industrial relations and agriculture. He involved himself in the coal industry only when it threatened a general strike, and lost interest again as soon as the strike had been defeated. Even as a guardian of the Constitution his concern was selective: if anyone could have restrained the ruthless exploitation by the Unionists of the protestant ascendancy in Northern Ireland in the twenties, it was surely Baldwin; but he, like the rest of Britain, had washed his hands of Ireland. It is entirely characteristic that his greatest personal triumph, the abdication crisis, concerned an issue not essentially political at all; for Baldwin's concern, to use Bagehot's terminology, was far more with the 'dignified' than with the 'efficient' working of the Constitution.

Baldwin was not at all the simple, stolid Englishman that he liked to appear, though that image was a creation of his own, not of Central Office. It represented one side, one aspiration, of his nature – that side of him that derived from his revered father. But he was at heart less his father's than his mother's son: to her Celtic ancestry, poor health and literary talent (she published four novels as well as ghost stories, children's stories and poems) can be traced the love of words, bardic imagination and sometimes debilitating nervous tension which so incongruously belied his bluff exterior. This mixture of influences gave to Baldwin's personality both its complexity and its resonance. Though his shrewdness to some seemed merely sly, what seemed sanctimonious to many struck others as true humility; his words could move by their sincerity even those who might suspect them to be hollow. It was his father whom Baldwin followed into business and then politics; his father's example that pointed out to him the path of duty; but at critical moments, and increasingly as he grew older and drew self-confidence from public praise, it seems that his mother's inheritance came to dominate. This duality may explain his power as a preacher and his skill as a political manager, and at the same time his weakness in action, his reluctance to follow through his own words. He was in all things, though he would have hated the word, a dilettante: he was a weekend countryman, not a farmer; his love of scholarship was similarly superficial – he dipped and browsed in books, fingered and sniffed them, rather than read deeply. So it was also with politics. He liked the flavour of the House of Commons. But he never, for all his love of its institutions, could be bothered to go to the heart of his country's problems. He was, in sum, a thoroughly decent man, kindhearted, lovable, full of vague goodwill, gifted with great eloquence, but possessed of utterly conservative instincts, a good deal of self-satisfaction and no ideas – temperamentally quite unfitted for a job to which he had never aspired, the government of an advanced but failing industrial economy in the second quarter of the twentieth century'.

Notes

I have given specific references only to direct quotations. Baldwin's career is exceedingly well-documented in published biographies, memoirs and diaries to which reference could be made on nearly every page. The most essential are the following:

Keith Middlemas & John Barnes, *Baldwin* (London 1969).

H.Montgomery Hyde, *Baldwin: The Unexpected Prime Minister* (London 1973).

G.M.Young, *Stanley Baldwin* (London 1952).

A.W.Baldwin, *My Father: The True Story* (London 1955).

Thomas Jones, *Whitehall Diary 1916–1930*, ed. Keith Middlemas (Oxford 1969).

Thomas Jones, *A Diary With Letters, 1931–1950* (Oxford 1954).

Robert Rhodes James, *Memoirs of a Conservative: J.C.C.Davidson's Memoirs and Papers, 1910–37* (London 1969).

1. Baldwin to Asquith, 23 October 1926. *Baldwin papers* L2/161; quoted in Young, *op. cit.*, pp. 52–3.
2. Middlemas & Barnes, *op. cit.*, p. 18.
3. Baldwin, *op. cit.*, p. 71; Middlemas & Barnes, *op. cit.*, p. 41.
4. James, *op. cit.*, p. 36.
5. Middlemas & Barnes, *op. cit.*, p. 68.
6. Jones, *Whitehall Diary*, I, pp. 243, 255.
7. Hyde, *op. cit.*, p. 96.
8. Middlemas & Barnes, *op. cit.*, p. 123.
9. Middlemas & Barnes, *op. cit.*, p. 152.
10. Middlemas & Barnes, *op. cit.*, p. 212.
11. Marchioness Curzon of Kedleston, *Reminiscences* (London 1955), p. 191.
12. Birkenhead to Baldwin, 16 October 1928. *Baldwin papers* L2/163; quoted in Middlemas & Barnes, *op. cit.*, p. 488.
13. Middlemas & Barnes, *op. cit.*, p. 96.
14. Young, *op. cit.*, p. 40.
15. Jones, *Diary with Letters*, p. xxviii.
16. Lord Eustace Percy: *Some Memories* (London 1958), p. 127; quoted in Middlemas & Barnes, *op. cit.*, p. 487.
17. The Earl of Swinton, *Sixty Years of Power* (London 1966), p. 79.
18. B.B.C. broadcast, 9 May 1926, quoted in Middlemas & Barnes, *op. cit.*, pp. 414–15.
19. Speech in the House of Commons, 6 March 1925, quoted in Middlemas & Barnes, *op. cit.*, pp. 296–7.
20. Jones: *Whitehall Diary*, I, p. 230.
21. Young, *op. cit.*, p. 54.

22. Speech to the Royal Society of St George, 6 May 1924, printed in Stanley Baldwin, *On England* (London 1926), p. 6.
23. Rudyard Kipling, 'The English Flag'.
24. e.g. Jones, *Whitehall Diary*, II, p. 23.
25. Speech at the Queen's Hall, London, 17 March 1931.
26. Sir William Sutherland to Lloyd George, 8 September 1931, *Lloyd George Papers*, G/19/7/4.

Neville Chamberlain[1]

Alan Beattie

(Austen) has not the eagerness of temperament and inexhaustible
vitality of father, which kept him ever evolving some constructive
idea.... I believe I lie somewhere between the two.[2]

In the portrait gallery of twentieth-century Prime Ministers, the
pictures of Ramsay MacDonald and Neville Chamberlain have been
singled out for concentrated criticism, abuse, and disfigurement. The
political generations which succeeded them have found it difficult to
live with the pre-war past: 'the Man of Munich' and 'the Man of 1931'
provide a convenient and symbolic image on which to visit the alleged
failures of those times. To the historian of politics, such moralizing is
not merely irrelevant to his concern with understanding and
explanation, but also serves to distract attention from a neglected
aspect of the British political past: the various and individual kinds of
political leadership. The life of politics is, at least for some of its
practitioners, a creative enterprise; the politician's art of 'making
politics out of his own sensibility ... within the political arena where a
mark may be made'[3] is an activity more subtle and worthy of
dispassionate reflection than mere moralizing can allow. Although
creative, a political career is pursued in a world of an apparently
limited kind. A politician acts within the confines both of the past and
of the dispositions of his contemporaries. The typical portrait of
Neville Chamberlain is one which ignores the limitations of his
political world, and mistakes the nature of his political contribution.
That Chamberlain, as Prime Minister, inherited and maintained long-
standing policies and dispositions and was both limited and supported
by the context of democratic politics, is frequently overlooked. And
while such an exaggeration of the novelty of his ideas might promise
an informed appreciation of his distinctive political style, his political

individuality is more often reduced to a mere catalogue of private vices: Chamberlain – arrogant, ignorant and incompetent – is represented as inflicting his personal shortcomings upon a helpless and innocent political world.

In recent years, a number of scholars have done a great deal to rescue Chamberlain's foreign policy from the publicists and to establish him in genuine historical perspective.[4] But relatively little attention has been paid to the character of his politics: his antecedents and the limitations of his circumstances are now much better understood, but that Chamberlain's attempt to 'make a mark upon the world' produced a distinctive kind of politics is usually overlooked.[5] The precise character of the creative, individual aspect of Chamberlain's politics is important not only because an appreciation of the various styles of political leadership is of intrinsic interest, but also because such an appreciation illuminates many aspects of both Chamberlain's career and the times in which he lived. The key to Chamberlain's political character lies in its unusual combination of the qualities of the man of business and the man of imagination. The son of Joseph Chamberlain inherited much of his father's radical fervour, while combining it with an aptitude for the efficient dispatch of political business. While the former attribute is most apparent in his conduct of foreign policy, the latter pervades all his work as Prime Minister. Chamberlain's businesslike characteristics have often been interpreted in such a way as to represent him as little more than an authoritarian clerk; Earl Winterton, writing in a style reminiscent of a testimonial, concluded that 'fundamentally, he was a sober, intelligent, very able businessman turned administrator and Prime Minister in his later years.'[6]

Yet Chamberlain was aware of his own character, and the man of business was put to the service of the man of imagination in a way which created a Prime Minister far removed from either mere administrative competence or authoritarianism. It is this unique resultant of the characteristics of efficiency and imagination which makes it impossible to fit Chamberlain into any of the usual categories employed to describe the office of modern Prime Minister.

1 Ministerial Career

It amuses me to find a new policy for each of my colleagues in turn. As you will see, I have become a sort of Acting Prime Minister – only without the actual powers of the PM.[7]

Neville Chamberlain became Prime Minister on 28 May 1937 at the age of 68. Of the previous nineteen years of continuous membership of the House of Commons, eleven had been spent in ministerial office. He was generally recognized as Baldwin's successor by 1935, a recognition founded upon his ministerial experience, administrative ability and parliamentary presence. Chamberlain brought to the prime ministership an attitude subtly different from that of the politician accustomed to adopting the standpoint of the departmental minister: his departmental ability was undoubted, yet his political horizons were much wider. Any Chancellor of the Exchequer holds a position which involves him in the work of government as a whole, and Chamberlain's tenure in the years 1931 to 1937 covered an especially critical period in the development of domestic and external affairs. Even in the narrower role of Minister of Health (1923 and 1924–9), the relaxed and unobtrusive nature of Baldwin's prime ministership allowed Chamberlain to act as the work-horse and initiator of programmes for the ministry as a whole. Throughout Baldwin's career as Conservative Leader, Chamberlain's role was much more than that of the departmental minister; he was required (and willing) to act as a sub-Prime Minister', without prejudice to the different abilities which Baldwin brought to the office itself. This departmental and quasi-prime-ministerial experience was supplemented by a long-standing interest in Conservative party organization and, above all, by his interest in the political world of his times. His father's radicalism bequeathed a lifelong interest in social reform,[8] and his half-brother Austen's tenure of the Foreign Office (1924–9) made foreign affairs a familiar part of his political world.

The major part of Chamberlain's ministerial career was spent under Baldwin's prime ministership, and this is crucial to an understanding of his own conception of the office of Prime Minister. The role of Prime Minister within the Prime Minister' became progressively less acceptable to Chamberlain as his view of political circumstances eroded his belief in the relevance of Baldwin's unique political skills. Although overtly loyal to his leader during the internal Conservative divisions of the late 1920s, he sympathized with those Conservatives who saw Baldwin as lacking the necessary qualities of leadership.[9] As Prime Minister, his view of Baldwin's limitations combined with an awareness of his own character to lead him to invoke Baldwin as an object-lesson to those unwilling to accept the consequences of his own political style.

II   Chamberlain as Prime Minister

Neville (said) that he himself possessed some of the qualities S.B. had, but he had also qualities which S.B. had not. He intended to take a new line. He wished all his Ministers to be in the closest touch with him, to tell him their difficulties, to inform him not only about their immediate plans in their departments, but what they were planning for the future.[10]

Chamberlain's impatience with Baldwinian habits clearly revealed itself in Cabinet. Baldwin's habit of reflecting in an almost metaphysical manner on the heavy burden imposed by such prime ministerial decisions as the choice of ministers and the compilation of the Honours List seemed to Chamberlain a manifestation of an inappropriately unbusinesslike manner. The Prime Minister, in Chamberlain's view, had a primary responsibility to extract the maximum amount of effective work from his ministers. Such a conception did not entail that the Prime Minister should or could, for the most part, do the work of his ministers in addition to his own. Chamberlain had been accustomed to the task of keeping ministers on their departmental toes while serving under Baldwin, and his accession to the prime ministership thus required little change in his outlook. To Chamberlain, the ability of a Prime Minister to promote diligence in his ministers, and to assess their departmental competence, required knowledge both of the matters generally relevant to their work and of their own individual proposals:[11] one of his first acts as Prime Minister was to ask his ministers to submit plans indicating their departmental intentions for the following two years. He became a master of the details of government business to an extent which surprised his colleagues and subordinates.[12] He read Cabinet papers thoroughly, chaired all important policy Cabinet committees, and was especially active on the Committee of Imperial Defence.[13] Throughout his prime ministership, he attempted to keep in touch with government business as a whole: in the midst of his later involvement in foreign affairs he could still find time for a consideration of the importance of programmes for industrial recovery.[14] The knowledge of current and future governmental activities which he regarded as essential to the role of Prime Minister was facilitated by his use of Sir Horace Wilson,[15] both to keep him informed about departmental actions, and to provide invaluable administrative assistance in rendering a mass of information to the coherence necessary for effective supervision.

Chamberlain's impatience with ministers who did not appear to be 'on top of their job' is revealed both in his communications with his less effective colleagues[16] and in the recollections of his con-temporaries. One of the latter relates that on occasion Chamberlain would send ministers out of the Cabinet room to seek answers to questions to which they had been unable to provide a ready answer.[17] Having little of Baldwin's ultimately sceptical tolerance of inactivity and vagueness, he placed a high value on the qualities of clarity, diligence, willingness to take decisions, and reliance upon preparation and articulated programmes. In this respect, he was the radical successor to the Whiggism of Baldwin.

Chamberlain's determination to mould his ministerial team into an effective and hard-working group of departmental supervisors explains (in part) his choice of ministers. He preferred individuals who either were or could become effective in Whitehall to those whose claims rested on parliamentary or popular appeal. In January 1939 he noted that

> The press have had their attentions drawn to the fact that the three new men I have introduced have been the man who knows all about organization, the man who knows all about defences and the man who knows all about agriculture.[18]

In peacetime circumstances, he preferred a Ministry of Administrative Competence to a Ministry of All the Talents.

Chamberlain's ambition to stimulate the diligence and effectiveness of his ministers did not, outside the field of foreign policy, create any sort of prime-ministerial domination. His emphasis on ministerial competence was to a great extent the consequence of a recognition that the Prime Minister could not do the work of all his colleagues, a recognition reinforced by his increasing involvement in foreign affairs. The temptation to see some of his ministers as mere executors of particular prime-ministerial plans was one from which Chamberlain was no more immune than any other British Prime Minister; but on the whole, his relationships with ministers differed from Baldwin's not in any attempt to deprive ministers of the initiative, or to override departmental authority, but in his belief that the Prime Minister had an obligation positively to promote and assess the diligence and effectiveness of his ministerial team. The need for an informed and active Prime Minister did not arise solely from the presence of incompetent or lazy ministers. The prime-ministerial role was seen to involve encouragement as well as advice and admonition; a Prime Minister could not defend even able colleagues in Whitehall and Parliament unless well versed in the issues involved.[19]

Chamberlain's emphasis on ministerial diligence and effectiveness did not lead to an indifference to the importance of other factors. He shared with most Prime Ministers an unwillingness to undertake frequent Cabinet reshuffles, an unwillingness partly based upon his recognition of the importance of harmonious personal relations, and the extent to which governmental effectiveness depended upon the Cabinet's quality as a working group. He wrote of his War Cabinet:

I constructed my War Cabinet on no theory or role governing its size or the nature of its composition or otherwise. My sole purpose was to find a Cabinet that would work, which means that *personalities* must be taken into account.[20]

It was, for example, precisely Sir Thomas Inskip's lack of dramatic initiative which made him, in Chamberlain's view, a more appropriate coordinator of the highly sensitive and sectionalized field of defence than more flamboyant (and hence divisive) individuals such as

Churchill.[21] Considerations of Cabinet harmony could lead to the retention of ministers unsatisfactory from the administrative standpoint, especially if (as Chamberlain believed to be the case in his circumstances) there existed little hope of securing a more competent replacement. All Prime Ministers tend to hesitate before rearranging ministries which are to some extent a reflection of their own initial judgement, and in Chamberlain's case reluctance to make what could be represented as a public admission of unsound judgement was accompanied by a personal distaste for the business of dismissal.[22] His treatment of Morrison[23] illustrates his unwillingness to press prime-ministerial warnings and criticism to the point of replacement, and reveals the personal affection and willingness to give another chance which often accompanied the emphasis on administrative efficiency.[24]

Chamberlain's conception of the office of Prime Minister was 'personal' in a sense rather different from that often supposed. He was sceptical of proposals to reform the 'machinery' of the Cabinet, believing that formal procedures were less important than the individual qualities of ministers and success in maintaining harmonious relations. His resistance to the fundamental changes urged by critics such as L.S.Amery in the period immediately before and after the outbreak of war stemmed partly from this attitude.[25] Chamberlain also believed that the effectiveness of a Cabinet ultimately depended more upon the competence of the Prime Minister than upon formal Cabinet arrangements. Such arrangements were no substitute for the pressure of an assiduous and well-informed Prime Minister: 'Sure of himself and his programme, he was convinced that he could make almost any ministers work well in his Cabinet.'[26]

On the other hand, his interest in the efficient despatch of business led him to amend the Baldwinian character of the Cabinet. He announced upon his accession his intention to make use of an 'inner Cabinet', and both the Foreign Policy Committee and, later, the 'Big Four' of Chamberlain, Simon, Halifax and Hoare to some extent fulfilled this role.[27]

Chamberlain's management of the Cabinet and its committees had none of the characteristics of mere personal domination. He seldom spoke first on any item of business, reserving himself for a summing-up which was usually notable for its lucidity, order and grasp of essentials:

I knew of no-one who could listen to a long discussion and sum up a situation better than Chamberlain. Such men have a mind like a searchlight.[28]

Ministers and witnesses in committee were usually visited with sharp and relevant questions from a Prime Minister whose command of the subject under discussion was variously a source of wonder, admiration, fear, resentment or encouragement:

You cannot know [wrote Ernest Brown] what a comfort it has been to hard-pressed departmental ministers to know that, when their subjects have to be discussed, whoever else had not read their papers and disgested them, one man had – the Prime Minister.[29]

Chamberlain was conscious of the need to keep junior ministers in touch with their Cabinet colleagues, and held weekly meetings to this end until the pace of the world of Munich and beyond made even full Cabinet consultation increasingly difficult.[30]

Chamberlain's qualities as a man of business were fully evident in his relations with his Cabinet, but his previous and quasi-prime-ministerial experience under Baldwin gave to his prime ministership an outlook other than that of the pure administrator. If willingness to take the initiative and to substitute his own judgement for that of others is a plausible (although misleading) interpretation of Chamberlain's role in foreign affairs, such an interpretation cannot be sustained over the remaining fields of government business. Here, Chamberlain's conception was coherent and far removed from mere personal domination. Much influenced by his views of Baldwin's weaknesses, he brought to the Cabinet a greater emphasis on ministerial activity and prime-ministerial knowledge than his predecessor. The 'personal' aspects of his Cabinet role were restricted to a belief in the superior importance of individual competence (including his own as Prime Minister) to considerations of 'machinery' or formal procedures, It was in this manner that Chamberlain the man of business was combined with Chamberlain the imaginative politician in a way which defies description in terms of either the clerk or the commissar.

III   The Politics of Character

In what is Chamberlain Tory? Perhaps most notably in his reluctant entry to politics to prove himself, his clear aspiration to govern, to take charge, despite the irresistible 'nausea and revulsion' which 'the drudgery, humiliation and pettiness' of the public life produced in him. And there is also the 'exact correspondence between intimate thought and public deed', the reluctance to develop style.[31]

In his approach to democratic political institutions Chamberlain was an educated, rather than a natural, politician. Lloyd George and Winston Churchill could never have been anything other than politicians, and Baldwin (who could have been something else) absorbed the lessons of political life by a process of unconscious osmosis which revealed a characteristic aptitude. Chamberlain, on the other hand, arrived at a political understanding through diligence, determination, and periodic stock-taking of his position. A political world which was to others either immediately or innately intelligible was to him an unpromising environment whose contours would yield only to a determined act of will, and which would be harsh in its retribution on those who failed. On the path to the prime ministership, Chamberlain had learned his statemanship by cumulative experience, but the lesson was more strongly absorbed by the head than by the heart: his appreciation of the demands of free politics remained somewhat formal. He was as aware of the need to retain parliamentary and electoral support as Baldwin had been, but was unable and unwilling to achieve it by similar methods. It was impossible for Chamberlain's active, restless character to absorb the atmosphere of the Commons by frequent and idle attendance on the benches or in the company of the smoking-rooms: the intricacies of party management were left almost entirely to David Margesson, the Chief Whip.[32] His formal conception of the demands of political conciliation is revealed in the importance he attached to including National Liberal and National Labour elements in his government.[33] In a similar way, although recognizing the importance of electoral support, Chamberlain had none of Baldwin's almost reverential attitude to 'public opinion', and laid no claim to have inherited his predecessor's alleged 'feel' for the workings of the English mind. As the only twentieth-century Prime Minister not required to fight an election, evidence as to Chamberlain's detailed views on the importance and strategy of electioneering is necessarily confined to his previous ministerial career and the scattered reflections which he entertained while Prime Minister, unaware that war would postpone elections to the indefinite future. Such evidence confirms the view that elections and public opinion did not play the important part in his political life they had assumed in Baldwin's.

That Chamberlain's character and his somewhat formal appreciation of the demands of democratic politics produced a prime-ministerial style quite different from that of Baldwin is obvious; that it was less effective or coherent is a matter more often assumed than illustrated. Chamberlain was more conscious of the nature of his abilities and limitations than those who emphasize his merely businesslike characteristics will allow. This awareness of himself as a politician was accompanied by a reading of his circumstances which made his individual qualities appear particularly appropriate, and provoked a series of actions in which it is possible to discern an imaginative and creative political strategy. It is in his conduct of foreign policy that Chamberlain's political imagination and moral fervour are most in evidence. The politics of appeasement after 1937 are an example of the way in which a politician goes about 'making politics out of his own sensibility' in the attempt to convert what might otherwise have been limitations into positive advantages.

IV Foreign Policy

I believe [that peace] must be wanted too by Germans, Italians, Russians and Japanese. But these people are in the grip of their governments. ... [These governments] pay no heed to reason, but there is one argument to which they will always give attention and that is force ... [but] the English realise that we are in no position to enter lightheartedly upon war with such a formidable power as Germany, much less if Germany were aided by Italian attacks on our Mediterranean possessions and communications ... therefore, our people see that in the absence of any powerful ally and until our armaments are completed, we must adjust our foreign policy to our circumstances, and even bear with patience and good humour actions which we would like to treat in a very different fashion. The dictators are too often regarded as if they were entirely inhuman. I believe this idea to be quite erroneous. It is indeed the human side of the dictators that makes them dangerous, but on the other hand, it is the side on which they can be approached with the greatest hope of successful issue.[34]

Recent historians have demonstrated the extent to which British foreign policy in the later 1930s was conducted within inherited limits.[35] From the Treaty of Versailles to the early 1930s the British pursued a foreign policy whose ambivalence was either unrecognized or made tolerable by the apparent absence of urgency. British participation in the First World War and the Peace Treaties had involved Britain in European interests more extensive than before. To this general sense of obligation towards the post-war European order was added a more specific concern, arising out of a national economic interest in the revival of international trade through the creation and maintenance of a stable systm of currencies. Such stability was seen to depend, in part, upon the establishment of friendly relations between France and Germany and was the basic context of British actions over such questions as reparations. On the other hand, the British were unable and unwilling to concentrate on Europe to the exclusion of Imperial connections, and they did not see themselves as part of the European order in the same way as did the French: it was at this point that a dilemma was posed. To the French, a settled relationship with Germany would be possible only if concrete guarantees of her future security were extended by the British. The British were in general unwilling to enter into such a commitment, and fearful in particular of its potential effect upon a Germany for whose position the British had considerable sympathy, and in whose economic and political revival they had a positive interest. Unwilling either to appease the Germans to the point of ignoring French claims or to support the French at the expense of Germany, the British fell back upon a policy of diplomatic mediation and the limitation of European commitments. The British view of the League was consistent with this general position. Its arbitrational and consultative aspects were congenial to the policy of mediation, while its potential as an enforcer of sanctions in the event of aggression was sceptically underplayed. The British had insufficient faith in the military and economic strength of the League to look favourably upon participation in 'peace-keeping' enterprises, nor did they relish the prospect of relinquishing their freedom of action to a League endowed with Wilsonian idealism but deprived of American membership. The League's action over the Japanese invasion of Manchuria in 1931 was seen by the British as appropriate: discussions and negotiations had taken place over an episode in which the Japanese were by no means entirely in the wrong, and realism dictated a course of conciliation when military adventures were neither defensible nor easily undertaken.[36]

The success of the policy of mediation was generally acknowledged until the early 1930s. Reason had ultimately prevailed in the matter of the French occupation of the Ruhr, and the Locarno Treaty of 1925 was widely acclaimed as the symbol of a peaceful Europe. Such signs of the relaxation of tension served both to confirm the British in their avuncular role and to weaken their incentive to penetrate beneath the surface of European amity. The political context of British foreign policy in the 1920s provided little scope for policies of a different kind. Unpopularity was more likely to accrue to governments which undertook foreign commitments than to those which shared Bonar Law's preference for concentration on domestic affairs at the expense of foreign adventures. Economic depression in post-war Britain both deflected public attention away from external questions and provoked an economic policy whose emphasis on the limitation of public expenditure was inconsistent with the high defence expenditure implicit in foreign commitments. Few dissented from the view that since the arms race had caused the First World War, in disarmament lay the best hope for peace. Fewer still could see a potential aggressor on the horizon or agree among themselves as to who such an aggressor might be. Sympathy for the alleged German humiliations suffered at Versailles was widespread; France rather than Germany provoked deep suspicions on the left; and the potential threat posed by Japan was, for the most part, ignored. On balance, the fact that the governments of the 1920s took considerable interest in European affairs owed more to a sense of political duty than to public pressure.[37]

By 1933 a reappraisal of policy was taking place.[38] The relative calm of the age of Locarno had been replaced by the rise of National Socialism and rearmament in Germany, by fear for British interests in the Far East aroused by the Japanese, and by bellicose language from Mussolini. Moreover, the Disarmament Conference which met in 1932, and on which many British hopes had been placed, broke upon the rocks of French unwillingness to disarm and German accusations of the failure of other nations to meet the disarmament promises allegedly made at Versailles. Mussolini's invasion of Abyssinia in 1935 confirmed British scepticism about the effectiveness of the League from the standpoint of military and economic sanctions, and reinforced existing doubts about the adequacy of British military strength. The Abyssinian crisis also threw light upon the confused and divided state of British public opinion with respect to both British commitments abroad and the possibility of honourable appeasement. Alive to these dangers to their interests, the British began to reconsider the adequacy of their policies and their defences, and from this reconsideration a number of conflicting possibilities emerged. The Labour party ultimately evolved a policy combining support for the League with unilateral disarmament; others embarked upon a campaign for a major rearmament programme and collective action to deter future aggression. The National government, under Baldwin, evolved a policy of appeasement which identified Germany as the most important long-run threat (although Japan was seen to constitute a more immediate problem), and combined an emphasis on armed deterrence with a willingness to negotiate both the removal of specific and legitimate grievances and a general European settlement.

In the evolution of this policy Chamberlain, as Chancellor of the Exchequer, played an important part. His support for rearmament was such as to provoke charges of 'warmongering', and in his distaste for the character of the German government and his awareness of the threat posed by Germany he was second to none. In the election of 1935 in which the National government appealed, *inter alia*, for a mandate to re-arm, Chamberlain urged that rearmament be made the primary issue. Although differing from some of his National Government colleagues over the precise nature and relative importance of the threats to British interests, and the specific rearmament programme necessary to meet them, there can be no doubt that after 1933 Chamberlain was a convinced supporter of British rearmament and more concerned than most with the threat posed by Germany.

The 'double line' policy of combining rearmament for deterrence with a search for peaceful settlement contained within itself a variety of problems, potential inconsistencies and differences of emphasis. As the policy gradually established itself after 1933, its internal difficulties were acknowledged and debated by members of the National government, especially during the Abyssinian crisis which began in 1935. The plurality of British interests, the precise form which both deterrence and conciliation should take, and the relationship between each side of the 'double line' were urgent and recognized questions. The breadth and interrelation between British interests in the Far East, Western Europe and the Mediterranean constituted the major difficulty. Given that the British were unable simultaneously to defend all their interests, a resolute defence of any one interest might provide an opportunity for potential aggressors to act adversely towards the others. The desirability of conciliating Japan and Italy in order to concentrate on and combine against the danger from Germany could be balanced by the possibility that a firm stand against Italian aggression in Abyssinia might at the same time act as a deterrent against future German expansion. Such a consideration was but a particular illustration of the general extent to which the ideas of deterrence and conciliation were subtly interrelated and even potentially incompatible. An emphasis upon negotiation and compromise might reduce the credibility of rearmament and collective action as a deterrent. Alternatively, an emphasis on deterrence through rearmament and cooperation with France, Italy and the League might produce an arms race and German resentment in which all hope of peaceful settlement would be lost.

Within each of the lines of British policy uncertainties existed. German intentions were unclear, and the possibility of creating and maintaining a common front against potential German aggression was fraught with difficulty. The 1920s problem of French sensitivities with respect to Germany loomed again. Britain's emphasis on conciliation and settlement might arouse fresh suspicions about the genuineness of Britain's commitment to the balance of power in Europe, while willingness to cooperate closely with the French involved the possibility that Britain might lose her freedom of action to French governments in whose judgement she had little confidence and whose European interests were more extensive than her own. Moreover, in the context of Franco–German suspicions, cooperation with France might reduce the apparent sincerity of British efforts to take German grievances seriously as a subject for settlement. The deterrent element in the policy of the 'double line' had additional difficulties. The adequacy of British defence preparations could only be judged in the light of estimates of the likely sources of aggression and (more problematical) the international cooperation which the British would require (or could expect) in response. Such estimates related to matters which were neither within the complete control of the British nor entirely independent of their actions. British defences had to be discussed in the light of what others might do, but the actions of others (either friendly or otherwise) would be influenced in turn by the strength and policies of the British. Moreover, British rearmament after 1933 proceeded in the context of a public opinion whose reluctance to support either a major rearmament programme or extensive British commitments abroad was continually encouraged by the Labour and Liberal opposition.[39] Expenditure on rearmament had also to take account of the limitations imposed by economic circumstances, and by the political difficulties which would follow any concerted attempt to alter the structure and practices of peacetime British industry in pursuit of a significant improvement in defence. Finally, there was uncertainty about the institutions through which the policy of the 'double line' was to be pursued. Judgements about the effectiveness of the League, and the extent to which regional and/or bilateral cooperation could or should be represented as consistent with League obligations, were both generally cautious and subject to disagreement. The British response to the unsettled international scene of the early 1930s was subtle, cautious, and not easily reduced to coherence. The Abyssinian crisis showed that important differences of emphasis could emerge within the British response to one event. In addition, there were changes of emphasis between one event and another, as in the case of the relationship between British participation in the 'Stresa Front' and the subsequent Anglo–German Naval Agreement.

It was a world in which everything was interrelated, and of which almost everyone was unsure. Vansittart's description of the Abyssinian crisis as an event in which 'there was a terrible lot to be said on both sides . . . we were all in a muddle, and it is hard to keep track of opinions when the owners are not sure of them'[40] could easily have been extended to the British position as a whole. In such circumstances, differences of opinion arose from subtle differences in the relative importance attached to a shared variety of considerations or estimates. The subtlety and complexity of British policy placed a high premium upon those who could think carefully about the appropriate response, whose grasp of the situation would be sufficient to enable them to see their way through tangled international negotiations, and whose diplomatic skill would be sufficient to avoid dangerous misrepresentations of British attitudes. Inadequate coordination of British efforts and lack of the finer diplomatic skills could result in the kind of situation in which Hoare found himself during the negotiations with Laval over Abyssinia. The Hoare–Laval agreement was not obviously inconsistent with British policy as it emerged after 1933, yet was subtly different from the precise course favoured by Baldwin, Eden and Chamberlain, and thus appeared to them as a major departure from original intentions.[41]

Chamberlain, as Prime Minister, inherited a situation in which most of the relevant considerations had already been established, and in which the appropriate balance between such considerations was a matter of dispute, confusion and subtlety. The limits on his freedom of action were even greater than is usual in the case of newly established Prime Ministers. At the same time, the nature of the inherited situation was such as to instil in Chamberlain a belief that his individual abilities were peculiarly appropriate. Between 1933 and 1936 Chamberlain had supported the policy which identified Germany as the major long-run threat, and which supported increasing the forces of deterrence to a point where Britain could consider German claims from a position of strength. By the time he became Prime Minister his views had undergone a significant change, as a result of which the element of appeasement was given considerable priority over the element of deterrence in British foreign policy.[42] Chamberlain had been conscious, in the years before his accession to the prime ministership, of the element of confusion and drift in British policy. He was aware of the subtleties and strengths of all the points of view which had constituted the National government's reconsideration of British policy after 1933, but he was more concerned with the potentially dangerous consequences of allowing the debate to continue in such a cautious and apparently endless manner. Chamberlain was character-istically disposed to respond to such a situation by reflecting upon the various alternatives, selecting that which seemed most promising, and pursuing it with firmness and consistency. His instinctive belief that, in politics, certainty and clarity often won the day was reinforced by his reading of the circumstances. His awareness of an increasing German danger instilled in him a sense of urgency which led to the belief that war was more likely to be the accidental result of continuous debate and uncertainty on the British side than of the bold adoption of clear and consistently pursued policies: the debate had gone on long enough.[43] Moreover, he was aware that the combination of over-subtlety, compromise and caution which had, in his view, characterized Baldwin's leadership, had provoked dissatisfaction and uncertainty both at home and abroad. Chamberlain's belief in the virtues of boldness and certainty struck a responsive chord in many of his contemporaries:

> I was not dismayed when [Chamberlain] said with a smile: 'I know you won't mind if I take more interest in Foreign Policy than S.B.' We both knew that no-one could have taken less.[44]

The emergence, under Chamberlain, of a policy of appeasement in which the satisfaction of legitimate grievances was given a considerably higher priority than the maintenance or extension of the deterrent, represented a shift in his own position which was not the result of a random choice between alternatives. In Chamberlain's view, the realism of the policy of the 'double line' had been weakened by a number of developments which had affected the deterrent side of the balance. First, the possibility of concentrating the deterrent upon illegitimate German expansion had been much reduced by developments in the Far East and the Mediterranean.[45] No satisfactory agreement had been made with the Japanese, and the USA had been unwilling to adopt a sufficiently positive policy to allow the British to regard their interests in the Far East as secure. In view of Britain's obvious inability alone to defend herself in that area, Japan remained a perpetual distraction from the European scene. Efforts to supplement British defence by cooperation with the Dominions had failed, and the Abyssinian affair had divided the 'Stresa Front' without diminishing Italian ambitions. Cooperation with France, which had been an important element in the Baldwin–Eden interpretation of the 'double line', was regarded as less possible (and less desirable) in the light of continued French vacillation and military weakness. The Abyssinian crisis had revealed the League to be dangerously non-collective in the matter of security, ultimately weakened by the absence of the USA and by its dependence upon France and Britain, whose actions could not, in the last resort, successfully be coordinated. Finally, the degree of British rearmament which would be necessary to support a unilateral British attempt to apply the 'double line' to the German problem was seen as economically and politically impossible. Rearmament had already been the subject of intense inter-party dispute, and any major increase in the rearmament programme would require a degree of social cooperation (from the trade unions in particular) which all the evidence indicated would not be forthcoming.

There is a sense in which Chamberlain's appeasement involved the representation of necessity as a virtue. If the possibility of collective deterrence had been reduced, then to act on the assumption that Germany might be satisfied by concessions to legitimate demands, backed by an attempt to detach Italy from the German orbit by similar concessions, might offer the only remaining hope.[46] And if the rearmament appropriate to unilateral British action was out of the question, then British military preparations might best be regarded as existing for ultimate defence against direct German aggression, rather than as assets available for a collective deterrent. Chamberlain, who had been as alive as anyone to the potential conflict between the two lines of British policy, was prepared to accept the consequences of all this. If it had always been the case that undue emphasis on either deterrence or conciliation might prejudice the chances of peace or containment respectively, then a situation in which the possibility of effective deterrence was regarded as greatly reduced necessarily implied that public emphasis would have to be placed on the importance and possibility of conciliation. To the extent that this policy staked a great deal on the possibility of appeasement, it was supported by the consideration that emphasis on the deterrent side of the 'double line' would be likely to destroy foreign belief in the possibility of a settlement without providing in compensation anything more than a bluff which, if called, would enormously increase the likelihood of illegitimate expansion.

> Again and again Canning [laid down] that you should never menace unless you are in a position to carry out your threats.[47]

Tom Jones put one aspect of the issue crudely, but not entirely inaccurately:

> Eden himself thinks the Cabinet very weak and the armament programme far in arrears. On the other hand, he seems to agree that we can't do business with Germany until we are armed – say in 1940. This assumes we can catch up with Germany – which we cannot, and that Hitler takes no dramatic step in the meantime, which is unlike Hitler. We have spurned his repeated offers. They will not be kept open indefinitely. All this [Chamberlain] sees and says.[48]

This shift in emphasis was not necessarily inconsistent with a concern for rearmament. Rearmament necessarily remained less important to Chamberlain's policy than would have been the case if either the 'double line' policy had been continued unchanged, or the view that war was inevitable had been accepted. But the establishment of armaments adequate at least for defensive purposes would constitute something to fall back upon if appeasement failed. In practice, Chamberlain's belief that Britain's weakness in defence could only be repaired over a longer period than was (in the light of foreign developments) available, reinforced his search for a speedy settlement.

Chamberlain's appeasement also had other, and more positive, origins. He shared a general contemporary belief that a second world war could only arise from international misunderstandings. The horror of a second war would be such that no statesman could be imagined who would contemplate it as a means of pursuing his objectives. A war in which no-one's gain was predictable and in which loss by all seemed the more likely consequence would predispose all rational (and even occasionally rational) men to negotiation and compromise.[49] To this belief in the importance of removing misunderstandings by personal initiatives taken against a background of a common interest in the avoidance of world war was added another, also widely shared by his contemporaries. That a re-armed Germany under National Socialism was a danger to British interests was taken more for granted by Chamberlain than by many of his contemporaries; but appreciation of such danger should not, in his view, lead to the indiscriminate rejection of all German demands. The post-war sympathy for Germany's alleged ill-treatment at Versailles was not easily discarded by Chamberlain's generation, and a distinction was made between German actions in pursuit of legitimate grievances and those which might reasonably be regarded as presenting a threat to the European balance of power.[50] Admittedly, it might prove difficult to recognize the point at which consecutive actions of the former kind might imperceptibly and cumulatively produce a situation of the latter sort. But it was precisely on the question of German intentions that necessity, morality and the need for personal diplomacy were most obviously identified: scepticism about the existence of an effective deterrent combined with belief in the importance and effectiveness of personal initiatives to discover (and influence) German intentions. Finally, the abhorrence of war rendered it the moral duty of the politicians concerned to exhaust all possibilities of peaceful settlement before inflicting devastation upon a society of which they were the elected guardians.[51]

Chamberlain's faith in his ability to make a personal impact on international politics made him less fearful (although not less aware) of the dangers than some of his critics. Such uncertainties and inconsistencies as his policies possessed would, he believed, cause less difficulty under his own style of leadership than that of, say, Baldwin. It is thus impossible to consider Chamberlain's foreign policy in isolation from the politics which accompanied it: the success of the one was to be effected by the character of the other.

V The Politics of Appeasement

I can't do all the things that S.B. did, as well as the things he didn't do, and I consider that at present at any rate the latter are more important.[52]

Chamberlain's relations with the politicians and political institutions of his day were shaped by the importance which he attached to the pursuit of clear, bold policies. This emphasis was to some extent the expression of his character, but was also entailed by his perception of the needs of the contemporary world. He was a man of firmness, nerve and initiative, and he saw about him a country which could be rallied in support of such qualities:

It was so long since our people had heard a real fighting speech that they went delirious with joy and I don't remember hearing the cheering so prolonged as it was when I sat down. The Chief Whip says he has never known such enthusiasm over the lead the Party is getting and of course that is not surprising when you remember that for fourteen years they have had only S.B. and Ramsay.[53]

What so often appeared as mere intolerance of opposition and a dangerous willingness to act outside orthodox channels was not a simple expression of personal arrogance. The policies pursued by Chamberlain were no less persuasive and well grounded than those of his opponents. His impatience was reserved for those (such as members of the Liberal and Labour parties) whose attitudes he saw as irrelevant or inconsistent, and (more important) for those whom he regarded as fertile in their reservations about his policies but bereft of an equally clear and positive alternative of their own. The latter critics and doubters were often to be found among his own party colleagues.[54] To Chamberlain, most of these were anxious to prolong a confused and diverse debate which had already continued dangerously long, and from which unanimous agreement was unlikely to emerge. Taking such criticisms or reservations too seriously would have the same effect as giving undue emphasis to the deterrent side of the 'double line': it would destroy his policy without offering any more hopeful alternative than a return to the Baldwinian years of uncertainty and drift.

The policy of putting an end to the previous debate on foreign policy, by choosing one of the various alternative courses and refusing to be deflected by the reservations of his critics, had implications of which Chamberlain was fully aware:

> Hacking, the party chairman, told me that he had never known the party so united, but on the other hand he thought my outspokenness and precision had probably frightened the rather weak-kneed Liberals who felt safe with S.B. I expect that is true ... but it was inevitable. I can't change my nature and I must hope to make up for Liberal defections by greater enthusiasm in our own party.[55]

He ran the risk of alienating the support of colleagues such as Eden, who possessed both political stature and a sympathetic awareness of his difficulties; and it rendered impossible (and indeed, irrelevant) the Baldwinian strategy of leaving open the possibility of future collaboration and agreement between the National government and the Liberal and Labour elements in opposition.[56]

On the other hand, Chamberlain's assumption of the firm base which could be constructed for his political leadership was by no means unfounded. His clarity of mind and his willingness to take firm decisions in confused circumstances were qualities long recognized by many of his contemporaries. His accession was initially welcomed by many of those (including Eden)[57] who shared his impatience with the Baldwinian style of politics. Within the Conservative party, respect, admiration and support for his leadership were undoubted, and he possessed the almost unreserved allegiance of such senior Cabinet figures as Hoare, Simon and Halifax, all of whom were at one time or another intimately concerned with foreign affairs.

The Consequences of Leadership. That Chamberlain's political strategy might have divisive consequences was recognized by many of those most sympathetic to him. His refusal to be diverted from his course by the reservations of others drove some of his colleagues to the choice between unconditional support and an open breach. The risk of alienating the 'moderates' or 'centre' within the Cabinet was real; his occasionally undisguised impatience with those who seemed willing to query but afraid to decide might easily undermine the internal harmony of his government:

> When Chamberlain became Prime Minister he seemed at once to crystallize all the fluid forces in the Cabinet. His clear-cut mind and concrete outlook had a stringent effect upon opinions and preferences that had hitherto been only sentiments and impressions. As soon as he succeeded Baldwin, I became increasingly conscious of two distinct points of view in the Cabinet. For the time being, the general relief at the advent of a very efficient and vigorous Prime Minister preserved its outward unity.[58]

Chamberlain's manner of conducting foreign policy in Cabinet was not dictatorial,[59] but circumstances conspired to give some less senior ministers the impression of being helpless spectators of disturbing events.[60] Early reliance upon the Foreign Policy Committee of the Cabinet later gave way, under pressure of events, to reliance upon an inner Cabinet of Simon, Hoare, Halifax and Chamberlain, and ultimately, during the 'Munich period', to almost exclusive attention on Chamberlain himself. Unlike Baldwin, Chamberlain as Prime Minister was unshielded from his critics.[61] His willingness to commit himself personally and unreservedly to the policy of appeasement inevitably gave rise to an over-simplified identification of the Prime Minister with the major issues of the day. In Cabinet and Parliament he constantly rejected the arbitrational role which had been an important source of Baldwin's relative anonymity and immunity from attack. The replacement of Eden by Halifax as Foreign Secretary in February 1938 meant that on the most sensitive aspect of policy the government's spokesman was in the House of Lords. Chamberlain was thus obliged (and was the reverse of unwilling) to bear the major burden of parliamentary defence.[62] In diplomatic fields, his readiness to use unorthodox procedures and amateur emissaries provoked accusations of incompetence and interference with professional traditions. Chamberlain's relations with the opposition parties were characterized by continual and mutual hostility. Baldwin's earlier willingness to respect the feelings and dignity of his opponents was replaced by a fierce parliamentary debating style with which the logic, responsibility, and intelligence of opposing members were mercilessly attacked.

It is somewhat surprising, in view of Chamberlain's present low reputation, that the divisive consequences of his political manner have not been more widely exploited: attention has been concentrated upon the alleged misjudgements in his policies rather than upon the consequences of his politics. It would be easy to build a superficially plausible explanation of Chamberlain's alleged failure upon an examination of his political methods, representing him as a man ultimately responsible for his own downfall. Having alienated a significant section of his own party and the entire official opposition, he might be seen as inevitably lacking the support necessary to continue when the policy with which he over-identified himself failed in its avowed object of averting war. It cannot be doubted that Chamberlain's fate was settled by some of these considerations. But to rest content with an appreciation of his politics as the inevitable harbinger of failure is to miss the complexity, the self-awareness, and the political judgement which lay behind it and which gave it a (frequently underrated) coherence and effectiveness. Chamberlain's failure to reconcile in a Baldwinian manner either his official opponents or his discontented colleagues was less real, less important, less avoidable, and less the result of political incompetence than might be supposed.

Complaints by ministers who feel strongly about alleged lack of consultation have occurred under all Prime Ministers (including Baldwin) and were in Chamberlain's case as much the result of the pressure of events as of an intention to exclude. Moreover, Chamberlain's perception of his political world was such as to instil in him a scepticism about the effectiveness of the 'Baldwinian style'. The creation of political harmony through reconciliation would take time, and the urgency of contemporary circumstances deprived a political leader of the necessary span.[63] Even in more 'normal' circumstances, more relaxed methods of leadership had not always brought success. Both Balfour and, on occasion, Baldwin had earlier taken the road to reconciliation to the ultimate end of uniting almost their whole party against them in a demand for firm leadership. To Chamberlain, certainty might often be welcomed even by those against whose views it was directed. Finally, agreement might only be purchased at the cost of adopting erroneous causes; Churchill had not been alone in criticizing Baldwin's willingness to postpone what he thought to be right out of respect to the sensitivities of democracy.

In a tactical sense, Chamberlain was by no means convinced that, in so far as unanimity was possible and desirable, the methods of tolerance and compromise were necessarily the best way to achieve it. His (and Churchill's) frequently expressed impatience with Baldwinian methods sprang not from any indifference to democratic values but from a different view of the relationship between government and people. Baldwin was seen[64] as having taken the opinions of others as relatively fixed, and as incapable of change by the exercise of firm leadership. The lessons of events, rather than the exercise of political initiative, were what changed the minds of men. Such a view entailed the politics of good timing: statesmanship was the art of formally registering the marriage of events and public opinion. Chamberlain was neither as optimistic about the ability of men to learn from experience nor as pessimistic about the possibility of political leadership. He deplored the tendency to think, 'not, "is this right?", but "how would this affect the House of Commons or my constituents?" My method is to try and make up my own mind first as to the proper course, and then try and put others through the same course of reasoning.'[65] The world of politics was there to be changed by the efforts of those who had the necessary courage; to act as a 'broker' between the opinions of others was a dereliction of moral duty. To convince others, by action and argument, of the merits of one's own policies was, to Chamberlain, a sign of responsible statesmanship rather than of dictatorial methods. Democratic politics involved the removal of those who failed to convince, but it did not entail the suppression of honest and reasoned conviction.

Those who pointed to the dangers consequent upon such firm leadership (the possibility of being in error, the risk of public division) received the reply that any sort of political leadership (especially in the circumstances of the 1930s) involved risk-taking.[66] In this respect, Chamberlain recognized what many of his critics did not: that the only way to avoid risks and responsibilities was to stay out of politics altogether. The life of the statesman was not for those whose appreciation of the necessity to choose and of the risk of failure reduced them either to impotence or to keepers of the nation's conscience. Gilbert Murray's view that, in contrast to Chamberlain,

> Lord Baldwin once admitted frankly that events in Abyssinia were to him 'a bitter humiliation', and that one phrase took the sting out of opposition criticism. His sympathies were on the right side, and that made all the difference

stung Chamberlain to observe that

> It is that sort of spirit that makes me hate and despise the 'Liberals'. ... I suppose Gilbert Murray's ideal is Archie Sinclair who abounds in 'uplift' and drivels of his devotion to high moral standards. ... Archie infuriates me with his hypocritical cant.[67]

The Prime Minister, more than any other politician, was responsible for the political fate of the nation.[68] It was consistent with this view to distinguish, as Chamberlain did, between those of his opponents (such as Churchill) who were deemed to possess the necessary nerve, and those who were scorned as mere boys among political men.

Personality in politics. Chamberlain, then, consciously embarked upon a hazardous course in a situation and in a profession where no other sort of enterprise was seen to be possible. The foreign policy involved was a product of informed judgement, and it was inseparable from Chamberlain's political manner: to say that Chamberlain was arrogant is to generalize about a character whose complexity defies such glib assertions. A politician's personal defects are related to his public activities in a manner at once indirect and subtle. The character of public men is always created and artificial to a degree which renders the moral judgements of everyday life more difficult to apply; the judgement of politicians involves the judgement of a public performance rather than a private morality. Politics is not an activity characterized by the humility of its practitioners, and Chamberlain's public self-confidence was not, in the context of his times, ill founded. That he was ignorant of foreign affairs is simply untrue: his foreign policy was founded upon a view of the international scene no less informed and perceptive than that of most of his contemporaries. His knowledge of the internal politics and dispositions of the states with which he had to deal (especially those of France and the USA) was such as to insulate him from the wishful thinking often identifiable in critics such as Eden and Churchill: Chamberlain's parochialism is a fabrication of the uninformed. To the extent that criticisms of his judgement in international affairs rest upon the invocation of some abstract ideal of statesmanship they are irrelevant; in so far as they rest upon relative comparisons with his contemporaries they are unconvincing. The cabinet from which he drew such firm support included at least three ministers (Simon, Hoare and Halifax) whose familiarity with such matters is unquestionable, and opposition from diplomatic professionals was neither unanimous nor peculiar to Chamberlain's prime ministership. Few elected politicians (including Eden) have escaped allegations of incompetence and interference from their professional advisers. Those professionals (such as Vansittart) who have been taken as representative of professional feelings were sceptical of politicians in general rather than of Chamberlain in particular; in Vansittart's case Chamberlain's impatience was widely shared by his contemporaries. Criticisms of Chamberlain emanating from such sources can be offset by the admiration and respect of men like Cadogan, whose professionalism and knowledge are presumably to be taken for granted. There was no resentment of Chamberlain and his policies by 'the professionals': the professionals lacked both the collective agreement and the certainty necessary to sustain such a generalization.[69]

On the other hand, Chamberlain's willingness to supplement and circumvent the orthodox procedures of British diplomacy was particularly marked. This emphasis on personal initiatives[70] (of which the Munich negotiations were the culmination) arose in part from a perception of the circumstances which was not peculiar to Chamberlain: his individuality lay rather in a greater willingness to surrender to temptations which predecessors such as Baldwin had experienced equally strongly.[71] Diplomacy by personal initiative was a tendency visible in a post-war world in which suspicion of the procedures and personnel of pre-war diplomacy was widespread, and in which a democratically accountable foreign policy was often regarded as a primary aim.[72] Such views were especially prevalent on the British left, and formed the background to personal initiatives such as those of MacDonald in the 1920s. Chamberlain and Baldwin were more impressed by the nature of the circumstances than by considerations of democratic accountability and suspicions of the 'old diplomacy'. The emergence of the dictators represented a degree of personal rule which served to render traditional diplomatic channels less effective; in so far as a knowledge of Hitler's intentions was vital to British policy, diplomacy by personal confrontation seemed implicit in the situation. Chamberlain was more willing to undertake and less keenly aware of the dangers in such a course than had been the case with Baldwin, but self-confidence in the superior nature of his own abilities was not the only consideration. His willingness to challenge the views and procedures of many of his professional advisers was never carried over into his dealings with the military, for whose strategic advice he sometimes showed an exaggerated respect. Chamberlain's personal diplomacy owed more to his view of the implications of dictatorial rule than to an unwillingness to admit the existence of professional diplomatic expertise.[73]

A final consideration is the extent to which Chamberlain's willingness to take burdens upon himself was a reflection upon the competence of many of his colleagues. Here again, to dwell upon his personal arrogance is an insufficient explanation. Chamberlain's view that the office of Prime Minister itself entailed certain inescapable obligations has already been noted, and in his case there were a number of additional, circumstantial factors to be considered. He saw himself as the most articulate and forceful public defender of a policy which was firmly supported by the bulk of his parliamentary supporters and his Cabinet. In so far as his emphasis on the need for leadership emerged from a belief that political talent was thin upon the ground,[74] such a belief had been shared by MacDonald and Baldwin, and his confidence in his own abilities was widely shared by his contemporaries. Arrogance was certainly present, but it was based on a view of his abilities and of his circumstances not peculiar to himself. It was precisely the reality of, and the wide recognition accorded to, these abilities and circumstances that enabled Chamberlain (like MacDonald before him) to avoid the absurdity and pathos which are the dividends of mere private arrogance. Contempt and ridicule for Chamberlain and MacDonald were more likely to be indulged in by the mediocrities among their contemporaries and by the unhistorical moralizers of future generations than by the statesmen of their own times. From the latter, both men received admiration, respect, opposition or hostility: responses more appropriate to men of political substance than those of mere ridicule or indifference.

The management of opposition. Chamberlain's pursuit of appeasement incorporated a politics based upon the assumption that there existed, actually or potentially, widespread support for his kind of leadership and politics. In addition, Chamberlain saw his opponents as falling within three broad categories. First, there were those of his colleagues who combined a willingness to criticize with an inability to suggest effective alternatives (a description which embraced such Ministers as Stanley, Elliot, and De La Warr).[75] Second, there were opponents of character and nerve who commanded his respect despite their alleged errors or their unacceptable desire to prolong the debate about foreign policy. Churchill was perhaps the most constant member of this category,[76] although Eden was extended intermittent membership.[77] Finally, there were those whose motives, intelligence, knowledge and judgement were such as to deserve no serious consideration. The Labour and Liberal opposition parties were generally regarded in this light,[78] although the attitudes of Conservative backbenchers such as Ronald Cartland often provoked Chamberlain to visit them with a similar contempt.[79] Chamberlain responded to these various opponents and critics in a manner quite different from the conciliation, tolerance and respect so characteristic of Baldwin. He was aware that his temperament was such as to render the Baldwinian style impossible and he believed that in any case his abilities were both more effective and more appropriate to the circumstances.[80]

The National government supporters were to be the basis of Chamberlain's politics. Both those who understood and wholeheartedly supported appeasement, and those who might waver, were alike to be retained in the ranks and driven along by the Prime Minister's continual, articulate and vigorous defence of policy in parliament and the country. He revelled in 'those occasions when a leader, if he captures the right mood, rouses his followers to fresh enthusiasm and excites them to renew personal loyalty.'[81] Chamberlain had a rationalist's belief in the ultimate triumph of articulate and informed public argument, and a partisan's belief in the importance of continually defeating the arguments of his opponents as a means of maintaining ministerial solidarity. The weight of Chamberlain's reasoning and moral passion were to be brought to bear against opposition parties whose views were, for the most part, to be treated as no more than convenient Aunt Sallies. The element of malice towards opponents which often accompanied his strategy was calculated, but consistent also with a temperamental moral passion and partisanship which was increasingly fed by the impact of momentous events upon a man well past the prime of youth.[82] His willingness to bear the brunt of the defence of appeasement in the Commons and in the country was reinforced by the absence of colleagues of comparable stature. Neither Horace Wilson in Whitehall nor Halifax at Westminster could do for Chamberlain what Chamberlain had done for Baldwin in this respect:

> While S.B. was Prime Minister he had me to help him, but I have no-one who stands to me in the same relation, and consequently I bear my troubles alone.[83]

The prime-ministerial leadership which Chamberlain provided both arose from and was continually reinforced by this belief.

Such a strategy of positive leadership discounted in advance the possibility of cooperation with the opposition parties, and it concentrated responsibility upon the Prime Minister to a dangerous extent. It was a conscious alternative to Baldwin's policy of maintaining public unity and ministerial support by conciliation, gradualism and caution. To Chamberlain, the bases of this latter policy were either unconvincing or irrelevant. Both Baldwin and Eden based their maxim of respect for the Opposition partly on the view that it was essential to avoid partisan divisions which might prove dangerous in circumstances where war was unavoidable:

> I remember that Chamberlain once complained to me ... [that] ... I was not sharp enough with the Opposition. 'Why don't you go for them more ...?' he said, 'their position is utterly illogical.' ... I said that I agreed with the criticism, but ... I always had it in mind that one day I might have to go down to the House of Commons and tell the nation that it was at war.[84]

Chamberlain could counter this maxim with alternative considerations. The hostility of his Labour and Liberal opponents was established before he became Prime Minister, mainly as a result of his actions and speeches at the Ministry of Health and at the Exchequer, and was probably impossible to overcome. Chamberlain recalled an occasion as early as 1927 on which Baldwin had warned him about his parliamentary manner:

> I always gave him the impression, he said, when I spoke in the House of Commons that I looked on the Labour party as dirt.[85]

Efforts to overcome such hostility would entail a conciliatory politics in which the avoidance of acrimonious divisions could only be purchased (if at all) at the price of preventing a wholehearted pursuit of policies whose soundness was (to Chamberlain and to many others) undeniable, and support for which was widespread. Finally, Chamberlain was unconvinced by the consideration of unity for war. He did not share Eden's (and, possibly, the later Baldwin's) ultimate scepticism about the possibility of averting war. He believed, also, that unanimous public support for British engagement in war would be more likely when every possible effort had been made to avert it, than when allegations of missed opportunities for peace could plausibly be made.[86] The policy of averting war through appeasement entailed both a conscious refusal to pursue simultaneous and inconsistent policies of deterrence, and a determination to avoid a situation in which the normal confusions and uncertainties of democratic politics might lead to foreign misunderstandings about the policies to which Britain was committed. Chamberlain, staking almost everything on the possibility of averting war, was neither swayed by arguments addressed to a future wartime situation nor impressed by the likelihood of domestic divisions should his policy fail and war occur. The policy was admittedly hazardous, but it was seen to involve no greater element of risk than any other combination of actions, and to be based on a more realistic appreciation of British limitations than any of the proffered alternatives.

The view that the avoidance of war through appeasement was the only realistic policy was supported by Chamberlain's intensely held belief that a statesman had a moral obligation to engage in war only when all other reasonable alternatives had failed. He shared with many of his contemporaries an overwhelming horror of war, and was continually conscious of the burden of responsibility borne by those whose actions might lead to an armed conflict in comparison with which, he believed, the First World War would appear almost civilized. Awareness of his almost Gladstonian attitude to war led him to discount further the warnings of those who were alarmed by the personal consequences which failure might bring:

> I would like to have longer to see my policy through, and I believe that, if I am allowed, I can steer this country through the next few years out of the war zone and into peace and reconstruction. But an interruption would be fatal, and I should have then to leave it to someone else to try some quite different line.[87]

War would represent the failure of policies with which Chamberlain was inextricably identified, and his position might become untenable; but since he would probably not remain Prime Minister in such circumstances, the consideration was irrelevant.[88]

Many of the doubts about Chamberlain's political skills involve a misunderstanding of his priorities. His refusal to include in his government critics such as Churchill and (later) Eden, and his reluctance to disturb the procedures and practices of peacetime finance and administration by a radical reconstruction of the machinery of government, did not stem from petty revenge or thoughtless conservatism. Such changes were rejected because they would compromise a policy of appeasement whose only hope of success lay in a determined pursuit undistracted by rival and incompatible considerations. He shared Baldwin's earlier recognition that in circumstances where war seemed unavoidable, Churchill's presence would be both inevitable and desirable. But in advance of such circumstances, toleration of or compromise with his opponents could only involve either support for alternative policies offering no greater hope of success, or (and more probably) a continuation of the previous confusion and inconsistency which would be the worst of all possible worlds:

> [I am urged] to abandon my policy and adopt Winston's!
> Fortunately my nature is as L[loyd] G[eorge] says extremely

'obstinate' and I refuse to change. But if anything happened to me I can plainly see my successor would soon be off the rails and we should once more be charged with that vacillation which in the past has made other diplomats despair.[89]

He was aware that he had made a choice, and fear that the choice had been misguided hauntingly accompanied the consideration that even a wise choice might yet fail in its object.[90] Like MacDonald before him, he was for the most part successful in preventing such fears from undermining his resolution; but he came to share with MacDonald a belief that he was engaged in an enterprise whose ultimate end might be the sacrifice of his reputation on the altar of the public interest.[91] In such a politics, the line between nobility of conduct and the absurdity of self-delusion is too thin and too subtle to afford protection to posthumous reputation.

Chamberlain's strategy of creating and maintaining support among brave and timid alike by a vigorous refusal to compromise was not an obvious failure. From the point of view of overcoming the reservations of his colleagues and supporters, his role of Bonar Law to Baldwin's Balfour was a success. Few of the members of his Cabinet experienced Chamberlain's prime ministership without at one time or another undergoing doubt about his methods or his policies, yet only Cooper and Eden resigned in overt opposition to either. In the Commons, his overt Conservative critics never numbered (by their own account) more than forty,[92] and not until May 1940 were these restless groups prepared to offer public opposition of a more than individual or token kind. The reluctance of both Eden and Churchill actively to oppose the National government, or to cooperate with the Labour party,[93] clearly owed more to the concern for Conservative unity of the one and the desire for office of the other,[94] than to any conversion to Chamberlain's point of view. Yet the numerical weakness of such critics and the fear for party unity are in themselves eloquent witnesses to Chamberlain's success in retaining the loyalty of the great bulk of his parliamentary followers. Many of those Conservatives (Quintin Hogg and Richard Law, for example) who voted against the government in the Norwegian debate did so only after a prolonged and often agonizing struggle with their loyalty to and admiration for the Prime Minister:

> God bless you in your present trouble. Your country is and always will be grateful for your devoted service and your splendid courage ... whatever happens, you can be sure that you *have* your friends even amongst those who did not vote with you.[95]

Even in the case of the opposition parties, the adverse effects of Chamberlain's strategy can be exaggerated. The refusal of the Labour leaders to join Chamberlain's government after the outbreak of war was not entirely due to their admittedly implacable personal hostility, or to belief in his political weakness: fears of the likely reactions of the 'wild men' on the Labour back benches played some part.[96] Even by the time of the Norwegian debate, the Labour leaders were sufficiently uncertain of Chamberlain's ultimate parliamentary weakness as to move the division of the House only after the debate had begun. After his resignation as Prime Minister, Chamberlain remained an important member of the Cabinet and Leader of the Conservative party: Churchill's recognition of his qualities and of the extent to which he retained the loyalty of a large number of National government supporters in the Commons was clearly and frequently expressed.[97]

The Labour party and the forces it represented ultimately played a more important part in Chamberlain's fate than did his Conservative critics. Chamberlain lacked Baldwin's instinctive understanding of the Labour leaders' difficulties, and was both unwilling and unable to continue Baldwin's habit of protecting the Labour front bench against their own left-wing colleagues. He was unable to disguise his contempt for official Labour criticisms of a foreign policy whose alleged weaknesses he saw as the consequence of Labour's earlier and continuing refusal to support more effective and desirable alternatives. If Chamberlain failed to sense the internal difficulties of the Labour leaders, the apparent ignorance of the latter about the delicacy of foreign policy in a democratic polity was keenly felt by Chamberlain in return.[98] He expected his critics to realize that public statements about diplomatic affairs were couched with a foreign, as well as a domestic audience in mind. In so far as there was thus an inevitable gap between public statement and private intention, responsible opposition involved both an appreciation of this fact and a trust in the good intentions of those in office. Chamberlain was unshakable in his belief that Labour lacked the appreciation, and they for their part were unwilling to extend the trust. Chamberlain's indifference to the possibility of cooperation with his Labour and Liberal opponents stemmed in part from the logic of his foreign policy. He was aware that the cooperation of the Labour party and the trade unions would be essential to any radical change in the structure of the peacetime economy, and to any successful prosecution of war. He was sceptical (and continually confirmed in his scepticism) about the possibility of any leader's securing such cooperation unless the danger of war was overwhelming. And since his policy placed a secondary emphasis only upon domestic reconstruction, the role of labour remained for him an hypothetical and relatively unimportant question:

> I am not prepared for the sake of what must be a sham unity, to take as partners men who would sooner or later wreck the policy with which I am identified.[99]

If war came, the necessary cooperation would emerge either from a recognition of common peril or, should personal animosities prove too great, from his own removal. In either case, the political strategy of appeasement in the pre-war situation could consistently relegate its Labour and Liberal opponents to a position as little more than the anvil on which National government solidarity was to be forged under Chamberlain's hammer.

Chamberlain's substitution of the strategy of rallying his colleagues and followers for the Baldwinian emphasis of the placation of opponents extended to the electoral arena. His thoughts upon the election (which, in the event, he was never called upon to hold) were characteristically bold. He assumed that any election fought under his prime ministership would turn upon his policies and upon his politics,[100] and he proposed to defend them in his usual uncompromising and vigorous manner. In elections, no less than in parliament, the prizes would go to leaders whose personal impact, moral passion and intellectual capacity were superior. Yet Chamberlain was a genuine parliament man.[101] It was in the Commons rather than in the country that he preferred to fight his battles, and a degree of disunity which might be tolerable in the House was, to him, inappropriate among the voters. In part, this view rested upon his conception of the public as a passive element in politics. Nothing, ultimately, could be done against their overt opposition, but everything, initially, depended upon the politicians who were responsible for their welfare. The people could be rallied or they could remain unmoved, but in either event it was no business of the parliamentary politician to abdicate his responsibility and judgement to them.[102]

VI Munich[104]

In my view the strongest force of all ... was that unmistakable sense of unaminity among the peoples of the world that war somehow must be averted. ... Ever since I assumed my present office my main purpose has been to work for the pacification of Europe, for the removal of those suspicions and those animosities which have for so long poisoned the air.

The path which leads to appeasement is long and bristles with obstacles. The question of Czechoslovakia is the latest and perhaps the most dangerous. Now that we have got past it, I feel that it may be possible to make further progress along the road to sanity. ...

Let no one think that because we have signed this agreement ... at Munich we can afford to relax our efforts in regard to [rearmament]. ... While we must renew our determination to fill up the deficiencies that yet remain in our armaments and in our defence precautions, so that we may be ready to defend ourselves and make our diplomacy effective – [interruption] – yes, I am a realist – nevertheless I say with an equal sense of reality that I do see fresh opportunities of approaching the subject opening up before us. ... It is to such tasks, the winning back of confidence, the gradual removal of hostility between nations ... that I would wish to devote what energy and time may be left to me before I hand over my office to younger men.[105]

The Munich agreement is central to Chamberlain's political

reputation: to the moralist, it is proof positive of his ignorance and error, while to the historian it is a concentrated source from which to draw a deeper understanding of his dilemmas.

Hitler's claim to the Sudeten or 'German' areas of Czechoslovakia was one event in a series which had begun with the Japanese invasion of Manchuria in 1931, and which continued through the Abyssinian crisis, the occupation of the Rhineland, and the invasion of Austria. Every incident in this series had presented problems for Britain, since on each occasion there were both compelling reasons for avoiding too firm a response, and factors which made it impossible for Britain to appear indifferent. Considerations of limited liability, military weakness and the legitimate grievances of the aggressor state mingled with unease in the face of overt contempt for diplomatic procedures and apprehension about the cumulative implications of such incidents. As Prime Minister, Chamberlain attempted to establish a European settlement by the appeasement of legitimate German demands through duly negotiated agreements. The Czech question was thus seen as a crucial test of British foreign policy. Chamberlain saw no reason to change his existing policy of acting on the assumption that a negotiated settlement could be reached: every consideration pointed in the direction of avoiding a rigid or bellicose response to the German position. All of the factors which had earlier convinced him of the difficulties of pursuing the policy of the 'double line' were present in a stronger form at Munich. Military advice reinforced his own belief that the state of British armaments ruled out the possibility of effective intervention in Europe; France was clearly unwilling (and probably unable) to adopt a firm position, and Russian military assistance for Czechoslovakia would be impossible in view of the attitude of Rumania and Poland to Russian intervention, even if one believed (as Chamberlain did not) in the realiability or sincerity of Russian offers of assistance. The Dominions would not be willing to participate in a policy of firmness, and fears that the Japanese would take advantage of British involvement in Europe remained. Finally, an established reluctance to undertake commitments in Eastern Europe was combined with the assumption that domestic public support would not be extended to any British actions which appeared to be defending Czechoslovakia at the expense of Britain's own security. For all these reasons, Chamberlain's presence at Munich was, in part, a continuation of the role of international mediator in which the British had cast themselves since 1918. On the other hand, although these considerations led Chamberlain to reject in advance the possibility of adopting a bellicose position, his actions at Munich cannot be accurately represented as the mere consequences of a negative recognition of weakness: Munich had, for him, a more positive significance. Britain's concern with German demands on Czechoslovakia stemmed from an interest in the possibility of a general European settlement and, more specifically, from a recognition that if the French blundered (or were forced) into war as a result of their treaty obligations to Czechoslovakia, then Britain might not be able to avoid involvement. It was in this sense that Britain, at Munich, combined the roles of referee and player.

Some (Hore-Belisha, for example) took the view that, since Britain had no Eastern European interests, it might be preferable to jettison the role of mediator and avoid any British involvement in the Czech question: that in the East European game the appropriate role for Britain was that of a spectator. Chamberlain was unable to accept this view. At the very least, British interests were at stake from the standpoint of the actions of the French. In addition, British indifference might encourage Hitler to further expansion. Finally, and perhaps most important of all, the Czech question could be regarded as an opportunity to investigate German intentions, and even as an occasion on which to establish a general European settlement. The latter consideration – the pursuit of the policy of appeasement – was alone quite incompatible with a merely passive British attitude. German interest in the Sudetenland was not in itself illegitimate according to the established criteria of appeasement. Hitler's incitement of Germans in Czechoslovakia could not be regarded as clear evidence of an absence of spontaneous national feeling among the latter, and after Versailles no British statesman could easily deny the force of the principle of national self-determination. Much depended on the nature of Germany's aims: the approach to the Munich negotiations and the possibility of optimism about a successful outcome hinged, ultimately, upon judgements of Hitler. German claims on Czechoslovakia could be represented as legitimate only if taken in isolation and at their face value. If in fact they formed part of a general plan for German expansion then both British tactics and optimism about a general settlement might have to be reconsidered: although even then Chamberlain could not drastically have changed his approach. Considerations of military weakness and doubts about the directness of British interests in Eastern Europe would still have counselled a relatively cautious approach.

Chamberlain's ultimate optimism during and immediately after the Munich negotiations stemmed from his belief that the die had not been finally cast. There was room for doubt about German intentions, and (equally important) there was a possibility of affecting these intentions by personal contact. At the very least, the Munich agreement could be regarded as having cleared the air. For the first time, Hitler had been induced formally to state the limits of his territorial demands in Europe: one way or the other, his actions after the Munich agreement would help to settle the question of Germany's ultimate aims. In short, Chamberlain saw no advance indications that a general settlement was impossible, and believed that the fate of the Munich agreement would at the very least settle the course of British policy in the future.

Munich and domestic politics. British criticism of the Munich agreement was muted in comparison with the relieved reaction of the majority of politicians. What is of more interest is the fact that many of Chamberlain's critics shared his assumptions about the considerations relevant to the Czech question. The opposition to Chamberlain and to the Munich agreement was thus a more complex and subtle matter than is often supposed. With the possible exception of some members of the Liberal and Labour parties, his critics agreed with Chamberlain's assumptions that the defence of Czech sovereignty could not in itself constitute a ground for British involvement in war, and that action to defend Czechoslovakia would inevitably have escalated into (at the very least) a general European war. The defence of Czechoslovakia was not, for most politicians, the point at issue. Further, only Duff Cooper can plausibly be represented as having recommended, at the time, that Britain should have been willing to engage in such a war.[106] The Munich agreement was accepted by most of the critics as a regrettable necessity. Criticisms of Munich, for the most part, reflected an uneasiness about the wisdom of Chamberlain's handling of Hitler, and a corresponding fear that Chamberlain's future actions would be equally misguided.[107] Some critics considered that Germany was demonstrably bent upon European domination. The Government was urged by such critics to institute immediately a policy of accelerated rearmament and a search for allies, either in preparation for an inevitable war or to provide the means for bold policy of deterrence. Others, such as Churchill, appeared to believe that at Munich the mere threat of firmness would have been sufficient either to preserve Czech sovereignty or at least to deter Hitler from the general domination which he would otherwise inevitably pursue. This latter view was compatible with the criticism that Chamberlain's handling of the Munich negotiations had made war and/or German expansion more and not less likely, by giving Hitler the impression that Britain was prepared to concede any German demands provided that the necessary minimal formalities were undertaken. Nearly all of the critics were agreed that the only lesson to be drawn from Munich was that appeasement must be reversed, and that a policy of alliances and rearmament should thus replace the previous emphasis on the possibility of negotiated settlements.[108]

Chamberlain failed, both during and after the Munich negotiations, to reassure his critics about his present and future actions. The cause of this failure lay partly in Chamberlain's refusal to accept in their entirety his critic's conclusions about Munich, a refusal which was in turn related to his uncertainty about the best course to pursue. While convinced that to act on the assumption of the possibility of a peaceful settlement both of the Czech question and of Europe in general was the only course open to Britain, his public optimism concealed serious private doubts about Germany's aims. When the *Sunday Times* described him as 'a man at peace with himself', Chamberlain commented:

I was glad I was successful in giving that impression, which is what I try to do. But it hardly represents my real frame of mind, for I confess that I do sometimes feel terribly discouraged. I am continually getting reports that 'Hitler is still most anxious for friendship with England ...' but how can you reconcile that with

the daily poisoning of the wells by Hitler's propaganda department?[109]

At the time of Munich, Chamberlain's awareness of the still
unsettled state of Europe led him eagerly to welcome what might
well be the last chance to clarify this fundamental question. As he
explained to George VI:

> On the one hand, reports are daily received in great numbers, not
> only from official sources, but also from all manner of individuals
> who claim to have special and unchallengeable sources of
> information. Many of these (and of such authority as to make it
> impossible to dismiss them as unworthy of attention) declare
> positively that Herr Hitler has made up his mind to attack
> Czechoslovakia and then proceed further east.
>
> On the other hand, your Majesty's representative in Berlin has
> clearly maintained that Herr Hitler has not yet made up his mind to
> violence.
>
> In these circumstances, I have been considering the possibility of a
> sudden dramatic step which might change the whole situation.[110]

Far from exaggerating Hitler's rationality Chamberlain shared the
view of many of his contemporaries that Hitler was near to lunacy;[111]
the Munich meeting was partly designed to test this impression. In so
far as the element of irrationality was confirmed, personal contact with
Hitler might create the sort of atmosphere in which common sense
might prevail, and in which Hitler's intentions might be discovered
and influenced. In so far as Chamberlain at Munich came near to
casting himself in the role of psychiatrist, everything depended upon
the extent to which, without the assistance of professional diplomats,
his nerve and the clarity of his appreciation of the situation could
survive the distractions and the drama of such crucial negotiations.
The strains imposed by such a situation and by Chamberlain's private
uncertainties sometimes overcame his normal clarity and persistence.
Lord Templewood wrote perceptively of the difficulties involved:

> Like [Chamberlain] and, I imagine, my Cabinet colleagues, I had
> been caught up in the toils of a critical negotiation. The longer it
> went on, and the more serious the issue became, the more anxious I

grew to see it succeed. This is almost always the course of negotiations. As they proceed the parties concerned in them become increasingly obsessed with the need to prevent their final failure. If they are to continue, it is necessary to make concessions, and one concession almost inevitably leads to another. ... Throughout the Munich discussions, I often asked myself whether the slide into surrender had not started.[112]

Much of Chamberlain's earlier policy had depended on his ultimate ability to make a significant and sure-footed impact on such personal negotiations. But the extent to which, in the course of the Munich meetings, such balance was almost impossible to maintain is indicated by the extent to which the earlier policy of the 'double line' was intermittently and unconsciously revived. Uncertainty made him vulnerable to the promptings of Halifax, in particular,[113] and his determination to avoid the threat of force occasionally wavered. His belief that reason alone (in the appropriate setting) would dictate to Hitler that Britain could not be indifferent either to forcible and arbitrary absorption of the Sudetenland or to a general German intention to dominate Europe was overwhelmed, on occasion, by a need to supplement reason with firmness. Chamberlain believed that a firm British attitude had in fact averted a German advance into Czechoslovakia in May,[114] a belief not easily assimilated to his Munich fears that a firmer attitude could only have been a horrifyingly dangerous bluff, and might (given Hitler's temperament) have made a German resort to force more likely.[115] His defence of Munich was neither totally optimistic nor a surrender to pessimism. His emphasis on the need for rearmament revealed his recognition of the possibility that the Munich agreement might fail,[116] while his refusal to go to the lengths of the administrative, economic and defensive reconstructions demanded by his critics reflects his belief that it might yet succeed. Sir Henry Page Croft recorded a conversation with Chamberlain in the period after Munich, in which Chamberlain stated that 'Hitler's words rang absolutely sincerely, never from anyone have I had assurances so emphatic.' On the other hand, rearmament was necessitated by the fact that Hitler was 'a man of intense cruelty and I was obsessed with the fact that if in a year or two he changed his mind he would be so ruthless that he would stop at nothing.'[117]

Chamberlain's policy changed after Hitler's breach of the Munich agreement, but in a way which failed to satisfy his critics. He was convinced by then of the existence of a German plan for general expansion, but wavered between three alternative courses. War might now be inevitable, in which case every effort for preparation should be made. Alternatively, it might still be possible to negotiate a settlement, although any such negotiations would now overtly include the threat of force. Finally, the threat of force might be invoked in response to future German actions without any accompanying offer to negotiations. On balance, Chamberlain preferred the near-revival of the policy of the 'double line' implicit in the last two possibilities. His optimism was such as to make him reluctant to adopt the first view, but not so great as to rely wholly upon the second. His reflections on these possibilities misled many of his critics into believing that his earlier appeasement was being maintained.[118] The final irony perhaps lies in the fact that the response of Chamberlain's critics to his firmness in the matter of the guarantee to Poland in September 1939 was a vocal relief which overrode the question of why Britain's traditional refusal to undertake commitments in Eastern Europe had been reversed.

VII   Resignation

Labour refused to join my Government and thereby rendered impossible all the interference with the liberty of the subjects and the press that now go through without opposition.[119]

Chamberlain resigned as Prime Minister on 10 May, three days after the Commons began to debate the failure of the Norwegian campaign. The Labour party's decision to divide the House had resulted in a reduction of the National government's normal majority of 240 to 81; 65 National government supporters abstained or were absent unpaired, and 41 voted against the government. It is possible to construct an interpretation of this debate and its consequences in terms of the failure of the Norwegian campaign, and the final eruption of pent-up bitterness on the part of those who had opposed (or who now regretted) Chamberlain's pre-war policy of appeasement. Chamberlain's resignation might thus be seen as the result of the Norwegian failure and the delayed reaction to appeasement, producing a revolt within his own party. These factors are undoubtedly essential to any explanation of his resignation. No-one was more inclined than Chamberlain to see the outbreak of war as representing the failure of his policy, and such a general reaction gave his Conservative critics an obvious psychological advantage. In addition, the failure of the Norwegian campaign, soon to be followed by the German invasion of Holland and Belgium, constituted a major strategic reverse. On the other hand, there was much more to the opposition to Chamberlain and to his resignation than is implied in this interpretation.

Chamberlain's resignation owed much to the attitude of the Labour opposition, and too great an emphasis on the Norwegian failure distracts attention from more general influences on Parliamentary opinion. The importance of the Labour opposition did not reside merely in its obvious ability to weaken the general prosecution of war by symbolizing the extent to which Chamberlain's National government lacked unanimous and unreserved public support. A more precise consideration was the extent to which the administrative and industrial changes necessary to an effective war effort required the wholehearted cooperation of organized labour. Chamberlain had more experience than most of the veto which the unions could exercise in this respect,[120] and while such lack of cooperation could be discounted in terms of Chamberlain's pre-war policies, continuation of uneasy relations with labour into the war itself was a different matter. The opposition represented both a sizable proportion of the electorate and the power of the unions, and thus held the initiative both during the Norwegian debate and with respect to Chamberlain's own position.[121] Chamberlain was fully aware that he was ultimately dependent on the attitude of the Labour party. His desire, after the Norwegian vote, to have Labour's refusal to join his government expressed in a clear and public form stemmed from the need to explain his resignation to a Conservative party which was still, in general, prepared to support him.[122] The timing of the Labour decision to issue an overt challenge to Chamberlain was decided by the Norwegian failure and by Conservative divisions revealed in the debate; but the strategic political importance of the Labour party was, in the long run, an independent and decisive factor.

The great importance attached to the cooperation of organized labour can be understood only in the light of a widespread criticism of the National government in the early months of the war. The foundations of this unrest lay not so much in strategical failures, but rather in the alleged lack of governmental urgency as expressed in administrative defects. Few politicians supported L.S.Amery's desire for an almost dictatorial form of government,[123] but many were impressed by evidence of shortages in supply. By the time of the Norwegian debate a considerable proportion of the Commons was serving in the armed forces, and many were inclined to echo the stories of shortages of, and defects in, vital equipment which had for some time been the major concern of Labour leaders such as Dalton:[124] it is significant that Admiral Keyes, for example, attended the debate in uniform.[125] Considerations of defects in supply were crucial in persuading Conservative members such as Hogg that although they had been right in their support of Chamberlain's pre-war appease- ment, the policy rectitudes of the past could not ultimately override the administrative shortcomings of the present. The parallels with the situation during the first war were present and recognized: .

> Macmillan says that the reason why young Tories in uniform voted with us against the Government was because in the army their loyalty to the King overcame their loyalty to the old man [Chamberlain] ... it is, he says, like 1915 when old Asquith told Parliament that there were plenty of shells and soldier MPs came back from the Front and said 'That's a bloody lie. We only had 3 shells a day at Festubert.'[126]

In both wars, military and strategic considerations were a peg on which to hang a combination of past political grievances and demands for more effective government: in 1940 Amery appears as a lesser Carson. In the context of the demand for administrative reconstruction and urgency, the pivotal role of the Labour party and the trade unions which it represented was clear. Once the Labour party had issued its overt challenge, Chamberlain's position was untenable.

IX Conclusion

The criticisms which ultimately undermined Chamberlain's position as Prime Minister were addressed to failings which were to some extent the inevitable consequence of his earlier decision to stake almost everything on the possibility of appeasement. He had always recognized that the relegation of the deterrent side of the 'double line' to the status of a relatively secondary consideration ran the risk of increasing the ultimate likelihood of war and of decreasing Britain's ability to engage successfully in such a war. It was in this sense that his foreign policy was based upon a conscious choice. Chamberlain's political stature depends, in the last resort, not so much upon the validity of his expectations as upon the character of his response to his political world. Assessments of the relative superiority of alternative choices that might have been made are inevitably hypothetical, and must remain in the realm of mere opinion. Chamberlain himself saw the onset of war as representing the failure of his policies. The combination of optimism, realism, and vision on which his policy of appeasement was based had failed in its avowed object. At Munich, the certainty and sureness of touch which were central to Chamberlain's politics ultimately failed entirely to prevent the re-emergence of the difficulties and complexities of the earlier policy of the 'double line'.

The fascination of Chamberlain as a politician lies in his recognition that politics is characterized by the necessity of choice, and in his creation of a politics of leadership in which reason and moral vision were combined in a manner appropriate to and inseparable from the policies pursued. There is a coherence and vision about Chamberlain the politician which defies attempts to reduce his public *persona* to the everyday level of private and personal shortcomings, and a stature which survives his ultimate failure to triumph over the tides of political fortune. The imposition of character upon political circumstance is an enterprise which pervades the whole of Chamberlain's public life, and no-one was more disposed to see, at the end, the ultimate victory of a life-long adversary: the intractable world of politics. He brought to the office of Prime Minister a style which was sufficiently individual to be clearly distinguishable from both the mere man of business and the manipulator of personal power. Recognition of his leadership and of his identifiable political character with respect to the policy of appeasement need not be purchased at the price of conceding the claims of those who were (and are) prepared to visit the entire responsibility for that policy upon Chamberlain alone. The confused range of alternatives from which Chamberlain attempted to create a coherent foreign policy was not of his making. His policies were widely supported by his contemporaries, and few contemporaries of comparable political stature and experience could proffer alternatives whose plausibility and minimization of danger could confidently be regarded as superior, even by the proponents themselves.[127] Chamberlain has been, in company with MacDonald and Baldwin, a victim of a long-standing political myth. The reputation for mediocrity fastened upon British Prime Ministers of the inter-war years owes much of its force to the effusions of those who either supported or later glorified the Lloyd George coalition which collapsed in 1922. From this termination of 'the reign of the great ones' followed, we have been told, 'the reign of the pygmies, of the second-class brains'.[128] It is upon such a confusion between genuine political character and style and the brilliant facade of the political jerry-builder that the consignment of Chamberlain to the status of a 'pygmy' has rested.

Notes

1. The author's view of Chamberlain's politics was considerably changed by the cumulative impression produced by a reading of his private papers. He is therefore greatly indebted to Mr and Mrs Stephen Lloyd for their kindness in making the papers available. A debt of gratitude is also owed to Sir Reginald Dorman-Smith, Sir Alec Douglas-Home and Viscount Stuart of Findhorn who, by private conversations and/or correspondence, sharpened the author's perception of his subject. It should not be necessary to add that the above persons bear no responsibility for the interpretation of Chamberlain presented in this essay.
2. Quoted in Sir K.Feiling, *Neville Chamberlain* (London 1946), p. 287.
3. J.H.Grainger, *Character and Style in English Politics* (London 1969), pp. 1 and 4.

4. See W.N.Medlicott, *British Foreign Policy since Versailles* (London 1968); K.G.Robbins, *Munich* (London 1968); D.C.Watt, *Personalities and Policies* (London 1965); A.J.P.Taylor, *The Origins of the Second World War* (London 1961).

5. Although J.H.Grainger, *op. cit.*, Sir K.Feiling, *op. cit.*, and Lord Templewood (formerly Sir Samuel Hoare), *Nine Troubled Years* (London 1954) are noble exceptions.

6. Lord Winterton, *Orders of the Day* (London 1953), p. 260.

7. N(eville) C(hamberlain) to H(ilda) C(hamberlain), October 1932, and 23 March 1935. Quoted in I. Macleod, *Neville Chamberlain* (London 1961), p. 165.

8. See the perceptive account in C.B.Pyper, *Chamberlain and his Critics* (London 1962), p. 14 *et seq.*

9. A.J.L.Barnes and K.Middlemas, *Baldwin* (London 1969), p. 568.

10. Hore-Belisha's Diary, 25 May 1937. Quoted in R.J.Minney, *The Private Papers of Hore-Belisha* (London 1960), p. 16.

11. Templewood, *op. cit.*, p. 376.

12. *Ibid.*, p. 376.

13. *Ibid.*, p. 330.

14. Feiling, *op. cit.*, p. 307.

15. Chief Industrial Adviser to the government; seconded to the Treasury to assist the Prime Minister in 1935; Head of the Treasury 1932–42.

16. One such communication (to Duff Cooper) was accompanied by the remark: 'He is not dealing with S.B. now.'

17. Information supplied by Sir Reginald Dorman-Smith.

18. N.C. to I(da) C(hamberlain), 28 January 1939. The references are to Anderson, Chatfield and Dorman-Smith respectively.

19. See the gratitude expressed in this respect, by Hore-Belisha: Minney, *op. cit.*, p. 77.

20. N.C. to H(ilda) C(hamberlain), 17 September 1939.

21. Macleod (*op. cit.*), p. 193.

22. N.C. to H.C. 17 May 1938.

23. W.Morrison, Minister of Agriculture 1936–9, Chancellor of the Duchy of Lancaster 1939–40.

24. N.C. to H.C., 6 April 1940.

25. N.C. to I.C., 3 February 1940.

26. Templewood, *op. cit.*, p. 387.

27. Chamberlain, *MSS Diary*, 5 May 1937. It is ironic that Chamberlain, who was later to be criticized for failing to depart from traditional Cabinet practices, was also accused of using 'the inner circle' to circumvent the Cabinet. Arrangements originally introduced to facilitate the efficient dispatch of business could thus be regarded, alternately, by his critics as

evidence both of personal domination and of an undesirable degree of consultation.

28. Lord Swinton, *I Remember* (London 1949), p. 265.

29. Quoted in Feiling, *op. cit.*, p. 303.

30. N.C. to I.C., 22 October 1939.

31. Grainger, *op. cit.*, p. 230.

32. Lord Stuart, *Within the Fringe* (London 1967), p. 83.

33. For example: Chamberlain, *MSS Diary*, 17 January 1937 and 19 March 1937.

34. N.C. to Mrs Morton Prince, 16 January 1938. Quoted in Feiling, *op. cit.*, p. 323.

35. See f.4.

36. R.Bassett, *Democracy and Foreign Policy* (London 1951), *passim*.

37. See the perceptive account in J.F.Kennedy, *Why Britain Slept* (London 1940), especially ch. 1.

38. Barnes and Middlemass, *op. cit.*, chs 27 and 28.

39. See the speeches of Baldwin, Samuel and Attlee as reported in *The Times*, 14 November 1935.

40. Lord Vansittart, *The Mist Procession* (London 1958), p. 544.

41. Barnes and Middlemas, *op. cit.*, p. 30.

42. D.C.Watt, *Essays*, Nos 4 and 8 in *Personalities and Policies, op. cit.*, and 'Appeasement, The Rise of a Revisionist School' in *Political Quarterly* (April–June 1965).

43. Templewood, *op. cit.*, p. 258.

44. Lord Avon (formerly Sir Anthony Eden), *Facing the Dictators* (London 1962), p. 455. See also the reaction of Walter Citrine (Lord Citrine), *Men and Work* (London 1964), pp. 366–8.

45. Watt, *op. cit.*, f.42.

46. Macleod, *op. cit.*, p. 208.

47. N.C. to I.C., 11 September 1938.

48. T.Jones to Lady Grigg, 24 October 1937. Quoted in T.Jones, *A Diary with Letters* (London 1954), p. 370. Chamberlain was unwilling to relegate rearmament to the entirely insignificant position favoured by Jones, with the result that he was later criticized by the latter for an insufficient sense of urgency and for an unwillingness to carry the appeasement of Germany to 'absurd lengths'. (Jones, *ibid.*, p. 396.)

49. F.S.Northedge, *The Troubled Giant* (London 1966), p. 482.

50. As, for example, in his broadcast of 27 September 1938. Quoted in Feiling, *op. cit.*, p. 372.

51. Northedge, *op. cit.*, p. 543.

52. Quoted in Feiling, *op. cit.*, p. 306.

53. N.C. to H.C., 9 April 1938.

54. Cf. his reaction to Oliver Stanley's fears about the consequences of Eden's resignation (Chamberlain, *MSS Diary*, 19 February 1938).

55. N.C. to H.C., 9 April 1938.

56. Dalton recorded an account by Harold Nicolson of Baldwin's remarks at the latter's farewell dinner: 'Never try to score off the Labour party, or to be smart at their expense. Never do anything to increase the sense of bitterness between the parties in Parliament. Never go out of your way to irritate or anger the Labour party. Remember that one day we may need them.' *Dalton Papers* (British Library of Political and Economic Science), f.18, Box 1937–40.

57. Avon, *op. cit.*, p. 445.

58. Templewood, *op. cit.*, p. 257.

59. Oliver Stanley (frequently regarded by Chamberlain as one of the 'doubters' in his Cabinet) found that Chamberlain 'never resented honest differences, and indeed welcomed and encouraged expressions of opinion. In Cabinet he was cool, decided, clear and above all never complacent.' Quoted in Feiling, *op. cit.*, p. 306.

60. Duff Cooper, *Old Men Forget* (London 1953), p. 210–11.

61. N.C. to H.C., 5 March 1939.

62. Templewood, *op. cit.*, p. 290.

63. *Ibid.*, p. 277.

64. As is revealed by the excellent portrait in Barnes and Middlemas, *op. cit.*, Chamberlain shared with most of Baldwin's contemporaries a tendency to underestimate the subtlety and effectiveness of his predecessor's political style.

65. Quoted in Feiling, *op. cit.*, p. 311.

66. N.C. to I.C., 11 September 1938 and 12 March 1939.

67. N.C. to H.C., 6 March 1938. Murray's article appeared in *The Times*, of the same date.

68. See his views as recorded by Halifax: Lord Birkenhead, *Halifax* (London 1965), p. 457.

69. Both Dalton and Eden recognized this; they located the discontent with Chamberlain mainly in the younger and junior ranks. See Dalton, *MSS Diary, op. cit.*, 24 September 1938; Avon, *The Reckoning* (London 1965), p. 3.

70. Templewood, *op. cit.*, p. 291.

71. Barnes and Middlemas, *op. cit.*, pp. 749–50.

72. Medlicott, *op. cit.*, p. 91; Robbins, *op. cit.*, p. 283.

73. His reliance upon Sir Nevile Henderson, for example, was based upon his recognition that 'the man on the spot' must be taken seriously: I.Colvin, *Vansittart in Office* (London 1965), p. 241.

74. Feiling, *op. cit.*, p. 387.

75. N.C. to H.C., 27 March 1938.

76. See the perceptive and very sympathetic portrait of Churchill in N.C. to H.C., 4 May 1940.

77. It is significant, in this respect, that Eden shared Chamberlain's view that the efforts of Simon and others to avert the resignation of the latter (in 1938) by suggestions of compromise solutions, showed their fundamental misconception of the issues at stake: Avon, *Facing the Dictators, op. cit.*, p. 600.

78. Stuart, *op. cit.*, p. 83.

79. N.C. to I.C., 5 August 1939.

80. N.C. to H.C., 4 May 1940.

81. N.C. to I.C., 19 November 1938.

82. Cf. his willingness to encourage the constituency parties to act against his Parliamentary critics: N.C. to I.C., 5 August 1939.

83. N.C. to I.C., 17 December 1938.

84. Avon, *Facing the Dictators, op. cit.*, p. 486.

85. Quoted in Macleod, *op. cit.*, p. 203. For a Labour confirmation of this impression see Dalton, *MSS Diary, op. cit.*, 8 May 1940.

86. Macleod, *op. cit.*, p. 267.

87. Quoted in Feiling, *op. cit.*, p. 412. For the view that the National government's members were, as a whole, 'essentially a peacetime Ministry', see Templewood, *op. cit.*, p. 341.

88. Diary of Lord Halifax, 11 May 1940; quoted in Birkenhead, *op. cit.*, p. 457.

89. N.C. to I.C., 8 January 1939.

90. According to Dalton, Chamberlain was prepared 'to freely admit that we are often haunted by fears like this': *Dalton MSS Diary, op. cit.*, 17 September 1938.

91. N.C. to I.C., 12 March 1939.

92. Avon, *The Reckoning, op. cit.*, p. 38.

93. Dalton, *MSS Diary, op. cit.*, 12 October 1938.

94. See, for example, the approach to Hore-Belisha recorded in Minney, *op. cit.*, p. 130.

95. Quintin Hogg to Chamberlain, quoted in Macleod, *op. cit.*, p. 290.

96. Dalton, *MSS Diary, op. cit.*, 9 April 1940.

97. N.C. to I.C., 11 May 1940; W.S.Churchill, *Their Finest Hour* (London 1949), pp. 23–4.

98. N.C. to I.C., 17 December 1938; N.C. to H.C., 14 May 1939.

99. N.C. to H.C., 15 October 1938.

100. N.C. to H.C., 5 August 1939.

101. Feiling, *op. cit.*, p. 304.

102. For his criticisms of Baldwin in this respect, see *ibid.*, pp. 312–13.

103. See, for example, H.Dalton, *The Fateful Years* (London 1957), pp. 198–9.

104. In the section which follows, references to 'the Munich negotiations' should be taken to refer not merely to the meeting at Munich on 29 September 1938 but also (as a generic phrase) to the earlier meetings with Hitler at Berchtesgaden (15–16 September) and Godesberg (22 September).

105. *H.C. Debates* (3 October 1938), vols 48–50.

106. Cooper, *op. cit.*, p. 225.

107. Avon, *The Reckoning, op. cit.*, p. 30.

108. L.S.Amery, *My Political Life* (London 1953) III, p. 288.

109. N.C. to H.C., 15 July 1939.

110. Quoted in Sir J.Wheeler-Bennett, *George VI* (London 1958), pp. 346–7.

111. N.C. to I.C., 11 September 1938.

112. Templewood, *op. cit.*, p. 311.

113. A.J.P.Taylor, *op. cit.*, p. 223.

114. Feiling, *op. cit.*, p. 354.

115. *Ibid.*, p. 354. The latter view was forcefully urged by Henderson in Berlin: Colvin, *op. cit.*, p. 240.

116. R.Higham, *Armed Forces in Peacetime* (London 1962), p. 189.

117. Lord Croft, *My Life of Strife* (London 1948), p. 168.

118. Taylor, *op. cit.*, p. 288.

119. N.C. to H.C., 17 May 1940.

120. As early as 1936, the crucial limitations imposed upon administrative and manpower policies (in pursuit of rearmament) by lack of political agreement was recognized: K.Hancock and M.Gowing, *The British War Economy* (1949), p. 62. A meeting between Chamberlain, the defence Ministers and the TUC in March 1939, at which the unions showed clear hostility to the industrial implications of accelerated rearmament, is described in Templewood, *op. cit.*, p. 388.

121. Dalton, *The Fateful Years, op. cit.*, p. 308.

122. N.C. to I.C., 11 May 1940.

123. Amery, *op. cit.*, p. 362.

124. See, for example, the entries in Dalton, *MSS Diary, op. cit.*, 18 September 1939 and 7 March 1940.

125. Dalton noted that Duff Cooper was 'ostentatiously in uniform' (*ibid.*, 8 May 1940); Chamberlain himself was aware that 'the serving members were acutely conscious of various deficiencies': (N.C. to I.C., 11 May 1940).

126. Dalton, *MSS Diary, op. cit.*, 16 May 1940.

127. Dalton recorded Vansittart's doubts, at the beginning of Chamberlain's prime ministership, 'whether any good positive policy can be made just at

this moment', *ibid.*, 4 November 1937.

28. The phrases quoted are those of Professor Mowat: C.L.Mowat, *Britain Between the Wars* (London 1955), p. 142.

Index